MW00640145

Penned from the Heart

Volume XIV

Compiled and Edited by
Fran Pratt

Son-Rise Publications
51 Greenfield Road
New Wilmington, PA 16142

Thank You!

Sincere appreciation is extended to those who helped in the
preparation of this book!
They include my husband, **Don Pratt**,
Gloria Clover, Evelyn Minshull, Pan Sankey,
and **Audrey Stallsmith,**
who spent hours checking the manuscript before it went to press.
Thanks should go, too, to **Florence Biros** without whom the book
would never have been published and **Jim Jackson**, without whom the
book would never have been printed! Thanks also to **Debbie Schall**
without whom the book would not be mailed!
Perhaps the greatest gift to me was those who wrote that
they were praying for me. God heard their prayers!
The book is done and may God get the glory!
What would I have done without you!
God bless you all!
Fran Pratt

A Word from our Publisher

This 2008 Edition of **Penned from the Heart** features thoughts, spiritual insights, and Godly devotionals from people from all walks of life, all ages, and from all over the world.

You may find words capitalized that are not generally acceptable in literary circles today, but this has been deliberate, our choice to honor the Lord.

In addition, not all of our writers are professionals, but everything written here has been sincerely "penned from each loving heart" to the glory of God.

A list of our authors and location of their devotions is found at the end of this book.

It is our prayer that all who read this book will find the way to eternal life with Him in Heaven, and abundant life while here on earth.

Florence Biros

Scripture references are from the Holy Bible: *King James Version, New King James Version, New American Standard Bible, Taylor Living Bible, New International Version, Revised Standard Version, New Revised Standard Version, The Message,* Life Application Bible and *Websters Version.*

Son-Rise Publications
51 Greenfield Road
New Wilmington, PA 16142
© 2007 Son-Rise Publications
All rights reserved.
Printed in the United States of America

ISBN 10: 0-936369-75-2
ISBN 13: 978-0-936369-75-4

Penned from the Heart
2008 Edition

UNITY PRAYER FOR THE NEW YEAR

Gloria Clover   January 1

Father God, as the Lord Jesus prayed in the garden, so we pray this day for unity among those who believe in the Living Christ. As You are One – Father, Son, Spirit – so may we be one Body – united not in tolerance, compromise, and pretense, but truly united, possessing the mind of Christ, a sacrificial love for friends and enemies, and a faithful determination to press on to the end.

We thank You, Lord God, for creating Your church as the living Body of Christ, as branches connected to the Vine, bearing good fruit, as the Bride, pure and spotless. From these examples, we see that we are recreated as one and live as one in Christ, and we praise You.

Father, You are holy. Jesus, You are Savior. Spirit, You are strength and wisdom for Your people. Thank You for the shed blood that unites us as a people dependent on truth and grace. In Jesus' Name. Amen

GET A GRIP

Margaret Steinacker   January 2

Suggested scripture reading: Hebrews 10:19-39

"Let us hold fast to the confession of our hope without wavering, for he who has promised is faithful." Hebrews 10:23

I'm never tempted to consider climbing. My fear of heights stops any such notion. However, I've watched mountain climbers. Having the proper attire and equipment comes in as the number one require-ment. Climbers hold fast. They do this by wearing proper gloves or by apply-ing resin or some similar substance to their hands. Ropes also play an important part in the life of a rock climber.

Climbers grip to the mountain wall as if their lives depended on it, because they do. They insert their toes into the smallest crevice and use the foot-hold to cling strongly to the side of the mountain until another crack or fissure can be found for the next step. They climb with great patience and extreme perseverance gained by judicious training.

As we journey through life with God on our side, we do not have to fear the mountains of disease, death, divorce, disappointment, broken dreams, defeat, or depression. God supplies us with the correct amount of anti-skid compound to keep us from slipping. He is the Master Guide with a securely tied rope to keep us from falling. His

Word gives us footholds to stabilize our climb, even in the midst of rocky, thorn-covered paths. Trust in His unfailing grace today.

"God knows our situation; He will not judge us as if we had no difficulties to overcome. What matters is the sincerity and perseverance of our will to overcome them." (C.S. Lewis)

KICKED IN THE TEETH

Susan Stitch   January 3

"For our light and momentary troubles are achieving for us an eternal glory that far outweighs them all. So we fix our eyes not on what is seen, but on what is unseen. For what is seen is temporary, but what is unseen is eternal."
2 Corinthians 4:17-18, (NIV)

Last night our seven-year-old son enthusiastically proclaimed that his twin brother had made him lose his tooth! Kevin didn't have any loose teeth, so I was concerned about how this had happened. Chris had kicked his twin in the mouth during a wrestling session, and both boys were laughing hysterically about it (as only boys can do). Kevin proudly put his tooth in a bag and positioned it under his pillow. His eyes sparkled at the prospect of a new, shiny quarter in return.

Later, I marveled at how Kevin ignored his pain in the excitement of the moment.

I often feel like I've been kicked in the teeth by the world, and I'll guarantee that I'm not paying attention to possible benefits to be derived from the experience. Yet God promises us that our momentary troubles allow us eternal glory that far outweighs the world! While I may not see the small joys that occur in times of trouble, I can know that Heaven will be a time of eternal joy. I hope I focus on my promise of Heaven with at least the same enthusiasm as Kevin held for the promise of a quarter from the Tooth Fairy!

A WALK WITH JESUS

Lorena Estep   January 4

"They asked each other, 'Were not our hearts burning within us while he talked with us on the road and opened the Scriptures to us?'" Luke 24:32 (NIV)

"You need to get back to walking," my husband reminded me. "With my work schedule it's hard for me to go with you."

"But it's so boring to walk alone," I argued. However, I knew he was right. I was working at being healthy in soul and spirit, but I was neglecting to keep my body in good working order. I decided it was time to take action.

I had signed up to be a prayer partner for our church. We received a monthly list that we were to pray for daily. I tucked mine in my pocket and headed off on a three-mile circle. I took out my prayer list and talked to the Lord about each item as I walked.

By the time I had prayed through it, I realized I was home already! My walk was completed, my prayer list covered, and I felt energized in body, soul and spirit!

I was reminded of the two men walking to Emmaus who were joined by Jesus, and how they later thought back to the way their hearts had burned within them while He talked with them on the road. I felt truly blessed that I, too, had been able to walk with Him and knew I could do it any time and any day.

Lord Jesus, help me to draw ever closer to You, walking with You every step of the way.

KINDNESS AND FORGIVENESS

By Glenda Race   January 5
**Let all bitterness, and wrath, and anger, and clamour,
and evil speaking, be put away from you, with all malice:
And be ye kind one to another, tenderhearted, forgiving one
another, even as God for Christ's sake hath forgiven you.**
Ephesians 4:31-32 (KJV)

As my friend and I sat at our high school cafeteria table, girls next to us tormented her because of her protruding teeth. We tried to ignore their jibes, but that never stopped their teasing. Then one day the character of my friend was tested.

One of the girls came into the cafeteria on crutches. Her friends were in another part of the room, so she told mine, "Hey, you. Get my lunch for me." Then my friend did what I didn't have the courage to do. She took the girl's money, waited in line, and brought the lunch. The girls never called my friend names again.

She could have spoken bitterly, but she chose to act kindly, reminding me of the great love of Jesus when He asked His Father to forgive the people *"...for they know not what they do...."* (Luke 23:24)

Christ's kindness is the model for Christians to follow. It is through His forgiveness we learn to put away bitterness and replace it with a tender and forgiving heart.

ASK, LISTEN, RESPOND

Christopher Griffin   January 6

*"If someone strikes you on the right cheek,
turn to him the other also."* Matthew 5:39 (NIV)
*"Ask and it will be given to you; seek and you will find; knock
and the door will be opened to you."* Matthew 7:7 (NIV)

One day a couple of friends and I gathered in the lunch room and discussed Jesus' teaching on turning the other cheek. Suddenly, Jesus became real to me! This was where the rubber met the road! While the discussion continued, my mind wandered. *How could you possibly receive a slap and not deliver one back?* I thought.

It wasn't long before I found out! It happened to me! I was slapped on the cheek and I felt belittled and reduced to fine sawdust! My heart and mind burned with rage. Yet – instead of sinning – I found myself turning the other cheek! I immediately prayed for the offender who is also my brother in Christ!

This event started with me asking questions – and that led, through faith and trust, to the answers. I realized that God is merciful and kind and that He is God and we are men. I learned to be careful what I ask – because God is always listening!

PEACE AMONG THE BROKEN PIECES

Karen Welborn   January 7

I'm sure we have all broken something we value, and then tried to glue it back together. When I was 12 years old, my parents and I went to Colorado to visit my brother. On a sightseeing tour, I begged Daddy for a large Kewpie doll bank. Being the indulgent parent that he was, he bought it. I still have it – 48 years later, but it is of no monetary value. It wasn't long before I knocked it off my dresser and broke it into many pieces. It now resembles a jigsaw puzzle.

We live in a world permeated by anger, hatred, jealousy, greed, and prejudice. Lives are broken. Even if they can be mended, dreadful scars remain. This has been a problem since the beginning of time. Humans cannot seem to live together in peace. Can broken lives be mended? Can an individual have tranquility amongst the turmoil? Is it possible to have peace in your heart and mind when you pillow your head at night? I believe it is.

Jesus said, *"Peace I leave with you; my peace I give you. I do not give to you as the world gives. Do not let your hearts be troubled and do not be afraid."* John 14:27 (NIV)

We can rest in Him, knowing that He will be with us, and guide us through whatever problems we are facing.

GOD'S WAY IS BEST

Donna J. Howard   January 8

"When Pharoah let the people go, God did not lead them on the road through the Philistine country, though that was shorter. For God said, 'If they face war, they might change their minds and return to Egypt.' So, God led the people around by the desert road toward the Red Sea." Exodus 13:17-18 (NIV)

Verse 21 says: *"By day the Lord went ahead of them in a pillar of cloud to guide them on their way and by night in a pillar of fire to give them light...."*

We need to remember that when we face a trial in life, God does not always lead us through it by the easiest way or the shortest way. He leads us in the way that is best for us, and He will bring us safely through – even though His route may take us through the Red Sea!

GET READY

Valerie Joyce Chambers   January 9

Are we living in the day Jesus spoke of long ago?
Of the times and the seasons – are they meant for us to know?
The disciples asked that question,
don't you think that we should, too?
Is preparing in advance what Jesus wanted us to do?
We've been drawn into deception by men claiming they are Him
With promises of "the good life" while we continue in our sin.
There have been so many wars – and rumors they are rising –
Jesus said that this would happen, so it shouldn't be surprising.
We have seen the devastation of the powerful earthquake
And wonder deep within our hearts,
how much more can this world take?
The seas, they have been roaring, causing perplexity to man
For all of our natural disasters, we can't begin to have a plan.
We have lost the love that we should have for one another
We have turned against our parents – our sister and our brother.
We've become a land of pleasure and forsaken the love of God
We continue in our wickedness and expect from Him a nod.
Like the pains of a woman in labor, the signs are coming faster
But if you put your trust in God you will miss the "great disaster."

Jesus said to watch the fig tree; when you see it begin to bloom
Your generation will not pass away,
So, Bride – G*et ready for your Groom!*

STONE COLD

Paul Soderberg   January 10

"And I will give them an undivided heart, and I will put a new spirit in them; I will remove from them their heart of stone and give them a heart of flesh." Ezekiel 11:19 (NIV)

Arctic wood-frogs freeze as hard as stone during the winter. There is no heartbeat, and all brain activity ceases. In fact there is no cellular activity at all. For all intents and purposes, they are dead. But, come spring, they thaw – and within 15 minutes the heart beats, and the blood pumps, and they are jumping around!

What a great reason to leap! We as Christians, being born again, should display such exuberance for our rejuvenation in Christ. We experience life anew with a clean slate and the awesome promise of eternal life, body and soul. Let us leap for joy!

Thank You, Jesus, for taking my heart of stone and giving me a heart of flesh and a new spirit, because the old is gone. Thanks for the second chance. Let me leap and jump as my new heart pumps out love for you. In Jesus' great and powerful name I pray. Amen

OUT OF THE BOX

Jennifer Kanode   January 11

"Do not store up for yourselves treasures on earth…but store up for yourselves treasures in heaven… for where your treasure is, there your heart will be also." Matthew 6:19-21 (NIV)

Where my husband and I used to reside, there was a barn about five minutes away. Within the two years that we lived there, the owner had built another one much bigger than the original. It was interesting to see the barn go up. But it made me think about the parable of the rich fool in Luke 12:13-21. He had so many crops that he built himself a bigger barn. Then he decided to take it easy, eat, drink and be happy. God was not happy with him, however, because he did not share with others who might be in need. In fact, God said to him, ***"You fool! This night your soul is required of you; and who will own what you have prepared?"*** Sure enough, that night he died!

God calls us to help those in need and to give to the poor. We need to remember the orphans and widows. We tend to get too comfortable.

Lest God calls **us** "fools!" let's step out of the box and away from our comfort zone. That's when the true adventure begins!

Lord, help us to put others before ourselves. For when we do that, we will be truly blessed. Amen

BEGINNING AGAIN

Joseph Smart   January 12

"But I trust in your unfailing love; my heart rejoices in your salvation. I will sing to the Lord for he has been good to me."
Psalm 13:5-6 (NIV)

Like David of the Old Testament, I have suffered great losses and have been blessed with great consolations. But whatever life may give me or take away, this is the simple wisdom that will always light my way. I have loved passionately and fearlessly with all my heart and soul. I have been loved in return.

Recently, I have faced a major set back. But with God's help, my life can begin again. What has been taken from me will not cause me grief. What the Lord will give back to me is enough. The sun will come up tomorrow and the day after that.

Dear Lord, You have been good to me and I have learned the value of love. Now I turn all my tomorrows over to You. Amen

EVERYTHING IS POSSIBLE

Janice May Harris   January 13
Read Mark 9:14-32.

"'If you can'?" said Jesus. "Everything is possible for him who believes." Mark 9:23 (NIV)

Kathy was what you might call a baby Christian, one learning to walk with Christ. She knew of salvation, but understood little about faith, including healing. Kathy always asked God to help her believe and not doubt when she prayed.

Arriving at home one day, she found her cat, Roscoe, very ill and listless. When she got close to him an unpleasant odor indicated the animal was dying. Worried that he might not make it through the night, she acted quickly. Her first impulse was to lay hands on him and pray. As she appealed to God, Kathy could feel her faith building.

The next morning, Roscoe was up and playing with his favorite toy mouse. Today, ten years later, he is a healthy 15-year-old cat.

Thank You, Lord, for the gift of faith, and for caring for us – and our pets, too! Amen

TRUSTING GOD FOR YOUR FUTURE

Nancy Dearborn   January14

Read Psalm 139:13-16

"For I know the plans I have for you," declares the Lord, plans to prosper you and not to harm you, plans to give you hope and a future." Jeremiah 29:11 (NIV)

"Mom, I'm so glad you called!" my daughter Valerie told me. "I just found out that Christine is going to be gone all summer, so now I have no one to room with when I arrive back in the States from my exchange program in Mexico." She stopped to stifle a sob, "Then I called to check on my job, and I found out they forgot to save me a spot! So now I have no job, either."

What could I say to my daughter? What would lend her hope and comfort? I didn't know what other job she could get for the summer – nor with whom she could room – but what I did tell her was that God still had a plan for her life. That He was her hope and provider, and that she needed to look to Him for answers.

We need to cling to God when our way is unclear, our future uncertain. We can take great comfort and assurance in knowing He has a plan for every day of our lives.

Dear God, I do not know what tomorrow will bring, but what I do know is that You have everything under control. Help me to look to You for guidance and direction. Amen

A POWERFUL WORD

Mary A. Koepke   January 15

I find many levels of meaning in the words of Scripture when I take time to discover their hidden treasure. So it has been with that tiny word "let." It is used more than 1,000 times in the Old and New Testaments and its importance is amazing.

It first appears in Genesis 1:3 as the creator God says, *"Let there be light."* In that context it is His command – the beginning of creation. Later, "let" is a term of surrender or a request to permit positive accep-tance.

Jesus taught His disciples in parables such as *"Let your light shine before men."* (Matthew 5:16) He used it to teach, as in *"Let the little children come unto me."* (Luke 18:16)

Paul used it also with *"Let this mind be in you, which was also in Christ Jesus."* (Philippians 2:5)

We have sung "This little light of mine, let it shine…." in Sunday

School. Even the Beatles sang "Let it Be" that includes a reference to the Virgin Mary. And who isn't touched when singing "Let there be peace on earth and let it begin with me." (Jill Jackson and Sy Miller)

God's ways have many directions and our spiritual journey must grow through a lifetime of listening and learning from such small words. They express God's love and His gifts if we will "let" Him give them to us!

INVENTORY

Helen Kammerdiener   January 16

Read Psalm 19:1-14

"The heavens declare the glory of God; and the firmament showeth his handiwork." Psalm 19:1 (KJV)

If you shop in January, you may see people with hand-held scanners electronically recording the contents of the store. By the end of the day, they hold a complete inventory of everything scanned. Many cell phones keep a record of all transactions made, too. If you've used the phone to send social security numbers, credit card numbers, and other information, it's in there. Even though the user has erased it, if a professional has not totally cleared the memory, someone may still be able to retrieve personal information. Quite often, material you think you've deleted from computers is still retrievable by an expert.

Our hearts and minds likewise store information. Maybe January would be a good time for each of us to make an inventory of the past year's thoughts, words, and actions.

What good things have we recorded in our lives? What do we want to repeat and maybe expand in this new year? What have we done that we would erase if we could? How will we avoid repeating those things in the coming year?

Let's also make an inventory of all God has done for us in the past year. Psalm 19 can help get us started.

Thank You, Lord, for the blessings of the past year and for Your promises for the one that is about to dawn. Amen

TRUSTING IN GOD

Pat Collins   January 17

"Trust in the Lord with all your heart, and lean not on your own understanding." Proverbs 3:5 (NKJV)

Are there times in your life, as in mine, when things seem to get hectic, pile up, and overwhelm us? Do you suppose that maybe God is trying to get our attention? Do you wonder why at times God seems close and at other times, He seems so far away?

These could be our trusting and testing times.

I feel my faith is strengthened through trying times. It helps to endure hardships, knowing they are a testing of our faith. We must trust in every trial. In doing so, we take our minds off ourselves, and draw close to God. His love for us is everlasting and unconditional.

He does not always approve of our ways – but His love is forever!

Thank You, Lord, for Your love and understanding, and for being there through all my trials.

TIME, WORDS, OPPORTUNITY

Esther Bordwell   January 18

There is a saying, "These things, once used, can never be recovered: time, words, and opportunity."

This quote reminds me of a children's sermon I once gave at church. I held a Bible in one hand and a comic strip section of the newspaper in the other. I asked the children if they liked the funnies. All hands went up!

Then I said, "What if everything we said appeared in a box above our heads like it does in the funny paper? Would we be more careful not to say angry words, cross words, and words that insult others?"

Of course they agreed. Then I quoted the following Bible verses:

1 Peter 3:10-12: ***"If you want a happy good life, keep control of your tongue, and guard your lips from telling lies."*** (TLB)

Proverbs 12:18: ***"Some people like to make cutting remarks, but the words of the wise soothe and heal."*** (TLB)

Colossians 4:6: ***"Let your conversation be gracious as well as sensible, for then you will have the right answer for everyone."*** (TLB)

This lesson was applied to children, but what about us adults? As we have the time, let our words be gracious at every opportunity!

A PSALM FOR MORNING OR NIGHT

Dorothy Holley   January 19

I seek Your presence, O Lord, at night
And in morning light.
Then throughout the day
I distract myself
With worry, pain, regrets.

But You are still with me,
Your love sustains me.
Your words strengthen me
To relate to friends and family,
To tend the garden, to express
Life in poetry, e-mail, or journal.
And at the dawning of each new day
I start all over again.

GOD'S GRAND DESIGN

Ruth M. Baldwin   January 20
Read Genesis 1:1-31

As my father and I worked in the garden, he told me how he'd originally decided to become a farmer. He felt it was the only profession that would make him wholly seek the Lord – asking for rain at the right time, and the deliverance of his crops from storms. In the fall, he'd prayed for income for living expenses and seed for the next year's crop.

"You know, Girl (his name for me), I homesteaded this farm after the Civil War. It was prairie land – never been plowed – left like the Lord made it. I chose one field to never plow, a reminder of how God helps us," Dad explained.

I looked at that field, awed that we lived on land that was still part of the Lord's original creation! Even as a young girl I sensed His presence in a deeper way.

Today, I see evidences of the Lord's care for us, such as the variety of foods He has lavished upon us – so many fruits and vegetables! The many trees, plants and flowers provide beauty. Can you count the numerous species of birds, animals, and fish He created for this planet?

Yes, God's grand design displays His love for all of us. *Isn't He wonderful?*

OH, LITTLE STAR

Betty Redmon   January 21
"Then, God made ... and the stars also. And set them in the firmament of the heavens to give light on the earth.
Genesis 1:16-17 (NKJ)

Oh, little star, you twinkle bright
Way up in your home tonight,
Sitting in your sky of blue

With clouds that lend a softening hue
To all that bright expanse
That seems to blanket all the land.
Would that I had wings to fly,
I'd join you in your home so high
Where all's so peaceful and serene
And heavenly lights around you gleam.
I would stay there by your side
To laugh at wind and fickle tide,
As they played on sand and shore
And witness things not seen before.
Resting there, I'd gently sleep,
For this old earth no more to weep.

IN STEP WITH THE SPIRIT

Judy Barron   January 22
*"But the fruit of the Spirit is love, joy, peace, patience, kindness,
goodness, faithfulness, gentleness and self-control ...
Since we live by the Spirit, let us keep in step with the Spirit."*
Galatians 5:22, 25 (NIV)

How will I ever keep in step with the Spirit? I am so far out of step I think I am walking backwards! All the fruits of the Spirit seem to be on branches too high for me to reach! None of them appear easy to attain. I love, but – too often – I am impatient and unkind and I rarely have self-control.

I lack peace and joy when it should be the very air I breathe because God is all around me. I try so hard to be faithful, but too often I mistrust or have doubts about His presence or His willingness to answer prayer.

How will I ever display these fruits of the Spirit when I don't seem to be in step with the Spirit? I forget the words I read. Worse, the lessons I learn, I don't always obey.

O, Father, forgive my offenses and thank You for Your patience and graciousness toward me. I know Jesus promised the Spirit would come to keep and guide me, counsel and comfort me. Please, as I abide in the Vine, let the Spirit strengthen me so that I may display the fruits I so want to exhibit. In Jesus' name I pray. Amen

WHERE'S YOUR FOCUS?

Tonya La Course   January 23

Matthew 14:22-23

In order to jump a horse properly you need to check three things:
Are my heels down?
Am I squatting?
Am I looking up?
The last – "am I looking up?" – causes you to focus on your goal, and it also shows the horse you have confidence that he will do what you have trained him to do.

Downcast eyes, or diversion from the focal point, will cause the horse to wander off track!

When Jesus walked on water, He appeared in a great storm to show His disciples that He was with them.

Peter (the only one who appeared to react in faith) asked to be allowed to walk out to the Lord.

Then Jesus said, *"Come"*

When Peter trusted Christ's word, he walked on water. However, when he focused on the storm and took his eyes off Christ, he began to sink!

Just as focusing on our destination in jumping is essential, so is fixing our eyes on the Lord to help us run straight toward our goal.

The moment we take our eyes and thoughts off "cone," our horse drifts to the right.

When we take our sights off God, our world begins to fall apart.

Father, we want to head straight for the goal You have put before us. Like the Apostle Paul, help us to let nothing interfere with the outcome of our race. Amen

PRAYER TO THE MASTER ARTIST

Charles A. Waugaman   January 24

"In the beginning was the Word, and the Word was with God, and the Word was God. He was in the beginning with God. All things came into being through Him; and apart from Him nothing came into being that has come into being." John 1:1-3 (NASB)

God, You are the Water of Life. I, but a scratch of pigment. Brush over me with the wide wash of Your will. Free me to color my world with love; splash it with joy; moisten it with peace and tint it anew with hope.

I am a fixed speck. You do not push, but You inspire. You do not force, but release. Free me to flood Your beauty into both the bright and dark spaces of my world, into its wide vistas as well as the tight contacts of my daily living.

Lord, in You I am rich; ready to let Your presence bleed into the bleak and empty lands I touch. Thank You. Amen

GOD'S GUIDELINES

Mary Herron   January 25

"Trust God from the bottom of your heart; don't try to figure out everything on your own. Listen to God's voice in everything you do, everywhere you go; he's the one who will keep you on track." Proverbs 3:5-6 (The Message)

Years ago I heard a lady say she thought of the Ten Commandments as "God's Guidelines." You follow them and you avoid many pitfalls. If you choose to try it your way or do what you know is wrong, you can get yourself into mighty tight situations!

Through the years I've thought about that and watched people try to do it their way. Some even blamed God when they got themselves into trouble!

Most of us think of laws as something hard and forceful, but *guidelines* have a softer tone. If I follow "God's Guidelines" I avoid a lot of heartaches. If I choose to disobey God, I can get into many hurtful situations from which I may take years to recover. But it is comforting to know our Heavenly Father is always ready with open arms to help us when we ask.

However, even when we miss the mark, God can take our mistakes and give us another chance to obey. So I pray, *Lord, help me to learn to ask for Your help in the beginning. It will save me from years of backtracking and suffering unnecessary trials. Help me to obey You because You know what is best for me. Amen*

A CHANGE OF HEART

Derrick K. Osorio   January 26

Along life's sinful path of darkness I treaded
Straight for the "lake of fire" is where I was headed.
I hadn't a clue, nor the slightest notion
That my final destination was that fiery ocean.
Then I heard that still, small voice calling out my name.
"I love you, My son, and I'll save you from that flame!"
I fell down upon my knees to kiss His blessed feet,
As in my heart I truly longed my Savior to meet.

He reconciled me to Himself, in me He made a change
Now, old ways of living seem very strange.
No longer do I follow the lures of this wicked realm.
Instead, I just let Jesus take control of the helm.

THE VIEW FROM HEAVEN

Columba Lisa Smith   January 27

Read 1 Samuel 23:1-6

"Each of you should look not only to your own interests, but also to the interests of others." Philippians 2:4 (NIV)

King Saul, with his army, was seeking David's life. Hiding in a Judean forest, David had only 400 men with him. These were Israel's cast-off discontents, men drawn to David, the man of God.

Into their desperate situation came a call for help. The Philistines were attacking Keilah. David's Rescue Response Team was wanted again.

"*Right now, Lord?*" The idea of this browbeaten gang rescuing anyone was almost laughable. David's followers voiced their fears plainly. But "David inquired of the Lord." The Lord said to go and conquer! So, in their needy, desperate state, they won a victory. Imagine their change in outlook!

Got a problem today? As overwhelming as your situation may appear, God is not worried. What is He asking you to try today? Do you trust Him enough to leave the impossible in His hands and simply do whatever He puts on your heart?

He has a victory waiting for you!

Dear Lord, thank You for Your perfect plan for today. Help me to give You control if I begin to listen to my fears or worries. Help me to faithfully obey You, no matter what else is demanding my allegiance. Amen

BEAUTY FROM ASHES

Debbie Carpenter   January 28

Read Isaiah 61:1-4

"...to bestow on them a crown of beauty instead of ashes, the oil of gladness instead of mourning...." Isaiah 61:3 (KJV)

The date was January 28, 1986. As I stood in my family room folding clothes and watching the launch of the Space Shuttle Challenger I heard the disturbing words, "obviously a major malfunction." I dropped to my knees and began to plead with God on behalf of the lives of the Challenger crew. This was the shuttle that was to trans-port America's Teacher-In-Space, Christa McAuliffe, on what she termed "the Ultimate Field Trip."

My husband, Bob, had been closely connected with this expedition that was known as "51-L." He and one other teacher had been selected as Arizona's two Teacher-In-Space candidates for this history-making project. Christa McAuliffe, who was later chosen to take the journey, was a nominee from New Hampshire.

The year preceding the launch was full of excitement and anticipation for all of the candidates. They prepared to use Christa's voyage to reach children all over their particular states with assemblies highlighting the value of getting a good education. That January day, the balloon burst. The Challenger had exploded. The Lord would have to bring beauty from the ashes.

BEAUTY FROM ASHES (continued)
Debbie Carpenter   January 29

In the weeks that followed the disaster, I spent time in quiet reflection on the brevity of life and the need to serve God faithfully each day. I took comfort in God's absolute sovereignty.

Bob spent a hectic but rewarding year speaking to groups of fellow Arizonans both young and old. In many groups Bob was allowed to mention God's ability to take bad situations and use them for good. He also encouraged audiences to persevere when things didn't turn out the way they had expected. Many students pondered what they wanted to do with the rest of their lives and how to begin to plan for their futures.

Although nothing could ever change the fact that seven Americans had perished in the explosion of Challenger, Bob and I were witnessing the Lord at work comforting, soothing, restoring. Lovingly He was spreading His oil of healing over our wounded nation.

Again we were reminded that He is the source of all hope.

SAVORING GOD'S WORD
Lydia Harris   January 30
Read Psalm 19

Years ago, our Bible study group sang the words of this psalm. Following the descriptions of the "law of the Lord" came the refrain, *"More to be desired are they than gold, even much fine gold: sweeter also than the honey, and the honeycomb."* Verse 11 was the coda: *"Moreover by them is your servant warned, and in*

20

keeping of them there is great reward." (KJV)

It was easy to sing those words without considering their mean-ing. Now I'm taking a closer look.

First, I notice the variety of words David used to describe God's Word: *law, decrees, precepts, commandment, and ordinances.* Then I see the praiseworthy claims the psalm makes. It's *perfect, sure, right, clear, true, and righteous.*

I also discover the amazing impact God's Word makes in our lives. It *revives the soul, makes the simple wise, brings joy to the heart, enlightens eyes, and serves as a warning.* What other book can make such claims?

Personally, I need the wisdom, joy, and guidance God's Word provides. I remind myself of that chorus so the words are etched in my mind. But I want them to go beyond my mind and be evident in my life. I need to rediscover how sweet and precious God's Word is.

Forgive me, Lord, for the times I neglect Your Word. Grant me a daily desire to savor its sweetness and valuable truths. Amen

COME AND FOLLOW ME

Eric Dilmore (13)   January 31

While walking up along the beach
He turned to the water to see
Two fishermen, who clearly heard,
"Come and follow Me."
While teaching right beside a lake
He asked for a boat to teach
Two owners of the boat then heard,
"Come and follow Me."
While walking the streets of Jerusalem
He paid taxes to the king
The collector behind the booth heard,
"Come and follow Me."
Here and now the Savior calls
And shows us how to live.
Each and every one of us hears,
"Come and follow Me."

FEBRUARY

JUST ONE SMALL PIECE OF FRUIT....

Evelyn Minshull   February 1

Read Genesis 3:1-7 and Matthew 4:1-11

All of Eden's trees were laden with luscious fruit – ripe, fragrant, dewy. There were no insect bites in Eden, no wormholes, no rot, no bruise, no sour taste. Adam and Eve were free to eat from any – *except* – exce*pt* for the Tree of Knowledge.

When they could sample so many, why was that one tree in particular denied?

Of course, the serpent had an answer. And once the law was broken, the bond with God was snapped ... companionship withdrawn ... trust and sharing gone.

The serpent found a different scene when he confronted Jesus, for Jesus knew His Father well and cherished their togetherness.

Nothing would fracture that relationship. Not the exhilarating prospect of daredevil feats. Not a pledge of earthly power exceeding that of czars and emperors. Not crusty bread to appease an overwhelming hunger.

Food for the body – be it bread or Eden's apple – is only fleeting, but spiritual nourishment lasts for eternity.

Lord, we are no more obedient than our first parents, and we have less excuse. They were children – naive, easy prey for sly, sophisticated Satan. We have the advantage of millennia of examples; we know to resist temptation and yet we often fail. Give us the strength that Jesus proved in the wilderness. Amen

UNEXPECTED ACTS OF KINDNESS

Joy Bradford   February 2

"A kind man benefits himself, but a cruel man brings trouble on himself." Proverbs 11:17 (NIV)

Recently I learned that there is a week in February when we are encouraged to do Random Acts of Kindness. The RAK Foundation was formed in 1995, and has a web-site (www.actsofkindness.org) that features a variety of kindness activities for classrooms and communities.

The Bible, from Genesis to the New Testament, is full of instruction on being considerate. So why must we select a week to make us aware that graciousness is a precious asset?

22

We all can make a difference in the lives of others. Our children witnessed us saying "Thank you" each time a server brought our food at a restaurant. We said those *magic words* often during the meal. Now, our adult children say the same words with a smile. This small gesture perhaps lifts a weary waiter's spirit.

So, during February, the month of love, why not give additional thought to kindness – with a dash of compassion. If we are to become "God's hands and feet" maybe it will become a pattern for the rest of the year. Let's show His love by being considerate to others.

Father, thank You that when we are to kind to others our own spirits are lifted. Let Your grace flow from us as we meet their needs. We want to honor You with our actions. Amen

WAITING FOR THE "UPPERTAKER"

Joseph M. Hopkins   February 3

"Blessed assurance, Jesus is mine!
O what a foretaste of glory divine!"
(From the Hymn by Fanny J. Crosby)

Our former beloved pastor in New Wilmington, Pennsylvania, the Rev. Bill McCoy, was a mortician. But God called him out of the funeral home into the seminary to retool for the Christian ministry. Since I always enjoy a pun, I told Bill I had the perfect name for his autobiography: *"From Undertaker to Uppertaker."*

Languishing in nursing homes throughout the nation are two types of people: those waiting for the undertaker and those waiting for the *Uppertaker*. How sad to face death without hope! All of us who trust Jesus as Savior and Lord should not only hope but *know* that Heaven is our eternal destination. John gives us this "blessed assurance" in his first letter:

"I write these things to you who believe in the name of the Son of God so that you may know that you have eternal life." (John 5:13) Note this: Not *"will* have," but *"have"* (present tense). Eternal life begins *now* – just as soon as we penitent sinners open our hearts to receive Jesus as our personal Savior and Lord. Hallelujah! Praise the Lord!

Lord, I have no fear of the undertaker. I am trusting Jesus, my Uppertaker. Please help me to live out my days loving and serving You and others until, at Your appointed time, I am translated into Your glorious presence! Amen

FOUR-LETTER WORDS

Jana Carman   February 4

"Let your speech always be gracious, seasoned with salt."
Colossians 4:6 (NIV)

When the movie "Gone With the Wind" came out, many were shocked when Rhett Butler said to Scarlett, "Frankly, my dear, I don't give a d....!"

That's mild compared to what we now hear and see on TV.

The world must not be allowed to monopolize four-letter words! Let's emphasize these in place of the ones polluting the minds of our nation:

For example, character words, like Good, Best, Pure, Fine, Wise, Kind.

Or family words: Home, Love, Hugs, Care, Obey, Ours, Give.

Some prescribe the path to health: Walk, Rest, Slow Down, Wait, Read.

Some describe the good life: Grow, Save, Work, Play, Help.

Some point to our spiritual side: Pray, Soul, Free, Life.

Then, when we run out of four-letter words, there are some great five-letter ones: Smile, Build, Study, Serve, Learn, Share, Bible, Jesus....! You get the idea!

FROM SHINGLES TO SALVATION

Stanley Tune   February 5

(As told to Deborah J. Tune)

The view from atop the little country church was awesome as I labored to repair its leaking roof that brisk February morn. Sounds of joyful voices down in the sanctuary drifted up to me. Not able to quite make out the words, I busied myself with the task at hand.

Later, I proceeded to go inside. It was a beautiful church with light beaming in the windows as though God was smiling upon this small group of people. I had no clue the evangelist had called for a prayer meeting of the members – and it had started a revival! I was unaware that my life would be forever transformed.

That day, God smiled on me as I gave my heart and life over to Him. The evangelist told me to bring my family that evening. Little did I realize that my wife would also repent that same night!

It's been almost 20 years since that day. Our family now works in the ministry, touching many lives, even as that evangelist touched mine. Jail ministry, singing, spreading the Gospel – all serving God continuously, through both the good times and the bad – all because a little church had a leaky roof!

24

So be careful. It seems that when God wants something, He has a way to get the job accomplished. I'm thankful to this day that I was that volunteer. May God smile on you as He's smiled on me!

WISH PRAYERS

Annette Irby   February 6
"And He said to them, 'What do you want Me to do for you?'"
Mark 10:36 (NKJV)

Today cottonwood seeds flittered everywhere while I worked on the patio. I remembered how, as a child, I would catch the seeds in my fingers, make a wish, then let them go. Somewhere along the way, I began making prayers out of wishes. Now I vocalize my heart's desires as prayers to the One who can make them happen as I commune with Him. The Word says He will give us the desires of our hearts as we delight ourselves in Him. (See Psalm 37:4)

It had been a few years since I snatched a floating cottonseed from the air and made a wish, but today one landed in my lap! I felt the Lord was giving me permission to dream. So, I paused and considered what I'd love to see Him do as I try to serve Him. He's the One who gave me my longings, so He knows they're not just about me. They're about His Kingdom work. He's given you dreams, too, I imagine. Go ahead and turn those desires into prayers. Let God breathe on your dreams and watch what He does.

Father, let my wishes be Yours. Thank You that Your ways involve getting me excited about Your dreams for my life. I love You. Amen

SATISFIED, PROUD, FORGETFUL

Joanna Ronalds   February 7
"When I fed them, they were satisfied; when they were satisfied, they became proud; then they forgot me." Hosea 13:6 (NIV)

Satisfied...
When are you satisfied? Are you contented when you have a roof over your head, a job to go to, food on the table? Are you pleased when you and your family are healthy and happy?
Proud...
If you are honest with yourself, do you recognize that the things which satisfy you are not the result of how good you are? Your job could end tomorrow, and storm, disease or world events could take away the roof over your head and your ability to put food on the table. You can control your own health only to a certain degree, and the happiness of

your family does not ultimately lie with you. Be satisfied with what you have, but don't let pride trick you into thinking that the good things in life are all your doing.

Forgetful...

God gives you the ability to work, earn money, buy food and pay the mortgage. He gives you everything. Don't let pride make you forgetful!

DUST TO DUST

Kathy Johnson   February 8

"By the sweat of your brow you will eat your food until you return to the ground, since from it you were taken; for dust you are and to dust you will return."
Genesis 3:19 (NIV)

This text took on new meaning for me when my family visited our daughter out in California and toured the Nixon Library and birthplace. In the back of the Library grounds, Richard Nixon's boyhood home stands on the exact spot where his father built it. Only a few feet away, the former President of the United States is buried.

From beginning to end, Richard Nixon's life is encompassed in nine acres of Yorba Linda, California.

It reminded me of the shortness of our existence. I pondered the fact that we have an effect on many people, and we all come full circle from birth to death. May we use our time wisely to praise our Lord, magnify His name, and spread the Good News.

Lord, let us never forget that our lives on this earth are short at best. Help us to stay mindful of Your command to seek and to save the lost. Bless each of our days here on this terrestrial ball. Amen

POSSESSIONS

Jennifer Kanode   February 9
Read Matthew 19:16-24

"What good is it for a man to gain the whole world, yet forfeit his soul?" Mark 8:36 (NIV)

I never realized until my husband and I had to move just how much one could get attached to a house or possessions. We had to downsize a little, and it was amazing how much we had collected and how difficult it was to get rid of some things. I had to remind myself that they were just material possessions – and in the end I couldn't take them to Heaven!

I'm sure you can think of a time when you lost something or had to part with a trinket that had sentimental value to you. It can be a painful process. But I think God uses those times to remind us what is truly valuable. It's not the house we live in or all the possessions we have. It is the memories we have made, the times we spent with loved ones, or moments when we reached out and helped those in need. You know, just the little things in life.

So just remember, the next time you are called to give up something, you can't take it with you when God calls you Home!

Lord, help us to be thankful for the things You have given to us, and help us never to put them before You or others. Amen

STANDING FIRM IN THE FACE OF ADVERSITY
Julie Pollitt   February 10

Shock punches us in the gut. Its sharp fangs sink into us with disbelief, chomping down and carving out deeper wounds with each attack. Despair slithers in and grabs hold of our peace, not giving us warning, or a chance to come up out of the slimy pit for air.

Death of a loved one, loss of friends, divorce, and times when life is just too much to bear, force us into the arena of pain. Peace eludes us. To find it under such circumstances would be like finding a Cartier watch in a flea market – it's just not there.

How do we cope? What options do we have when devastation slinks up and knocks us off our feet?

Jesus is ready. He desires to step in and carry us out of the pit. He is there to lift us up and offer a new beginning. Only He can bring renewal into our lives. He takes the pain-ridden devastation and breathes new life into our souls. He is the rose blooming among the thorns. King David said in Psalm 51:12 ***"Restore to me the joy of your salvation."*** He is beautiful, and His compassion rekindles our joy, even when it seems impossible.

2 Corinthians 4:8-9 says, ***"We are hard-pressed on every side, but not crushed; perplexed, but not in despair; persecuted, but not abandoned; struck down, but not destroyed."*** (NIV)

Jesus is ready.

WHO DO YOU TURN TO WHEN YOU ARE OVERWHELMED
Betty King   February 11
"When I am overwhelmed, you alone know the way I should turn." Psalm 142:3 (NLT)

We may become hesitant when asked to choose because we are

uncertain as to what we should do. Life can be puzzling when we are confronted with perplexing issues.

We often leave God out of the equation. Even when we seek His will our prayers are not always answered in the time frame we desire. And the answers we want are not always the answers we receive. Sometimes it's hard to know whether they are truly coming from God, or if they are our own thoughts trying to convince us. So I sometimes pray for a sign.

Recently, I found myself wondering again, so I asked for a sign that would leave no doubt. I knew what I "desired," and what "seemed" best, but was still perplexed.

The next morning my sign came to me delivered by another person. It was not the answer I had desired or the one I thought best – yet there was no mistaking it was God's answer!

We often miss His replies because we don't see them, or we reject them. We overlook them, or they come in unexpected ways. Perhaps the timing is wrong. But we don't like it when God says *no*.

Ask God when direction is needed; He will send answers. Be sure to be open to receive their delivery, and to accept what He sees as best for you at the moment.

MUSIC

Jesse Koontz Sr.   February 12

"Speak to one another with psalms, hymns and spiritual songs. Sing and make music in your heart to the Lord." Ephesians 5:19

Movement in Jesus through music,
Uplifting my spirit to the sky,
Faith building sounds so sweet,
Now I see the light.

Lord, as I listen to Christian music, my spirit is lifted and it builds my faith. Thank You for Your words in Ephesians that encourage me to make music in my heart to the Lord. Amen

THE FRUITY CHRISTIAN

Debra J. Phenes   February 13

"But the fruit of the Spirit is love, joy, peace, longsuffering, gentleness, goodness, faith, meekness, temperance: against such there is no law." Galatians 5:22-23 (KJV)

The fruit of the spirit that I am presently struggling with is *patience* –

or as the Bible states it – "longsuffering." A patient woman is one who puts others above herself. That woman is like ripe, juicy fruit. No bruising or decay is found there. Just *pure freshness* for all who partake.

My heart aches with compassion and love for struggling unbelievers. I want to wrap my arms around them and tell them of Christ's love and help. Some seem to think my fruit inviting. But what about my other fruity side – the one that comes out when a driver cuts me off as I'm running late for work? Or when that pushy woman shoves in ahead of me in the ticket line – the same line I've been standing in for half an hour?

How about you? Do you outwardly give them your Christian smile (shiny, outward fruit), while inwardly seething with anger and frustration (rotten, spoiled, inward fruit)? I do sometimes. (Honestly, a lot more as of late.)

Lord, may I be the freshest fruit of Your Spirit that I can be. Ripen my heart and mind with Your longsuffering Spirit. Give me that tasty shine that only the fruit of patience brings. Amen

A CAPACITY TO LOVE

Lanette Kissel   Valentine's Day   February 14

"...for God is love ... By this the love of God was manifested in us, that God has sent His only begotten Son into the world so that we might live through Him." 1 John 4:8-9 (NASB)

On Valentines Day, our thoughts turn to hearts, flowers, and all things love-related. This holiday tends to focus upon romantic ardor. Regardless of how strong the chemistry and connection may be, romantic affection seems small and insignificant when compared to God's love for us.

God wants us to have loving relationships in our lives. Therefore, he blesses us with husbands, wives, families, and friends. We love them to the best of our ability – to the extent of which our human hearts are capable. Yet, our capacity pales when compared to God's.

His love for us is unparalleled, merciful, bountiful, irrevocable, and enduring. There is no greater devotion than that which the Father bestows upon us, His children. He loves us so dearly that He was willing to sacrifice His own dear Son. We are the desire of His heart, His magnificent obsession. And every day is like Valentines Day when it comes to His love for us.

Dear Father, thanks for loving us so faithfully. Amen

IT COULD HAPPEN HERE

Debbie Carpenter   February 15
"The effective, fervent prayer of a righteous man avails much."
James 5:16 (NKJ)

For weeks I eagerly anticipated the Sunday when my church would welcome a pastor from Uganda, East Africa as the morning's speaker. The day arrived and I sat captivated by all that this man had to say about his life in the 1970s during the reign of Idi Amin. I was stunned by the hopelessness that existed in that country during and after Amin's regime of violence. Apart from God, there would have been nothing but despair. But that was not to be the end of the story.

God's people in Uganda began to pray purposefully and fervently and God started to heal the wounds inflicted by the tyrannical government! It brought a resurgence of hope, faith, and trust.

Today, as the Ugandan prayer movement continues to enlist thousands more people across that country, the AIDS rate has decreased from 33% to 5% and crime is down by 70%. President Musevini and his wife dedicated that nation to the Lord in the year 2000!

As I listened to this story of transformation and renewal, I was excited by the thought that America could also receive a fresh touch from the Lord, if her people would take seriously the privilege of prayer. What might God accomplish in this land of ours if the pop-ulace united to pray, asking Him to work in powerful ways among and through us? We, too, might have fascinating stories to tell the world!

GOD SUSTAINS

Carol J. Lee   February 16
"...you whom I have upheld since you were conceived, and have carried since your birth. Even to your old age and gray hairs I am he, I am he who will sustain you. I have made you and I will carry you: I will sustain you and I will rescue you."
Isaiah 46:3b, 4 (NIV)

The dictionary lists several definitions for *sustain:* "...to keep supplied with necessities ... to provide for ... to support ... to strengthen the spirit ... to encourage."

When I retired, I wondered about the purpose and direction for this new phase of life. After some time of worry and anxiety, I read the above Scripture. God's words encouraged me with renewed hope. As I meditated on the verse, I realized that He has always been there for me. And He will be there for me now, even in this transition time.

God's sustains, but the importance of that seems to increase during transitional times when we feel more vulnerable. The transition could be moving to a new home, getting a new job, getting married, getting divorced, experiencing widowhood, children leaving home, etc. Life continues and changes happen, but God remains the same with His sustaining love, guidance, and presence.

Father God, thank You for knowing me, for always knowing me, and for being with me now at this time in my life. Increase my trust in You and Your sustaining power today in my current situation. Amen

TRYING TO CATCH THE UNCATCHABLE
Scott D. Noble   February 17

We run impatiently, the sky is blue all over,
Leaves glisten under the cooling sun,
The oak trees' arms elegantly sway in time with the wind's rhythm.
Here the pathway seems worn, nearly overcome,
Is it because it has been traveled so many times;
Or perhaps no one knows another way?
Home approaches over the hills of despair,
Yet the distance seems to grow,
As we try to arrive safe, secure, at peace.

ASK FOR WISDOM
Barbara Peer   February 18
"Ask and you will receive, and your joy will be complete."
John 16:24 (NIV)

Did you ever pose a question and have everyone laugh at you for asking such a dumb thing? Most of us have been embarrassed like this at one time or another.

It makes us hesitate to ask questions. But God will never find fault with us for that. James says, *"If any of you lacks wisdom, he should ask God, who gives generously to all without finding fault, and it will be given to him."* James 1:5 (NIV)

God gives wisdom generously! We can continue to ask Him whatever we need to know. God will never lose patience with us for needing His guidance. In fact, He *wants* us to rely on Him for all of our answers!

OUR "TALENTS"

Glenda Joy Race   February 19

Read Matthew 25:14-28
"His lord said unto him, Well done, good and faithful servant...."
Matthew 25:23a (KJV)

While my co-worker and I were shopping in a South Korean town, I
wanted to go to the grocery store where oranges were cheaper, while
she preferred going to the market. I yielded to her wish and soon we
came to a man with a missing leg who was selling oranges. His were
five for 1000 won (80 cents), whereas in the store they were *six* for
1000 won.

After making her purchase, my co-worker smiled and said, "We
made his day."

I realized I had a lot to learn from her example in spending money.
It is not meant to be "dug into the earth" as the third servant in Jesus'
parable of the talents did. We can be like the first and second servants
who traded with others to gain more to give back to their master. God
will bless talents that are invested in eternity, both in reaching the
unbeliever and encouraging the believer to grow in Christ.

*Lord, thank You for the talents You have given me to meet my daily
needs. Help me be more sensitive to the needs of others and invest in
eternity. Amen*

GO THROUGH IT!

Angelicia Roberts   February 20
*"When you go through deep waters and great trouble,
I will be with you. When you go through rivers of difficulty,
you will not drown. When you walk through the fire of
oppression, you will not get burned up,
the flames will not consume you."* Isaiah 43:2 (NLT)

How many times have you experienced things in life that were
overwhelming and beyond what you thought you could handle? Or have
you ever felt lyou were under some serious heat – you know, *pressure
and weight?*

Fear can be present and failure may seem inevitable. God provides
comfort in the above Scripture indicating that He's with us. We won't
drown nor will we get burned. God, being all-seeing, all-knowing and
all-powerful, is able to provide comfort because He has already seen it
all played out before time began!

He says in this passage "when" not "if" you go through trouble. And understand this: you'll overcome it! The most important words to apply to your situation from this Scripture are "go through" (it). Even when fear and overwhelming feelings of pressure are present, you still have to understand the importance of "just going through it."

Remember, this too shall pass as you keep moving forward, pressing on and believing that God is able, and through Him *you* are capable. Note, too, that as you pass through, you will see God's Word manifested and promises fulfilled in and out of your situation.

RACING TO THE FINISH LINE

Margaret Steinacker   February 21

Read Hebrews 12:1-12

"Therefore, since we are surrounded by such a great cloud of witnesses, let us throw off everything that hinders and the sin that so easily entangles, and let us run with perseverance that race marked out for us." Hebrews 12:1 (NIV)

In 60 AD, frequent races drew large crowds to Rome's Coliseum. As with today's Boston Marathon, the attendance was colossal. However, the "cloud of witnesses" are the saints in Heaven cheering us on, while Satan tries to foil us on earth.

As you read "so great a cloud of witnesses," consider a low-hanging cloud ready to burst. Think of this crowd cheering for you to get rid of anything entangling your soul and focus on Christ's teachings. Using weights at their wrists or ankles, joggers enhance their training. However, at a race, there are no weights. Runners focus solely on the finish line, knowing winning demands perseverance.

Christ calls us to "persevere," and to submit to God's training by daily reading His Word, praying, worshiping, and by serving as He guides us. *"...God disciplines us for our good that we may share in His holiness."* Hebrews 12:10b

I will never be the same again; I can never return,
I've closed the door.
I will walk the path, I'll run the race,
and I will never be the same again.
Fall like fire, soak like rain; flow like mighty waters, again and again.
Sweep away the darkness, burn away the chaff,
and let a flame burn to glorify Your name. (Geoff Bullock)

WAITING IN EXPECTATION

Judy Barron   February 22

"In the morning, O Lord, You hear my voice; in the morning I lay my requests before You and wait in expectation." Psalm 5:3 (NIV)

Dear Father,
You are the only One for whom we can wait in expectation and never be disappointed. Others will let us down. Circumstances will not happen as we anticipate. People will fail us; vacations will disappoint; weather will refuse to cooperate; family will ignore us; even church will not always provide what we need. Only You do not disappoint. Whatever You promise, You provide. When You judge, we know what we deserve and what to expect. Or do we? What we should expect is death or hell or nothingness. And what we get is life everlasting, love, peace, joy, fulfillment. Maybe these things don't come immediately, but they do come. They will come. You have promised and You won't forget. So I can lay my requests before You in the morning, or late afternoon, or bedtime – or the middle of a lonely night – and You will hear my cry. And I can wait in confident expectation. Thank You, dear Father. Amen

MEDITATION AT THE ABBEY

Lizzie Joy Lukens   February 23

"Do not remember the former things, or consider the things of old. I am about to do a new thing; now it springs forth, do you not perceive it?" Isaiah 43:18-19 (NRSV)

I am a baby butterfly
emerging from its tomb,
unfurling its wings.
I am awed by the sunlight
and the song of crickets
as I dance on the sunflowers.
I am giddy with the scent of God
wafting from the lavender
and drunk with the taste of manna.
I am not constrained
by the size of my wings,
only by the expanse of the heavens.

A MERRY HEART

Micki Roberts   February 24

"A merry heart maketh a cheerful countenance:
but by sorrow of the heart the spirit is broken."
Proverbs 15:13 (KJV)

One day on my lunch break I hurried into the grocery store, needing to pick up a couple of items to prepare supper that evening. I gathered the things required and rolled the cart up to the checkout line.

When it was my turn, the girl (and when I say girl I mean she was probably in her late teens or early twenties) at the register voiced the usual greeting, "Hi, how are you?"

To which I replied, "I'm good, how are you?"

I'll never forget what she said. "Today is the greatest day of my life."

Now, at that time I was already way beyond tired! You see, I have fibromyalgia and most days I push myself just to be able to function. So I was feeling rather grumpy and cynical.

I looked at her and asked, "What happened? Did you win the lottery?"

To which she replied, "No, I woke up."

Instantly, I felt very small as tears filled my eyes. "You have a wonderful attitude," I said.

She just smiled.

As I walked out the door, I still felt really tired. But my heart was filled with cheer. Now, when someone asks me how I'm doing, I'm going to think about that young girl in the grocery store. And hopefully I will respond, "Today is the greatest day of my life!"

A PLACE ON EARTH

Neil C. Fitzgerald   February 25

"And he said unto them, 'Come away by yourselves to a
lonely place and rest a while." Mark 6:31
"Blest are they who hear the word of God and keep it."
Luke 11:28 (NASB)

My mother-in-law lived by herself in her own home until she was over one hundred years old! This was made possible by the loving attention of my wife and some wonderful home-health-care providers. Ever alert, my mother-in-law lay down on her couch one day and fell asleep in the arms of the Lord – Who I'm sure had prepared a place for her in Heaven.

In the summer, while my wife prepared her mother's lunch, I would often wander out into the backyard and stretch out in a lounge chair in what was best described as a "square gazebo." There I was surrounded by my small garden, a mischievous neighborhood squirrel, and a host of colorful birds. In the house behind the yard lived a violin teacher. Noontimes – when no pupils were present – he would practice the various melodies he enjoyed. For me this completed a perfect reverie. I was reminded how Jesus would set apart time for prayer with His Father. I had my own corner to pause during a busy day and listen to God with my heart.

For my mother-in-law, this "place on earth" was a stepping stone to her "place in Heaven." For me, it is a reflection of God's benevolence, a beautiful reminder that peace and love and joy emanate from moments of contemplation and prayer.

STUPID ARGUMENTS

Janet R. Sady   February 26

"Don't have anything to do with foolish and stupid arguments because you know they produce quarrels. And the Lord's servant must not quarrel; instead he must be kind to everyone, able to teach, not resentful." 2 Timothy 2:23-24 (NIV)

It seems to be in some people's nature to argue. They dispute about anything and everything. When one of our daughters was a teenager, she questioned every rule we made. I always hoped she would use this talent as a lawyer. (No, she didn't become an attorney, but at her place of employment, she *does* argue for the rights of those who can't speak for themselves!)

God's Word instructs us as Christians to avoid "foolish and stupid" arguments. They stir up trouble which leads to years of dissension, and strife among families and friends.

We are to strive instead to be different from the world – to show the love of Christ. In this way, we may win someone who is lost and searching for the way to God.

Lord, help me to show kindness and love to those around me. May I be like You. Amen

LET GOD HEAL

Chet Weld   February 27

"He will respond to the prayer of the destitute; he will not despise their plea." Psalm 25:5 (NIV)

I used to be a counselor in Tucson, Arizona at a residential treatment center for men who were recovering from various addictions. One day I was crossing the street in order to get to the treatment center that was located in a house. In the backyard was a beautiful Irish setter who seemed to be in much discomfort. When I got closer to the dog, I could see that she was covered with cactus needles.

She was trying to pull them out with her teeth, but they were simply ending up in her gums. I wanted to bend down and remove the needles myself, but feared that because I was a stranger, the dog might attack me. I hoped that her master was somewhere nearby. Indeed, in a matter of moments, the owner, who was one of the residents, arrived on the scene. He gently stroked the setter's head, spoke in comforting tones, and began to remove the needles one by one.

I think of how often I try to extricate myself from troubles by my own efforts, making matters worse. How much better to simply look to Jesus! When I keep my eyes on Christ, He will bring comfort to me, removing the painful needles one by one.

SANCTUARY

Mary A. Koepke   February 28

There's no need
For public declaration –
My foolish foibles,
My unwitting mistakes,
My depressive guilt trips.
Freed from a blatant world
Into the listening silence
Of cloistered intimacy,
With transparent trust
I release them all to My Lord God –
Who lives in our secret sanctuary.

PRAISE AND WORSHIP GRAMMAR

Stefanie Grennek   February 29
"I will praise You, O Lord, with all my heart." Psalm 9:1 (NIV)

During a school chapel service, the man leading the singing stopped playing his guitar for a moment to talk to the audience.

"Praise and worship are verbs, not nouns," he said. "They're something you *do,* something you are actively involved in – not a thing or a style of music."

This statement made me think about my view of praising and

worshiping God. Many times I come to a chapel or church service preoccupied with the activities of the day. I attend the service, but instead of actively praising God, I sing the familiar songs thoughtlessly as my mind wanders back to my own concerns.

David pointed out a key to true worship in Psalm 9:1: "I will praise You, O Lord, with all my heart."

Truly praising God requires a choice to put aside all other thoughts and business, and to focus on the Lord with all of our hearts and minds. Our holy God is worthy of all of our worship and praise! *"Great is the Lord and most worthy of praise; his greatness no one can fathom."* Psalm 145:3 (NIV)

Lord, help us to see praise and worship as verbs, not as nouns. Teach us to forget everything else and spend time focused on praising and worshiping You. Help us to glorify Your worthy name actively with all of our hearts. Amen

MARCH
SECOND WIND DREAMS

Shirley Stevens   March 1
"Bless the Lord, O my Soul ... Who walketh upon the wings of the wind." Psalm 104:1-4 (KJV)

At a local retirement village I learned about a program called Second Wind Dreams. Like the Make a Wish Foundation, which fulfills wishes for terminally ill children, this group works on a smaller scale to grant wishes for the elderly who are ill.

At Passavant, people have arranged for seniors to ride the incline, go up in a plane, attend a local concert, go out for breakfast, and have a family reunion.

The friend who told me about this program had been on the committee to plan ways in which to fulfill other residents' dreams. Now that she is ill, she will be on the receiving end.

Perhaps each of us could be a part of fulfilling someone's Second Wind Dream without having a formal program or spending a lot of money. We might read poetry to a shut in, take a bouquet of lilacs to someone in a nursing home, deliver a surprise present like body lotion, or take a picnic lunch to share with someone who has had knee surgery.

Dear Lord, Help us to walk on the wings of Your wind today, making a difference in the life of someone who is in pain, bored, or lonely. Amen

LOVE IS SUPERIOR

Paul Soderberg   March 2

Read Psalm 105:15

"For all the law is fulfilled in one word. Even in this: Thou shalt love thy neighbor as thyself." Galatians 5:14 (KJV)

Throughout our lives we have to adhere to many laws or pay the consequences. Even Confucius knew that, "Without recognizing the ordinances of heaven, it is impossible to be a superior man." This is true with human laws as well as Scriptural commandments such as Galatians 5:14. We can go through our lives being obedient to the government, but still fall short of being a "superior man" in God's eyes.

In this instance, *Webster's Collegiate Dictionary* defines "superior" as meaning "refusing to give in to or being affected by."

Following this guideline, and trusting in the help of the Holy Spirit, we should not fall into temptation!

We need to make love our focus, for love conquers all – and the Word states that "it never fails!" (1 Corinthians 13:8) Following God's ordinance, our Holy Bible, we will become "superior men."

Lord God Almighty, lead me to be a man of love and integrity, following Your ordinances, commandments and laws so that, in Your eyes, I'll be the superior man You've intended me to be. Guide me in righteousness and love to spread seeds of fidelity in all my activities and speech. Fill me with your kindness, saturate me with the fruits of the Spirit which include love. Thank You, Lord, in Your most precious, potent, and powerful name I pray. Amen

CALM IN THE CHAOS

Angie K. Dilmore   March 3

"Today, if you hear his voice, do not harden your hearts as you did in the rebellion." Hebrews 3:15 (NIV)

In the morning, I sit to have my "quiet time" with God. As I open my Bible, the washing machine churns, the dishwasher hums, my neighbor mows his grass, the telephone rings, and I wonder why it's a struggle to focus on Jesus. Maybe I should get an earlier start?

I understand the importance of daily spending time in prayer and reading God's Word. It is a discipline and priority in my life, yet there are days it doesn't happen. I find that when I do take time with the Lord, the course of my day is smoother, less stressful. I'm more peaceful and confident in my decisions.

How can we listen for God in the commotion and chaos of our daily routines? If we carve out corners of quiet, where not only our environment is still, but our minds are calm and free of distractions, we are better able to hear the hush of the Holy Spirit. If we put aside our mental to-do lists, the dialogues of disagreements, and the worries over loved ones, our minds are open and receptive to the nudges of our Creator. We can listen for that still, small voice in the silence. What is He saying to you today?

Loving Father, Help us to be still and listen. We want to hear Your voice. Amen

UNDER HIS WINGS

Debbie Carpenter   March 4

Read Psalm 91

"He shall cover you with His feathers, and under His wings you shall take refuge." Psalm 91:4 (NKJ)

Inside my patio wall is a sheltered oasis I refer to as my "prayer garden." It is a lovely place to sit on a cool Arizona morning and commune with the Lord. Last spring there was a pleasant addition to this picturesque retreat.

I awoke one day to find a mourning dove couple building a nest in the hanging bougainvillea on my porch. The father bird diligently collected sticks of various sizes. The mother wove them into a cozy nest. In the days that followed, I was surprised to see that both doves were vitally interested in the care of two small eggs upon which they alternately sat. The nest was never left without a parent, except for a moment's time at the changing of the guard. The doves endured blowing dust, hot afternoons, and occasional showers, but they remained steadfast.

A couple of weeks passed and I noticed two feathery fledglings in the nest. The parental vigilance had yielded what appeared to be a healthy set of twins!

As I delighted in the sight, I thought of Psalm 91 and the promise God has made to give those who abide in Him refuge "under His wings." The Lord had provided me a visual image of His faithful protection.

VOICES

Basle Cox   March 5

A laugh, a cry
A song of cheer

A shout, a whisper in the air
Voices travel everywhere
Like thunder rumbling through the sky
Or soft and sweet in a lullaby
A baby cooing from the crib –
Or God telling us how we should live
Leaning down from Heaven above
He tells us of His pure, sweet love.

PRINCESS AT PEACE

Debbie Rempel   March 6

"Be sober, be vigilant; because your adversary the devil, as a roaring lion, walketh about, seeking whom he may devour. Whom resist stedfast in the faith...."
1 Peter 5:8-9a (KJV)

Once upon a time in a royal kingdom there lived a princess. One day, she was attacked by a wild animal. His name was Satan. He stole the princess for himself and she became frightened, discouraged, and sad.

While in her dungeon of despair, she felt a gentle touch and a voice said, "I'm here. Come, rejoice with the King!"

When she praised her Father, her joy returned and she was set free. Now, she watches for Satan's awful lies that ruined her love and joy. She is God's child, a daughter of the King – and always will be – whether her days are good or bad. Now, In her kingdom called *life*, at a cross with a crown, she goes to release her frustrations to her God and King. She's at peace.

I am that princess. I am from that royal bloodline. I eat and drink of His Word. I want my crown to be an "exclamation point life" to shine like gold! I have received healing for my wounded soul from the King Himself. I, the princess, will press on to reach the land of self-control. Still, Satan will try to get in my way. I will not let those negative thoughts dwell in me. The King is my Fortress, my dwelling place for all time.

THE FRUIT OF GENTLENESS

Kris Thayer   March 7

"The fruit of the Spirit is gentleness...." Galatians 5:22 (NIV)

Gentleness is a work of the Holy Spirit in us. It does not get angry, nor is it resistant, independent or rebellious. It is an inward manifestation of the character of Jesus. Perfect love casts out fear, and the

peace that results allows us to be gentle. As a lioness
tenderly carries her cub in her mouth, our powerful Father carries
His children. In Matthew 11:28, Jesus called on the people to learn from
Him, *"for I am meek and lowly in heart, and ye shall find rest for
your souls."* (KJV) And although it may seem a contradiction in terms,
Jesus, who has all power and authority, is gentle and meek in nature.

The Holy Spirit will work this in us also, using the awesome power
of a peaceful nature to bring others to Christ, as they see the love of
God reflected in us.

God can work in your life if you don't wallow in the anger and sin of
the past. Philippians 4:5 tells us to *"Let your gentleness be evident
to all."* Be ever so tender in all things, by simply speaking the truth.

Ponder, Pray, and Pursue: Are you gentle? We live in a culture that
encourages us to be abrasive, manipulative, pushy ... but rarely meek.
Gentleness will be seen as weakness by many around you, but it will
draw those who are looking for evidence of the reality of God.

CLIMBING THE HEIGHTS

Lorena Estep   March 8
*"The Sovereign Lord is my strength; he makes my feet like
the feet of a deer, he enables me to go on the heights."*
Habakkuk 3:19 (NIV)

"How much farther?" I whispered to my father when he stopped and
waited for me to catch up.

I was a teen, hunting with my dad on the first day of deer season.
We had been walking through a long valley, with steep rugged hills on
both sides, to get to a spot where he liked to hunt.

My heart sank when he pointed to the steep mountainous area on
our left. Without waiting for me to voice any complaints, he started up
the rugged terrain like a mountain goat. Shifting my rifle to a more
comfortable position, I began the torturous ascent, not wanting to slow
my father down.

We finally made it to the top and the area he had in mind. My
aching muscles were glad to stand for a while as my eyes scanned the
woods.

Now, as an adult reading in Habakkuk 3:19, I look back to that day
when my father climbed a steep hill, as fleet-footed as a deer, and I
trustingly followed behind. I can liken it to following my Heavenly Father
through valleys and up mountains, trusting Him for strength and feet
like a deer to enable me to go to the heights with Him.

*Heavenly Father, thank You for the strength You give us daily to do
Your work wherever You lead us. Amen*

GO DEEPER

Daisy Townsend   March 9

Read Luke 5:1-6

***"For my people have committed two evils: they have forsaken
me, the fountain of living waters, and they have hewn for
themselves cisterns, broken cisterns which cannot hold water."***
Jeremiah 2:13 (Amplified)

One of my least favorite memories of returning to my girlhood
home is the memory of the electric pump running endlessly, trying
futilely to pump more water. It was nerve-wracking!

Before we sold the old family homestead, my oldest brother
decided that we would have a deeper well dug for the new owners.
When he told us the depths to which the well diggers had gone, he said
joyfully, "These people will *never* need to worry about running out of
water!" I had never understood that what we needed was a deeper well!

Sometimes I wonder whether we as Christians have a similar
problem. As we pursue our busy lives, we are like the pump that runs
endlessly, but produces little in the way of living water to quench our
own thirst or the thirst of those around us. Often we are completely
unaware that what we need most is not more good deeds, but a deeper
relationship with Jesus Christ.

*Father, forgive us for being so busy that we fail to hear the voice of
Jesus urging us to "Come out into the deep." Show us how to come
deeper in our relationship with You. Amen*

Thought for The Day:
Spiritual activity is not synonymous with spiritual depth.

TALE OF A STINKY BOSS

Debra J. Phenes   March 10

This job stinks! How can I respect a hypocritical boss? Cassie
thought as she settled into her work cubicle. She plowed through work
until five o'clock.

"Thank God! I can go home," she muttered, heading out the door.

"Bad day, Cass?" her co-worker Sue asked.

"I'm fed up!"

"Really? Is that why you banged the keyboard?" laughed Sue.

"Sorry," Cassie grumbled.

At home, she complained to her mother who said, "Hold on, dear, I
have something for you," as she dug in her purse. "There it is," she
said, handing Cassie a card. "I picked up some 'blessing' cards. This

one really keeps me in perspective."

"Remember who you are and whom you serve!" Cassie read out loud. "I'm sorry, God. I forgot! Help me be a better Christian witness at work."

The next morning Cassie came across this verse as she read her devotional, ***"Servants, obey in all things your masters according to the flesh; not with eye service, as men pleasers; but in singleness of heart, fearing God: And whatsoever ye do, do it heartily as to the Lord and not unto men."*** 1 Thessalonians 3:22-23 (KJV)

As she opened the door to her office, she prayed, *"Lord help me be a servant today at work and remember that I work not just for my boss, but You, God, are my ultimate Boss. May Your Holy Spirit direct my actions and words so that I may draw my co-workers and boss to You."* Amen

LAUGHTER – PURE AND SIMPLE

Pan Sankey   March 11

"You have made known to me the path of life;
You will fill me with joy in your presence, with eternal pleasures
at your right hand." Psalm 16:11 (NIV)

My sister Jana once performed a skit with another accomplished pianist during morning chapel. The theme was, "The Body of Christ Working Together in Unity." They tried to demonstrate this by lashing a broomstick to one's right arm and to the other's left. Side by side on the bench, they attempted the morning offertory. Soon, with their skewered arms sticking out behind them like crossed bayonets, they began their own little happy dance!

Chaos erupted as the duo giggled to the point of tears, sending the cast, crew and captive audience into helpless, rolling-in-the-aisles laughter. Hopefully, the Body of Christ functions better than the skit portrayed. But later, around the supper table, we again experienced the hilarity it provided, which inspired the following poem:

We laughed until the tears ran down,
clasped our sides and gasped,
"I can't laugh any more!" But just then another wave of levity
Capsized our craft of dignity and plunged us
Once again into a sea of glee.
At such a time, do you suppose, that these poor earth-bound

Souls have caught a glimpse beyond the veil into Reality and Light –
Where mountains skip like springtime lambs and trees Clap hands in
pure delight?
Oh, Master, may we dance sometimes along this earthly path
In holy, glad response to Thee;
Discovering anew each day the joy You long to share,
That from Your presence emanates now and through eternity.

STACCATO OR LEGATO?

Sarah Lynn Phillips   March 12
"Let the words of my mouth ... be acceptable in Your sight."
Psalm 19:14 (NKJV)

I took a deep breath, then dialed the number. The voice that
answered gave the data I needed, but the short staccato-like tone left
me unsettled, cold, and feeling almost guilty. Although I made every
effort to keep this relationship in a major key, I still hoped I wouldn't
need to call again any time soon.

An hour later I compared that conversation to another – similar, in
that I asked for help. But the person answered with warmth, and even
called back with more information! She shared with a willingness that
left me appreciative and hopeful.

These two interactions played on my mind the rest of the day. One
individual related to me like staccato notes – in short, terse, abrupt
answers. The other reminded me of the smoothness of legato; she
connected with me in a harmonious way.

Then I thought of my own words. What do those around me hear?
Staccato or legato? Is my tone cold and short? Do I say what is necessary, but keep my distance? Or do I relate to others with a willingness to
help, a pleasant voice, and an aura of acceptance?

Colossians 4:6 says, *"Let your speech at all times be gracious
[pleasant and winsome].* (The Amplified Bible)

In music, there is room for staccato. But in my speech, I pray for
God's help to play legato on a consistent basis.

REFRESHING BREEZE

Margaret Steinacker   March 13
*"The wind blows wherever it pleases. You hear its sound,
but you cannot tell where it comes from or where it is going.
So it is with everyone born of the Spirit."* John 3:8 (NIV)

As I waited in the car, heat exhaustion seemed a distinct possibility.

In this humidity, I wished I'd stayed home and let my husband get the mulch! Then a refreshing breeze blew in the windows. I relaxed and basked in it. As a teacher, I had allowed year-end requirements to drain me, both emotionally and physically.

As the Scripture says, the wind blows where it will. I experience refreshment when I relax and enjoy it. Sometimes I sit by the river to have my devotions. When I do, I'm always refreshed physically by the gentle breeze and rippling water.

Like nature's zephyrs blow, the Spirit of God wafts into our lives. Sometimes I hear Him as I read Scripture and pray. Often I feel Him or see Him in others and this calms my soul. Throughout the four-month hospitalization and death of my best friend's husband, I saw the Holy Spirit refresh Sherry in ways only God could orchestrate. He continues to sustain her, almost two years later.

When I relax in the loving zephyr of God's grace, I find true refreshment. Even the hottest problems and the most humid circumstances can't destroy the refreshing breath of God in my life.

Suggestion: Take time today to relax, study the Scripture, and enjoy the soul-refreshing breeze of God's love in your life!

BROKEN

Paul E. Vander Wege   March 14

Read Romans 6:1-14
"Death has no power over Him."
Romans 6:9b (Life Application Bible)

I have never experienced the helplessness of being a slave, owned by someone else. I have, however, experienced the slavery of sin ruling my life. As a child, I spent many fruitless hours trying to break free from the sins of lying, cheating, and taking toys that belonged to someone else.

When I accepted Jesus as my Savior, I could say "Praise the Lord." That old liar, Satan, now has no power over me because on the cross Jesus broke sin's stranglehold. Where sin once reigned in my life, now grace abounds. All of my trespasses are forgiven; I stand guilt-free! Not only am I justified through Jesus, but I am also being sanctified through Him. So while I occasionally sin, I am free from its penalty – just as though I had never sinned.

May I then do wrong as much as I want since I am free of that guilt? The Apostle Paul emphatically says *no.* Because of Christ's death, we must no longer sin on purpose.

Father, thank You for giving Your Son of the Cross so I could be

free from the power of Satan and sin. Amen
Thought for the day: Live for Jesus today

GOD'S BREAD

Marjorie Gray   March 15

***"I am the living bread that came down from heaven.
Whoever eats of this bread will live forever"*** John 6:51 (NIV)

Three days before Aunt Ruthie died she stopped eating. The deathbed vigil with my father was similar, but he never stopped feeding on the bread of life. Dad drew his last breath as Mom was reading to him from *Just Give Me Jesus* by Anne Graham Lotz.

Beyond the idea that "seeing is believing," at a deeper level, believing is eating. Throughout our lives we come to know and trust the Savior more as the Holy Spirit energizes and synchronizes our hearts and minds to feed on Jesus.

Nutrition experts say, "You are what you eat." When we get sick, friends ask, "Was it something you ate?"

The more we devour the Living Bread, the more we become like Jesus, one with Him in His life, death and resurrection. But when we consume the dead bread of earthly heroes, our souls get sick.

Reading is like eating, too. Eugene Peterson, author of *The Message Bible*, wrote *Eat This Book,* about chewing on God's Word and digesting it into the marrow of our lives.

Old Testament appetizers such as the manna in the wilderness offer foretastes of vital Heavenly flavor. Jesus is the main course in Scripture's sumptuous banquet.

Living Bread, let more people throughout the world partake of You today. Amen

HOW DO I GET TO KNOW YOU?

Pamela S. Thibodeaux   March 16

*How do I get to know You, Lord?
Some say read the Word, others, speak the Word.
Walk the walk, talk the talk, live the life. It is so simple, yet complex.
How do I get to know You?
Is it on my knees in prayer, or standing with outstretched arms, hands up in the air, singing Your praises?
How do I get to know You?
I want to see Your face, hear Your voice, kneel at Your feet, hold You in my arms.*

How do I get to know You?

Intimacy is a mild word for the longing of my heart, the whisper of my soul, the cry of my mind. I want to know You, Lord!

As I sit staring out at the ocean, I know it's just a glimpse of Your majesty, the vastness, only an image of Your greatness.

As I contemplate this Good Friday, I wonder … what would I have done that day?

Would I have run or stood fast? How did I behave today? Are my actions today any indication of how I would have reacted that fateful day when You were crucified? I like to think that I would have stayed, stood by Your side through it all; but would I do that today?

Is it strength You want, Lord, or submission?

Honor and uprightness or humility?

I only want to know You, Lord … How do I get to know You?

A FRESH START

Brad Nelson   March 17

"Therefore if any man be in Christ, he is a new creature: old things are passed away; behold, all things are become new."
2 Corinthians 5:17 (KJV)

A man sits in a Jerusalem prison cell. He's a notorious thief, murderer and conspirator. He awaits his execution by crucifixion. His mind scans through a life filled with bad choices. If only he had one more chance, things would be different. But a fresh start is beyond the realm of possibility. He's a prisoner in a cage of his own making with no hope of freedom.

Suddenly, he's summoned. Unable to comprehend, he finds himself in the presence of the governor and an angry crowd. On his right is another man.

The governor makes a proclamation – he's going to set one prisoner free. Who? The thief is amazed when the crowd chants his name. "Barabbas, Barabbas!" His wish for deliverance is coming true! As Barabbas departs, he feels great joy at his newfound freedom, but knows it has come at the expense of another. He vows to live differently from now on.

This scene is portrayed in Matthew 27:15-23 as Barabbas is spared and Jesus condemned. It pictures a righteous transaction that takes place in the life of every believer. You are guilty of sin, and yet you are set free. Your liberty, however, comes at the price of another. Jesus has given you a fresh start. Live the rest of your life basking in the joy of this release! Live for Him who set you free!

Thank You, Father, for the high price paid for my salvation. May I live joyfully in the power of this redemption as I serve the One who set me free. Amen

FORGIVENESS

Annie Bruening   March 18

Ephesians 4:32

This verse tells us to be kind and tender-hearted to one another, forgiving one another, even as God for Christ's sake has forgiven us. If the Father can absolve us, can't we do the same for others? How important is forgiveness?

One evening while I was assisting a nursing home resident during dinner time, a program came on her television about a man who was severely injured in an accident and how he nearly died while on the operating table. He said to the audience, "You have not tuned in on this show by mistake. It is no accident you are listening right now. You are here by Divine appointment." Chilly bumps sprang up all over me!

He went on to tell how forgiveness is so important in the eyes of God. He said we are absolved to the degree we absolve others. The man didn't want us to miss out on all we could receive because there was unforgiveness in our lives. His words really impressed me.

On the 18-mile drive home, I started forgiving everyone I could think of in the precious Name of Jesus. I asked the Holy Spirit to bring to mind anyone who had ever injured, belittled, harassed, abused, or used me. I forgave them all and when I arrived home, I felt a whole lot better, like a big weight had been lifted from my shoulders.

Dearest Father, help us to forgive those who curse, hate, persecute and use us. Please let us know we don't have to be bound by hurt, if we forgive in Jesus' Name. Amen

CONTENT TO GRUMBLE

Michele L. Tune   March 19
"Not that I speak in respect of want: for I have learned, in whatsoever state I am, therewith to be content"
Philippians 4:11 (KJV)

The Apostle Paul spoke these words. We read the verse repeatedly, but do we really take it to heart? I, myself, am guilty of complaining about the state of my hair, that the weather is too hot or cold, or my day isn't going as planned.

One afternoon, I waited in the car for Mother to finish shopping at the hardware store. To pass the time, I watched folk walk by. They were in a hurry, too busy and preoccupied to enjoy the beautiful, sunny day God had graciously provided.

Then a young man on the loading dock caught my attention. I couldn't take my eyes off him. His body was crooked, and he walked with a limp. He must have been in pain, but one would never have guessed because of his radiant smile.

"It's a beautiful day today, isn't it, Ma'am?" he cheerfully commented as he carried a heavy bag of feed to his car.

"In whatsoever state I am, therewith to be content...." The words shamed my soul. How many times in my life had I failed to be content? I thought of how I'd fussed – just that morning – over petty things.

Here was someone with good reason to have a bad attitude, yet he was more pleasant than anyone around! I learned a vital lesson; I never want to be content to grumble!

HOLD ON

Valerie J. Chambers   March 20

What do you do when all is lost and
You've been called to carry your cross,
When your hopes and dreams have faded away and
darkness reigns in the middle of the day?
How do you live in the sweltering heat with
no water to drink and no food to eat,
When all that you have are the clothes on your back and
what you can carry in a small plastic sack?
You have lost all your cars and your homes and your stuff.
When it comes to sorrow, you've had more than enough.
Your children are crying and now so are you.
You have no idea what you're going to do.
The light of your future has faded away.
How will you make it the rest of the day?
My friend, there is Someone who has been there before.
He lost His palace and gained a dirt floor.
All of His stuff was taken away –
including His clothes – one fateful day.
He carried His cross in the sweltering heat.
He let them pierce His hands and His feet.
He was thirsty like you, so He asked for a drink.
He pushed on His feet so His back wouldn't kink.

50

He knows exactly what you've been going through.
He gave His life for me and for you.
If you listen closely you can hear Him say,
"Hold on, My child, I'm on the way!"

BEFORE EASTER DEVOTION

Joy Bradford   March 21

Every year I have good intentions of giving up something I care about during the period just before Easter. I desire to do this as a reminder to me of what Jesus did on the Cross. Sweets have been a good choice, as they are a weakness of mine. I've also tried eliminating television.

When it comes to considering this self-imposed "sacrifice," I am strong. But when it comes to carrying it through, I am weak. Once I slip, I consider it a failure – and go back to enjoying a slice of cake or an event on TV! Why can't I stay on mission and be more like Jesus?

While living in the human form, Jesus struggled and prayed on His journey to Jerusalem. Truly, I can relate to this. But He also remained steadfast in His journey to the Cross, knowing that His death would serve all mankind.

What Jesus did for us can be a source of renewal in our lives. I want to be a living message of love, hope and peace for those who may be seeking His Kingdom. Whatever it takes, I can't do this without being more aware of Jesus' life and sacrifice.

Father, I want to be a living sacrifice for You. As a Christian, I am called to serve. Help me to be stronger as I seek Your will. Let me use You, Jesus, as my example and help me be renewed during the holy Easter season. Amen

CONFESSION

Joseph M. Hopkins   March 22
"If we confess our sins, He (Jesus) is faithful and just and will forgive us our sins and purify us from all unrighteousness."
1 John 1:9 (NASB)

Only one thing is necessary in order for our sins to be forgiven: confession. And of course that means more than reporting our sins to the Lord. He already knows them! It means being genuinely sorry we have sinned, admitting our guilt, and earnestly seeking God's for-giveness. Jesus said, **"Unless you repent, you will all perish."** (Luke 13:4)

Former President Ford has been criticized for pardoning Richard Nixon for crimes to which he never confessed guilt! Jesus prayed for His murderers and the mob which hatefully mocked and spat upon Him as He hung upon the Cross. *"Father, forgive them, for they do not know what they are doing."* (Luke 23:34) I call this "Jesus' un-answered prayer," for without repentance there can be no forgive-ness.

"Confession isn't easy," wrote E. Stanley Jones, "(because) self-surrender means a basic change of the center – from self to Christ."

Sin is the hallmark of the self-centered life; righteousness, of the life that is centered in Jesus Christ.

Loving and gracious Heavenly Father, please forgive our sins of thought, word, and deed – or commission as well as omission. Help us to surrender our lives to Jesus, whose indwelling Holy Spirit alone can empower us to live obediently to Your will. This we pray in His holy name. Amen

"MY REDEEMER LIVETH"

Willie B. White **Resurrection Day** March 23
Job 19:25

Who is our redeemer? Jesus Christ was born of a virgin, ministered to the world as man and God, and then died on the cross at Calvary for the sins of the world. Why did Jesus die for humanity? We had broken our fellowship with God the Father, and were destined for eternal separation from Him.

Therefore, God the Father gave His only begotten Son to redeem or buy back men's souls from the clutches of Satan. We owe our lives, loyalty and gratitude to Jesus Christ for His redeeming work at Calvary. More importantly, He did not remain on the cross nor in His borrowed grave. The good news is that on Sunday morning our Savior rose with all power in His hands to heal the sick, mend broken hearts, comfort us when we are troubled, and provide salvation so that we may spend eternity with Him.

In the words of Job, *"I know my redeemer liveth,"* (Job 19:25 KJV) because He cares for our every need. He is there to lead, guide, and protect us in the midst of all life's struggles.

Finally, as we celebrate this Resurrection Day, we do so with the knowledge and gratitude that our sins have been blotted out by Jesus' redemptive death on the cross. We are compelled to sing praises to God. Christ is alive. Hallelujah! We have salvation!

CRUCIFIXION THORNS

Penny Deary   March 24

***"For since the creation of the world His invisible attributes are
clearly seen, being understood by the things that are made, even
His eternal power and Godhead,
so that they are without excuse."*** Romans 1:20 (NKJV)

His beauty and artistry embrace us.
Little brown birds dance in coastal sage;
Graceful red-tail hawk soars
Above splashy sycamore
And clinging chaparral.
Voices soften, awe abounds.
His creation attests to His magnificence.
Spirits awaken!
Crucifixion thorns tell the story –
The fall, the cross,
The sacrifice,
His rise to Glory.

*O Lord, open our eyes that we may see the story You tell in all that
surrounds us. You display Your power and magnificence for man to
see and acknowledge You as the great Creator! Amen*

FASTING OR FEASTING?

Joanna Ronalds   March 25

Read Zechariah 7:1-7

***"Ask all the people of the land and the priests, 'When you fasted
and mourned in the fifth and seventh months for the past seventy
years, was it really for me that you fasted? And when you were
eating and drinking, were you not just feasting for yourselves?***
'"Zechariah 7:5-6 (NIV)

Fasting appears to be referred to in the Bible more often than it is
talked about by Christians today. It's a practice that seems a bit unfash-
ionable, and has gone the way of sackcloth and ashes – a little too BC,
really. Or is it just that Christians who fast today don't talk about it?

I, for one, admit that I have never spent a day or even part of a day
fasting, let alone two months a year for 70 years (not that I have yet
lived that long). I have serious doubts that I would be able to abstain for
the right reasons. I think I would probably focus more on the weight that
I would hope to lose than on God.

So why is God questioning His people about fasting, through the prophet Zechariah? Because He doesn't want them to claim to be doing something for Him when really they are doing it for themselves. Fasting isn't about weight loss, nor about what other people think. Why would God care today about the motives behind our actions? Because whether we are fasting or feasting, it is all about Him.

THOUGHTS ON BEING YOUR HOME

Charles A. Waugaman   March 26

"Jesus replied, 'If anyone loves me, he will obey my teaching. My Father will love him, and we will come to him and make our home with him.'" John 14:23 (NIV)

Lord, the thought of my body being Your temple of residence is comforting and disconcerting.

The warmth of knowing You so near is lifting and reassuring. Your closeness keeps me strong against many of the "big" sins of human awareness, although certainly not all. And it does push me more quickly to remorse and confession.

But when I realize You feel each little fever of complaint, every chill of worry and fear, each unbalancing doubt, I grow apprehensive. As You must know, I try to ignore many of my doubts and wanderings, anxieties and negative ponderings. How can I confess what I won't admit? How can I reject faults I purposely keep invisible?

I pride myself that I am not so naïve as Jonah, going the other direction and thinking You don't notice. But pride is as silly as grief over a shrinking gourd. I don't think Jonah ever knew Your indwelling. Jesus taught us that. But maybe I'm as naïve, thinking You don't have ways to teach Your people except through Your written Word.

Help me not to measure against anything or anyone but Your own compassionate yardstick. Forgive my doubt. Create in me a willing heart. Lead me – from within – in the way everlasting. Thank You. Amen

A SELF-FOCUSED LIFE

Connie Ansong   March 27

"For the mind set on the flesh is death, but the mind set on the Spirit is life and peace." Romans 8:6 (NASB)

When we turn from the Lord, life becomes "all about us." And a self-focused life plants the seeds of its own destruction. God's goal is to transform us into His image/character. And, as we cooperate with His plan of spiritual metamorphosis, we train our minds to dwell on the things of God rather than on the things of the flesh.

The love we have from the Lord, is *"patient, it is kind, it does not envy; love does not boast, it is not arrogant, it does not behave rudely; it does not seek its own interest."* This passage in 1 Corinthians 13:4 teaches us that love should be number one on our spiritual priority list. The study of it will reveal a lot about our Lord's affection for us and since God is love, we abide in His love when we *walk* in it. Our focus and interest must be on God's Word and the Kingdom of God.

O Lord! You are our God; we seek You and our souls thirst for You. Please give us Your sense of order to stay focused and do Your will. Lord, give us the spirit of hearing, understanding and knowledge of Your death on the cross and Your resurrection. Lord, keep us close to You and help us to live for Your glorification. In Jesus' name we pray with thanksgiving. Amen

FATHER, FORGIVE US

Donna Arndt   March 28

Forgive us, Father, for doubting,
For becoming discouraged when our thoughts run astray.
For leaning on our own understanding,
And not remembering Your higher way.
Forgive us for not focusing on the awesome things You've done;
On the glory of Your creation, green trees, blue sky, warm sun.
We take so much for granted,
Our food, the clothes we wear.
We complain and say, "I hate this job.
It pays nothing, and it's taking me nowhere."
We forget there are people starving, and children with no bed.
There are those who would give their lives
For just a morsel of our bread.
Forgive us for not helping, or giving as we should;
For forgetting to share Your message, that all things work for good.
Forgive us, Lord, for questioning the trials You take us through.
Please help us, Holy Father, to turn our thoughts toward You –
And, dear Father – launch us out of our lethargy
And make us what we ought to be!

CHANGING THE UGLY

Bill Batcher   March 29

Imagine approaching a house of worship. Glancing up, you see the steeple is capped by a gallows! Or inside, hanging over the altar is a guillotine. Or one of the stained glass windows depicts an electric chair. Bizarre? Macabre? Yes. What religion would deliberately select as its primary symbol an object used for public, state-sponsored execution? What religion? Christianity.

There was nothing attractive or beautiful about a cross in the Roman Empire. It stood for torture and heavy-handed justice; it served as a morbid lesson of what happened when someone opposed the occupiers. The cross was even more shameful to the Jewish sensibilities, for the Torah taught that *"...anyone who is hung on a tree is under God's curse."* (Deuteronomy 21:23)

Yet Paul declared, *"The message of the cross is foolishness to those who are perishing, but to us who are being saved it is the power of God."* 1 Corinthians 1:18 (KJV)

Soon after Christ established His church, the cross, the object of scorn, became one of reverence. The crucifix, with Jesus' body on it, reminded Christians of His sacrifice, and the empty cross of resurrection. It was changed from something ugly into something beautiful!

That is how God works in the world – and in each of our lives – changing the ugly into the beautiful.

MY CHILD BRINGS LAUGHTER

Ruth Baldwin   March 30

"And whoever receives one such child in My name receives Me." Matthew 18:5 (NASB)

Mother liked to tell this story:

"Radio was a unique invention in my daughter Ruth's preschool days. She loved a program of Hawaiian music, and listened to it every time it was broadcast. When summer came, our church held Sunday evening services outside at individual members' homes. We hosted many of these services.

"One night as we were singing a hymn, I heard someone belting out a Hawaiian song at the top of her lungs. It was Ruth! I'd had no idea that she knew such a song. I don't recall the words, except the last ones; 'My hippy, hippy hula girl. MY-Y-Y-Y-Y hippy, hippy hula girl!' I was so embarrassed, but I laughed. Ruth's sister grabbed her arm and rushed her to the back of the house.

"'You don't sing songs like that!' she exclaimed. *'Especially in church!'*" Mother and Dad didn't scold me for singing that song. They thought it was just an innocent childish antic. They accepted me as I was. They loved me, and rejoiced that I brought laughter into their midst.

How like that is God's love! We don't have to earn it – in fact, we **cannot** earn it. He loved us first, and sent us His Son to bring us close to Him. I praise Him for this, and think that perhaps even God laughed when I sang that happy, melodious song!

IT'S THAT SIMPLE

Judy Barron   March 31

"My father, if the prophet had told you to do something great, would you not have done it? How much more, then, when he says to you, 'Wash, and be clean?'" 2 Kings 5:13 (NKJV)

So often we think that if we aren't asked to do something really difficult, the result is not worthwhile. For instance: We should exercise hard! Struggle mightily! Sweat and groan! Then we'll get the results we seek.

So when we're told, "Have faith and believe and you will be saved," we think it can't be that simple! We think we must perform great tasks or make great sacrifices to be worthy.

We never seem to learn that God's saving grace does not depend on our worthiness, but is totally independent of anything we can do. We must have faith and believe – God will do the rest! It really is that simple. Thank God that our salvation does *not* depend upon us!

Father, please help me to show others Your straightforward plan for salvation for all. In Jesus' name I pray. Amen

APRIL
MONEY AND GOOD WORKS

Annie Bruening   April 1

Read Nehemiah 5:1-19

"I also applied myself to the work on this wall; we did not buy any land, and all my servants were gathered there for the work."
Nehemiah 5:16 (NASB)

How many times have we hired Christian business people to do a job for us, and were ashamed and dissatisfied with their shoddy work? And we're from the same family! What do unbelievers think about Christians who perform like this? What message do we send others by our bad work habits?

As I work in a nursing home, do I pretend I don't see a room light on, or that I don't hear the room bells and emergency lights flashing? Do I ignore the food stuck hard on the floor or tray tables? Do I leave the stain on a bottom sheet for the next shift to change? Do I neglect work for which I am responsible so that others have to do it?

Who is watching us? We may never know until we get to Heaven and face a righteous God.

Dear Father, may we – at the end of a work day say – like Nehemiah, "Remember me, my God, for good, according to all that I have done for this people."

FAVORABLE OR UNFAVORABLE

Margaret Steinacker   April 2

Suggested reading: II Timothy 4:1-8

"...proclaim the message; be persistent whether the time is favorable or unfavorable; convince, rebuke, and encourage, with the utmost patience in teaching."
II Timothy 4:2 (NRSV)

Scripture tells us to expect both favorable and unfavorable times in life.

During college, I cleaned houses for a middle-class beautician and a rich woman whose husband had designed homes with Frank Lloyd Wright. Their social status had no effect on my job frustration. Both required repeated, boring cleaning. I had to psych myself into remembering that the monetary reward would outweigh the monotony. The bleached blond beautician had three rooms of tiled floors. Short and long hairs of every color and texture lurked in every seam and corner. That rich woman had a remodeled garage with large windows on three sides, covered with wooden Venetian blinds, which the owner required me to wash, dry and wax *every week.*

As we strive to live for Christ today, bothersome hairs and boring blinds will sneak into our daily existence. The hairs may come in the form of a volunteer job to help fold and collate the monthly newsletter or crease the weekly bulletin; a repetitious task with thanks from the congregation being nonexistent. The blinds may appear as meals delivered to shut-ins, when the repetitious route seems boring and the recipients critical. But when our goal is to show Christ to others, whatever the bother, we press on with patience and encouragement.

"But God has promised: strength for the day,
rest for the labor, light for the way,
grace for the trials, help from above,

unfailing sympathy, undying Love."
(Annie Johnson Flint)
"Yesterday is experience, Tomorrow is hope,
Today is getting from one to the other."
(Author Unknown)

A GUSHING SPRING

Lorena M. Estep   April 3

"Jesus answered, *'Everyone who drinks this water will be thirsty again, but whoever drinks the water I give him will never thirst. Indeed, the water I give him will become in him a spring of water welling up to eternal life.'"* John 4:13-14 (NIV)

We were experiencing a drought and our well was running low. With two acres of flower gardens that needed water, we had to find an alternative.

We gathered all the empty gallon jugs we could find, took them to a public spring several miles away, and filled them.

I was awed anew by the huge amount of water that continually gushed from the side of the mountain and out a pipe that had been installed. This constant flow had never ceased for as long as I could remember.

I thought of Jesus, who is referred to as a spring of living water in the Bible. I pictured his life-giving Spirit flowing through us as constant as that gushing spring, freshening and strengthening as we live our lives for Him.

Lord Jesus, thank You for being a spring of living water welling up within us, giving eternal life to all who seek You. Amen

HOLY CLAY

Charlotte Burkholder   April 4

A lump of clay became a man,
Fitting for the Creator's plan.
I, too, am clay, my life He holds.
With gentle hands He shapes and molds.
I smugly wait; the pressure's kind.
His hands have stopped! What did He find?
A piercing shard, like splintered glass,
An attitude before me flashed.
Quickly, Father, wash me, do –
Lest I pierce Your hands anew.
(Published in "Purpose" March 1992)

PERMEATING LIGHT

Paul Soderberg   April 5

Read John 1:1-9

*"That was the true Light, which lighteth every man
that cometh into the world."* John 1:9 (KJV)

Can you see in the dark? Back in the 1950s the military used the
M-3 sniper scope for that purpose. It was based on black light or
infrared. Infra is illumination below the visible spectrum and the brightness of heat. When you radiate warmth, you radiate light in that wave
length and the scope, which amplifies heat, allows you to see light in
the dark.

We live in a dark world. No wonder! Jesus said Satan was the
Prince of this world. (John 14:30) As a Christian I need to be an ambi-
ent light in the darkness, radiating as much brightness as I can into this
evil, wicked world. Also, I want to dawn like new morning sunlight,
chasing away the shadows of night.

Now, as a follower of Christ, I am indwelt by the invisible light of the
Holy Spirit. He helps me glow without an electronic device. His wave-
length is the power of the Almighty and can amplify beyond my wildest
imagination!

*Lord God Almighty, let me be a lighthouse exuding a visible light
into the world. Let me be like sparkling rays, bright with joy, hope and
happiness, diminishing the darkness through Your Spirit. Keep me
shining with Your light to guide me through the tempests of the world. I
pray this in Jesus' most precious name. Amen*

JESUS RESISTED

Evelyn Minshull   April 6

Luke 4:1-13

When the Holy Spirit led Jesus into the wilderness, it was not a
wilderness of fragrant pines and verdant ferns, but desert – hot and dry
and barren.

There Jesus hungered for forty days and forty nights and, because
He was famished, Satan urged Him to turn stones into bread. But
Jesus refused.

When the Holy Spirit led Jesus into the wilderness, it was not a
wilderness of bluebird song and busy squirrels, but desert – vast,
shadowed emptiness, and slithering lizards. Then there was Satan's
patient prodding, his insistent wheedling: *"Only worship me, and I will
grant You power."*

"Throw Yourself down from this high point – and let the angels catch You."

But although Jesus' body was weakened by hunger, although He was physically spent, He resisted each temptation.

O, God, temptations surround us each moment of the day. Help us always to remember that spiritual nourishment is to be preferred above bread, and that true power comes only through You. Amen

SHAKE THE DUST

Michele L. Tune   April 7

"But Jesus beheld [them], and said unto them, With men this is impossible; but with God all things are possible."
Matthew 19:26 (KJV)

This Scripture came to mind one afternoon as Mother read an ad for a Writer's Guild meeting in the newspaper. She said, "Michele, that meeting is next Saturday and you are going – regardless!"

"What?" I asked, awestruck.

"It's time that you do something with your writing talent," she said sternly.

"Okay," I agreed.

I'd always dreamed of being a "published author." But life and domestic violence reined my dreams to a screeching halt.

Days flew by, but Saturday arrived – and we went! The Guild's president assigned a quiz. "Write about an experience concerning which you never thought you'd say *'I'm glad I went through that.'*"

When it came my time to read, I was terrified! I felt vulnerable exposing my heart and soul to strangers. However, I read what I had written. When I finished, I looked around the table and noticed tear-filled eyes.

"Michele, that was beautiful!" one member exclaimed.

A little over a year has passed, and now I'm the president of our local Writer's Guild! Just like the Scripture says, **"...with God all things are possible...."** I know that in myself it's still impossible, but through Him all of my writing dreams are coming true!

Lord, shine on those who write for Your glory. Help us rise above our pasts, dig out our manuscripts, shake the dust, and submit! Amen

WHY IS IT?

Norm MacDonald   April 8

Read Romans 7:21-25

"What a wretched man I am! Who will rescue me from

this body of death? Thanks be to God –
through Jesus Christ our Lord...!" Romans 7:24 (KJV)

Why is it that we can be totally absorbed in one thing then –
suddenly – find ourselves wallowing in some activity we know is not
pleasing to God?

Why is it we can be at peace one minute and in total upheaval the
next? What was a blissful stream yesterday seems like brackish water
today.

There seems to be precious little justice in our world when this
happens. We want to punish ourselves beyond measure and subject
ourselves to all manner of insults. After all, what kind of Christian could
harbor such unpleasantness? What sort of mind could wrap itself
around Scripture in the morning and be selfishly sinful in the afternoon?

Oh, did I mention we are human? That might explain some of it.
Besides, we are in good company. The Apostle Paul found himself in
the same boat when he confessed "what a wretched man I am!"

Who can bring order to this kind of chaos? Who can get us off this
seesaw and restore balance? Thank God, the answer is in Jesus Christ
our Lord.

*Father, I wish I could say that my thoughts are always pure, my
desires always sincere, but they are not. My prayer is that You will help
me recognize that Christ has rescued me! I am no longer a victim, but a
victor in Christ Jesus. Amen*

AS FOR ME AND MY HOUSE
Joan Clayton   April 9
*"Thou shalt not bow down thyself unto them, nor serve them: for
I the Lord thy God am a jealous God, visiting the iniquity of the
fathers upon the children unto the third and fourth generation of
them that hate me."* Deuteronomy 5:9 (KJV)

I have come to know in a painful way the meaning of the above
Scripture. I worked with precious children for 31 years and I have seen
the devastation of sin and its effect on the lives of little ones.

Children are such treasures! It's heartbreaking to see them suffer
from someone else's sin.

Achan's entire family lost their lives because of his. (Joshua 7:24)

Eli sinned when he didn't restrain his sons, leading to dire consequences. (1 Samuel 3:13)

A happy home filled with the love of God is every child's birthright.
Children live what they see. What they see is what they become. I don't

62

want my children or grandchildren suffering because of my sins. I want young, tender lives built with love, faith, and trust in God because of my witness. I agree with Joshua when he said, *"As for me and my house, we will serve the Lord."* (Joshua 24:17)

Dear precious Lord, we praise and thank You today for the gift of children. May we seek Your wisdom and guidance daily in leading them. Amen

GOOD INTENTIONS TORPEDOED

Neil Fitzgerald   April 10

"It is idle to say God does not hear or that the Almighty does not take notice." Job 35:13 (NASB)

One summer during World War II when I was a young boy, my friends and I decided to have a lemonade stand. Since I lived on a main street a few blocks from a busy park and zoo, our business venture thrived.

At the end of the summer, proud of our accomplishment, we donated our profits to the local USO to buy cigarettes for our service men. Our actions even merited a picture and story in the local newspaper!

At the time we didn't realize what we did was damaging their health! One might say we were even aiding the enemy.

People often misjudge others by what they say or do. Thankfully, God always knows our intentions and the attitudes of our hearts, and that is all that really matters.

"WHAT, ME WORRY?"

Joseph M. Hopkins   April 11

This is the quote that made Alfred E. Neuman famous. Or was it vice versa? Anyway, it brings to mind *Mad Magazine's* famous cover boy. The implication of the cartoon is that normal people worry.

My mother was a fretter. When told not to brood, she'd reply, "I reckon I worry the least of any woman in Laurel. Facing facts isn't worry!"

Do you fret? I do. Yet the Bible tells us we shouldn't. Jesus said, *"Do not worry about your life, what you will eat or drink, or about your body, what you will wear...Who of you by worrying can add a single hour to his life?"* Matthew 6:25-27 (KJV)

Ian Maclaren observed, "What does your anxiety do? It doesn't empty tomorrow of its sorrow, but it does empty today of its strength. It doesn't make you escape the evil; it makes you unfit to cope with it when it comes." Another pundit likens worry to a rocking chair: "It'll give you something to do, but it won't get you anywhere."

So why do it? The apostle Paul admonishes, *"Do not be anxious about anything, but in everything, by prayer and petition, with thanksgiving, present your requests to God. And the peace of God, which transcends all understanding, will guard your hearts and your minds in Christ Jesus."* Philippians 4:6-7

Dear Father in Heaven, help me to refrain from worrying and to follow Paul's advice. Today I will trust You to solve all my problems as I surrender them to You for guidance and empowerment. Amen

BLASÈ

Lisa Hill   April 12

Although enamored by all things French, I despise the word *blasé*. Yet to my consternation, I found myself suffering from such apathy. Somewhere along the way, I just stopped caring. I stopped fighting, stopped striving and became complacent.

Since I'd been a Christian for well over two decades, my *Christianese* was flawless, and my lip-service passable, but my devotions were dry and unemotional. Somewhere deep in my soul, the Holy Spirit whispered, "You need help," but I ignored the small voice.

God didn't let me alone. He reminded me of all I was missing – the fellowship with Him, the secret revelations, and learning more about Him and His Word. Finally, my brain snapped to attention; I was ready to walk with God again!

I picked up my Bible, my devotionals, my prayer journal and did all the things I used to do – but didn't experience God. I began to panic, seek council and pray more, but still I made no progress.

My faithful God met me. He led me to a class about studying the Word. I went expecting to hone my study skills, and instead became refreshed by the Holy Spirit. Soon I was back on track, lost in the cares of others instead of my own selfish desires.

God showed me that we all change and my same old pursuit had become stale. What joy to break old habits and follow Him in a fresh, new way!

64

THE ENGRAVING

Lillian Lewis   April 13
Based on Isaiah 49:16 and Jeremiah 31:3

"You are engraved on the palms of my hands," God said.

Not my name, but me.
Who and what I am, my personality, my being.
Engraving is for remembering.
"I will not forget you," God said,
And engraved me on the palms of His hands.
He did the engraving with nails on the Cross
Where He died, remembering me.
Resurrected, He returned to glory
With me engraved on the palms of His hands,
Remembering me.
When He closes His hands, He holds me safe.
As He opens them, He sets me free to fullness of life.
Remembered still,
I am engraved on the palms of His hands.

FOUNDATION OF BLESSINGS

Violet Herlocker   April 14
*"Today you have completed the foundation for my temple,
so listen to what your future will be like. Although you have not
yet harvested any grain, grapes, figs, pomegranates, or olives,
I will richly bless you in the days ahead."* Haggai 2:18-19 (CEV)

My runner friends tell me that completing the race is the reason
they run. If they do not win the big prize, crossing that finish line is a
reward. Even the Bible stresses the importance of finishing the course,
or the work set before us.

The book of Haggai has a special word from God on this very thing.
God said, *"From this day I will bless you."* Was it the day that the
Israelites completed the temple? No, it was the day that they laid the
foundation and began the task of rebuilding the walls. It was the day
that they showed the commitment to work toward the goal, not the day
they reached it.

My charge is to work steadily toward the objective God has set
before me. Maybe I'll make the finish line, maybe I will not; but God will
bless my efforts along the way.

Father, give me a spirit of persistence. Even when I cannot see the

*finish line, let me never lose sight of Your promise to bless my faithful-
ness in continuing toward the goal. Amen*

LANTERN ON THE PLOW
Jana Carman   April 15

Road repairs on busy highways are sometimes scheduled for the
less trafficked, dark hours. Farmers trying to get their crops planted or
harvested work well into the night, thanks to headlights. In this day of
artificial lighting, it can be done. But what we can do easily in daylight –
work, walk – becomes difficult or impossible in the dark.

The old-fashioned phrase, "lantern on the plow," translates today
into headlights on the tractor. With them the work can be done, but not
as easily or as well. Jesus said, *"Walk while you have the light,
before darkness overtakes you."* John 12:35-36 (NIV)

Night is coming. There has never been a day without night.

But also, there has never been night without dawn! Often, another
opportunity will come. However, procrastination pushes today's work
into tomorrow's. Eventually something important gets left undone
because there is not enough time to do it. While you have the light,
walk, work, visit, witness, or .... You fill in the blank!

OTHERS, NOT OF THIS FOLD
Marjorie Gray   April 16
*"And I have other sheep (beside these), that are not of this fold.
I must bring and impel those also, and they will listen to My voice
and heed My call, and so there will be one flock
under one Shepherd.* John 10:16 (Amplified)

At eleven o'clock on a Sunday in spring
People gather to celebrate life with new zing.
In cathedrals, in storefronts, in homes or outdoors
They are meeting and singing of Christ's life restored.
What of others, the many not present today?
Without family some languish, with money some play.
Our divisions still multiply, tarnishing zest.
Good Shepherd Jesus, show us how to welcome guests.

REUNION
Dave Evans   April 17

Some have been gone for years,

Others more recently –
Now only fond memories live on;
Absence, an emptiness where once
Companionship, conversation, and love
Were shared
We long for the touch of their hands,
The soothing words from their lips,
The love from their hearts to ours;
All sorrowfully missed
But one day those in Christ
Will be our welcoming committee –
Beloved friends and family;
A receiving line to usher us into
The presence of the Father
And an indescribable reunion
Lasting forever!

"For now we see in a mirror dimly, but then face to face; Now know in part, but then I will know fully just as I have been fully known." 1 Corinthians 13:12 (NASB)

"…and He will wipe away every tear from their eyes; and There will be no longer be any death; there will no longer be any mourning, or crying, or pain; the first things have passed away." Revelation 21:4 (NASB)

THE RAINBOW DRYER

Leigh DeLozier   April 18

"Cleanse me with hyssop, and I will be clean; wash me, and I will be whiter than snow." Psalm 51:7 (NIV)

I opened the dryer door to take out the huge load of laundry – and stopped in my tracks. Red, blue and yellow streaks and spots covered all the clothes, and every inch of the dryer itself!

The culprits? Three crayon stubs melted onto the lint filter.

On their own, the crayons were innocent enough – just something to keep a child occupied and happy for a while. But the dryer's heat changed them completely – and affected everything around them.

The same is true for us, and for every aspect of our lives. Sometimes the smallest things have a much bigger impact than we expect. A sharp word can put a child in a grumpy mood all day and affect his schoolwork. But an extra bit of patience and a hug as he heads out the door can also affect him – in a much better way.

I spent the next couple of days experimenting to find the best cleanser for the dryer and laundry, and eventually got things unsmudged. The challenge for us as Christians is to do the same thing – watch for the spots and streaks in our lives and repeatedly go to the best Cleanser of all so He can wash us as white as snow.

FEAR OF POVERTY

Rose Goble   April 19

Read: Matthew 19:16-26 (NIV)
"It is hard for a rich man to enter the kingdom of heaven."
Matthew 19:23c (NIV)

Jesus said it was easier for a camel to get on its knees and crawl through a narrow gate than for the rich to make it into Heaven!

Why do we worship our money or hang onto it so tightly?

The prodigal son discovered that wealth buys only temporary friends and enjoyment. When it's gone, nothing is left but an empty heart. However, if God fills the heart, cups overflow.

The rich are afraid of being poor. They enjoy their position and rest in the security of its power. They haven't discovered the manna and quail that God provides to replace their life of plenty. So, how much does it take to make one rich? A child with a dime or toy finds it difficult to share his plenty. Tithing frightens those who have never discovered how God stretches the leftovers.

The giving of offerings is God's method for us to share our blessings and receive a multiplied blessing in return! God told us to test Him in Malachi 3:10: *"Bring all the tithes into the storehouse so that there will be food enough in my Temple; if you do, I will open up the windows of heaven for you and pour out a blessing so great you won't have room enough to take it in! Try it! Let me prove it to you!"* (TLB)

GIVE AND TAKE

Charles Harrel   April 20

Read: Job 1:8-22
"The LORD gave, and the LORD has taken away;
blessed be the name of the LORD." Job 1:21b (NKJV)

Give and take – an interesting combination! These two words are the same ones my mother used on my wedding day. She told me the best marriages were ones established by give-and-take relationships. She felt partnerships so based were more intimate and provided for stronger family bonds. The Lord had a similar relationship in mind for an individual named Job.

Satan intended to destroy Job's relationship with the Lord by causing embarrassment in Heaven, but Satan misjudged their bond. God had given much to Job over the years, but Job never based his relationship on what he received. Instead, he founded his affinity on trust, respect, and worship. So, when God allowed certain things to be taken away, Job's confidence never wavered. *"**In all this Job did not sin nor charge God with wrong.**"* Job 1:22 (NKJV)

He knew his relationship was being tested; God knew it was growing stronger and more intimate. In the end, God exalted and honored Job for his faith.

Try not to worry during seasons of unexplained misfortune. God might be building your faith for a stronger relationship with Him!

Thank You, dear Lord, for the giving and taking times in our relationship. I know You allow them both for a reason, and like Job, I will trust You. Amen

ASK, SEEK, KNOCK

Shannon Dubois   April 21
Read Mathew 7:7-11
"Ask and it will be given to you; seek and you will find; knock and the door will be opened." Mathew 7:7 (NIV)

Bang! Startled, I looked toward the noise. *Nothing but clear glass – I bet another bird just mistakenly crashed into our patio door.* When I explored further, sure enough, on the bottom rail of one of our outside chairs perched a brown sparrow, motionless. He looked dead, stunned probably, and no doubt succumbing to a headache that only an overdose of Tylenol could cure.

Unfortunately, this sparrow and I had a lot in common: running into closed doors. One of my deepest faults was barreling head-first into things, thinking hard work, determination, and energy were all I needed to be successful. No wonder my head hurt. Independence and stubbornness were as deceitful as a freshly cleaned window.

God doesn't want us to do it alone. We were designed to be dependent on Him, to ask for His help, to seek for His guidance – to *knock* at His door. He wants our neediness and our companionship. He wants to bless us. He wants us to come in.

Lord, help us to ask, seek, and knock in prayer as we travel through life. Amen

Thought for the Day

Do I ask for God's guidance and blessings first – or do I ask Him to pick up the pieces afterward?

SERVING AS JESUS DID

Lydia Harris   April 22

Read Philippians 2:5-11

"Christ Jesus made himself nothing, taking the very nature of a servant, being made in human likeness." Philippians 2:7 ((NIV)

While in college, I worked for a wealthy family. I cleaned, cooked, and served meals in exchange for room, board, and a small salary. Although I ate separately at the kitchen counter, I considered myself a family friend.

One day my employer asked me to help her married daughter with a dinner party. When the woman arrived, she said, "I'm here to pick up the maid." At first I wondered who she meant – then realized she meant me! The title of *"maid"* held a negative stigma, and I felt humiliated.

But Jesus didn't respond this way. Although He was God, he didn't cling to His status. No, He left all the glories of Heaven, took on the nature of a servant, and was made in human likeness. (verses 6-8) That's why God exalted Him and gave Him a name above all names. (verse 9) And one day everyone will *"confess that Jesus Christ is Lord, to the glory of God the Father."* (verse 11)

I hope I've matured since college and would no longer feel insulted if called "the maid." To be great in God's Kingdom, I must follow Christ's example and serve others. (Matthew 20:26)

Lord Jesus, forgive my pride and desire to be exalted. Help me to reflect Your attitude of humility, gladly serving others. Amen

LITTLE CLAY POT

Daisy Townsend   April 23

Read 1 Corinthians 1:18-31

"But we have this treasure in jars of clay to show that this all-surpassing power is from God and not from us."
2 Corinthians 4:7 (NIV)

Last summer God showed me clearly that He found His greatest pleasure in my willingness to be just a little clay pot that would not detract in any way from Jesus – the awesome Treasure that I carried within. I was so impressed by the importance of this concept that I began to search for a plain, little clay pot to put on my windowsill to remind me of my purpose.

To my amazement, it seemed that every one of the type that I wanted had a very large price tag on it – always a higher price than I was willing to pay! As God continued to work in my life, I began to realize that there is also a very high cost involved in becoming just a little clay pot – denying self, embracing the cross, and promoting Christ rather than ourselves.

In theory, most Christians would acknowledge the desirability of being just a little clay pot, but when faced with the reality, many discover that the price is higher than they are willing to pay.

Forgive us, Father, when our desire for recognition and praise outweighs our desire to bring glory to You. Amen

Thought for the Day

Vessels of clay are the most appropriate containers
for showing God's glory.

Prayer Focus: Those tempted by self-promotion

A WILLING HEART

Evelyn Heinz   April 24

"Know the God of your father and serve Him with whole heart and a willing mind." 1 Chronicles 28:9 (NASB)

Lord, like my father before me,
I choose to serve You.
I give my heart to You,
Use it as You will.
I yield to You my all,
Serving others in the best way I know.
Thank You, Lord,
For guiding me to those in need of You.

LET ME BE SALTY

Elouise H. Hults   April 25

"Salt is good, but if the salt has lost his saltness, wherewith will ye season it? Have salt in yourselves...."
Mark 9:50 (KJV)

It had been many years since I had made bread from scratch (dissolving yeast, kneading the dough, etc.) But I was drawn to attempt it again. However, just when the dough was ready to be placed into loaf pans, I realized I had forgotten salt! At that point, it was too late to add it.

So the loaves of bread were baked and eaten. They looked and smelled delicious, but were disappointing. Once more I made the same recipe. This time I was careful not to forget the salt. This bread was *m-m-m-m* good! What a difference seasoning makes!

As born again Christians, we represent Christ. If we live our lives without salt, our witness is bland. We must fill ourselves with the truth and boldness of Christ – become salty, tasty and appetizing. The saltiness we exhibit brings sanity and conviction to the world system. It draws unbelievers to us and inevitably to Jesus. All this attraction causes us to be – as old-timers used to say – "worth our salt" – a perfect loaf of bread.

Lord, season my life with Your Word. I want to be so flavored with salt that I will draw souls unto You. Amen

COMPLETELY ACCEPTED

Donna J. Howard   April 26

Read Mark 5:1-20

"And they came to Jesus and observed the man who had been demon-possessed sitting down, clothed and in his right mind."
Mark 5:15 (NASB)

A friend and I study the Bible together. In one lesson, about the demon-possessed man, we were asked to put ourselves in his place. I was sure I wouldn't be able to identify with the demoniac for I had never suffered the humiliation and inhumane treatment that he did. To my surprise, it was not as difficult as I expected. All I had to do was see myself standing before Jesus with all my sins in full view. In my mind's eye, I could "see" the scars and scabs of sin on my life.

Like the demoniac, I felt ashamed. I fell on my knees before the Lord and asked for forgiveness, cleansing and healing of my fragmented life. Just as He looked at the demoniac with love and compassion, I could see Him looking at me in the same way! I then felt the guilt and shame slide from me, and the brilliance of Christ's love flow over me. I felt completely accepted.

Are you feeling the pain of guilt and shame because of sin in your life? If so, confess your sin to the Lord and ask Him to forgive you. I promise you that He will!

BLOOMING HOPE

Elizabeth Van Hook   April 27

"The grass withers and the flowers fall, but the Word of our God stands forever." Isaiah 40:8 (NIV)

Dew glistens in the morning sunlight on the pink begonias in the garden. They remind me of a plant my sister once gave me – with instructions not to over-water! Its delicate flowers bloomed through

Thanksgiving! Temperatures dropped, and so did the petals. Only a stem remained. I couldn't throw it away. Life-threatening illnesses in my family had made me sensitive toward life in all forms. My sister faced surgery. One cousin had a mastectomy and brain tumor. Another suffered from pancreatic cancer.

All winter I prayed for them as I watered the withered stem. Suddenly, new leaves appeared – then a petal! It bloomed! I cried. When life seemed darkest, colors of life appeared.

Dottie is improving. George died, released from his pain. Patty continues to battle cancer, and had a stroke. She is now expecting her first grandchild and clings to life.

My life has changed, too. I gave my plants away when I moved. But the florist delivered one today from a suffering friend! A delicate butterfly – symbol of new life – centered the arrangement.

Each time I water my plant I am reminded to pray for the sick, to praise God for His healing, and to thank Him for peace as we go through the problems of life!

Father, help us not to take life for granted. I thank You for the flowers in Your creation that give us hope. Amen

HANG ON TIGHT

Annette Irby   April 28

**"For I know the plans I have for you, says the Lord.
Plans for good and not for evil. To give you a future and a hope."**
Jeremiah 29:11 (NKJV)

Today was the big day! I knew this morning that this was it, so I waited and waited for news. I tried to concentrate on other activities throughout the day, but my mind kept tracking back. It was so hard to be patient! Then, the news came! The baby had arrived! And it was a girl! Mom and baby were fine so I could relax again.

Sometimes God asks us to wait. He's working out His character in us. Patience. Long-suffering. Trust. The challenge is to trust God through the whole process, knowing by faith that what He promised He will do. He's faithful.

If you've been waiting on God, hang in there. Someday it'll all make sense, even if that someday isn't on this side of Eternity. He will not let you down. Even if things seem to go haywire, He will turn everything out for good. (Romans 8:28) Just hang on to Him.

Lord, please grant me the grace to cling to You while I wait. Amen

GOD STILL HEALS

Charles E. Harrel   April 29

Read: Matthew 8:13-17

**"And great multitudes followed [Jesus], and
He healed them there."** Matthew 19:2 (NKJV)

Some years ago, Paul, one of our residents at *HisPlaceOutreach,*
lay sick with a fever and his temperature was rising. He probably had
the flu. At the request of a staff member, I stopped by to pray for him.
Paul looked exhausted, and his face was flushed. After hesitation and
much doubt, I uttered an awkward prayer for his benefit.

Actually, I wouldn't call my words a prayer.

I simply said, "Fever, go away." I had no idea it would work, but it
did! God healed him instantly – no flu symptoms remained!

I hadn't realized God was still in the healing business! The church
I'd attended as a teenager had taught me that God no longer heals
today. This doctrine never made sense to me, yet I accepted it until that
day at *HisPlace.* Seeing a real miracle can change your beliefs fast.

Paul's healing was the first miracle I had ever witnessed. It started
me thinking –maybe God can heal others, too! In Jesus' name, I began
telling other sicknesses to "*go away,*" and they did.

Jesus paid for our salvation and healing on the Cross. The price
was costly, but His purchase opened a door of provision to all who
believe. This means that Jesus not only has the power to heal, He has
God's *authorization* to heal. In fact, Jesus enjoys making us whole, and
He uses some interesting methods as well.

Praise the Lord! Amen

CALM

Kathy Johnson   April 30

**"Without warning, a furious storm came up on the lake,
so that the waves swept over the boat. But Jesus was sleeping."**
Matthew 8:24 (NIV)

When my husband and I were first married we went on a camping
trip with his parents and younger brother. One day my husband, his
brother, and I went out in a motorboat on the reservoir to fish.

All of a sudden a storm came up and blew our boat closer and
closer to the dam! My brother-in-law was fighting to steer us, but it
wasn't helping – and eventually the motor died! We knew if we crashed
into the dam, we would be killed. As it loomed closer, my husband
jumped out of the boat, took a line and began to swim against the

waves toward shore. Amazingly, he was able to pull us close enough to land that he could finally stand and drag us the rest of the way in!

I know the terror the disciples felt, being on a boat when an unexpected storm rolled in. The Lord didn't calm our tempest, but He did grant the three of us peace. May the Lord's peace be yours as you weather your storms of life.

Lord, Your power is greater than anything we can imagine. Not only can You intervene in the natural order of things, You also grant peace to the troubled soul. Grant us Your peace today as we go on our way. Amen

FUTURE GENERATIONS

Jennifer Kanode   May 1

Read Galatians 6:7-10
**"Do not be deceived. God is not mocked.
A man reaps what he sows."** Galatians 6:7 (NIV)

I heard a song on the local Christian radio station the other day that talked about future generations. The artist sang about how she could either leave a blessing or a curse – and her descendants will reap what she sows. The next Sunday, the pastor talked about the legacy his grandfather had left.

Naturally that got me to thinking and asking the question, "What legacy am I going to leave for future generations? Do I want to sow a blessing or a curse?" I think now more than ever these questions are important to me, since my husband and I are expecting the birth of our first child.

No matter our background, with God's help we can choose to be a blessing to our children and those generations that come after us. We can learn from our ancestors' failures and ask the Lord to help us not to make the same mistakes. Let's leave a legacy of blessing for our children.

Lord, may we be a blessing to our future generations. Help us to leave a legacy of love, compassion and a firm foundation in You. May we sow a good crop, so we can reap a harvest of faithful followers of Christ. May future generations look back and call us blessed. Amen

MUSIC IN THE MORNING

Lorena Estep   May 2

"Look at the birds of the air; they do not sow or reap or store away in barns, and yet your heavenly Father feeds them. Are you not much more valuable than they?" Matthew 6:26 (NIV)

Having morning devotions outside by our large pond, I sat quietly at first, just listening as the birds tweeted their harmonious sounds. Then the bullfrogs croaked in with their deep bass voices and the younger frogs chirped with higher notes. Suddenly the serenade was disturbed by two blue jays squawking in a nearby tree. I glanced up to see them chasing a gray squirrel down to the ground, flying low behind it. When the jays had him far enough away, they returned to the tree, obviously protecting the nest they had constructed.

I realized that nature's tranquility can be broken by invading problems, just as our lives can. How often do we walk along singing, feeling all is well with our world, and suddenly a problem comes from an unexpected source? But just as the Lord has given animals an inborn protective instinct, God has given believers the indwelling Holy Spirit. We can turn instinctively and immediately to Him for help.

Sometimes the help is instant, but often the problem drags on, testing our faith. Then we have to rest in God's Word, which tells us not to worry, and remember that God knows our needs and will take care of us, even more than the birds over which He watches.

Lord, help us to trust totally in You, and not worry about what tomorrow may bring. Amen

THE PRAYER

Bill Batcher   May 3

Oh, Lord, You have given us a beautiful day. I pray that I may use it well. Boy, I sure wasted a lot of time yesterday. I must have spent hours looking for that receipt. Who left it down in the basement anyway? I really should get around to fixing those basement stairs. I wonder if Don might come over and give me a hand. Where's his phone number....?

Oh, uh, sorry, Lord, let's see, where were we?

Help me to use this day well. Bless the kids, whatever they're doing today, Lord. I don't know what they have planned. We never seem to hear from them. You'd think we didn't raise them right. Margaret hasn't called since last Thanksgiving. The latest picture we have of our grandson is from the Christmas before last. I should reorganize that photo album sometime. Nothing is labeled or dated, or....

Uh, excuse me, Lord. I guess my real prayer today is that You keep me focused, focused on Your grace, Your love, Your faithfulness. And thank You, Lord, that while I might forget that You're there, You never forget that I'm here!

ODE TO A LILAC BUSH

Amelia Chako   May 4

"...if some of the branches be broken off, and thou, being a wild olive tree, wert grafted in among them, and with them partakest of the root and fatness ... boast not ... thou bearest not the root, but the root thee."
Romans 11:17-18 (KJV)

For 32 years with her leaves pointed high, she grew –
becoming stately, majestic and tall. She made a lovely, lacy wall.
With beautiful spring blossoms of virgin white,
she surely was her proud owner's delight.
But the gardener eyed her free-growing frame.
Aha! he thought, *here's a wild one I'll tame.*
Out came his ladder and sharp pruning hook.
He climbed, lost his balance, then a trip his temper took.
Heart pounding, red-faced and raging,
he lowered her down to her starting dimension.
Then wilted and humbled with roots full of tension,
She clung to the ground for her very salvation.
The gardener, who was worn out and tired,
Contemplated his bruised, blistered hands
Foolishly thinking he had completed his plans.
But her being knows God's promise
and with tomorrow's beauty stands.
(Author's note: "She is now nine feet tall and just lovely!"
Praise God, He's the Master Gardener)

TO TRUST OR NOT TO TRUST

Sarah Lynn Phillips   May 5

"The king's heart is in the hand of the Lord, Like the rivers of water; He turns it wherever He wishes." Proverbs 21:1 (NKJV)

Over the years, my husband has often been in a position to hire employees. More than once, someone has sidled up to me, hoping to influence him. We all have goals and aspirations of what we want to accomplish (and where) or titles we'd like to claim. Though these desires are not necessarily wrong, what we do with them – and how we go about pursuing them – not only shows our true character, but reveals our level of trust in a sovereign God. Even in our "it's-who-you-know" society, to manipulate people and circumstances indicates a lack of trust in God. He ultimately holds the controls and has our best interests in mind.

"He who is faithful in what is least is faithful also in much; and he who is unjust in what is least is unjust also in much." Luke 16:10 (NKJV)

Let's be faithful where God has placed us and aim to establish credibility, a quality work ethic, exemplary behavior, and character. Then, when an opportunity arises, we can pursue it in a straightforward manner and leave the results in God's hands.

After all, He can even change a king's mind to fulfill His wishes for us!

THE FRUIT OF SELF-CONTROL

Kris Thayer   May 6

"The fruit of the Spirit is self-control." Galatians 5:22 (NIV)

Self-control is the ninth fruit of the Spirit, and is governed and guided by all the other fruits of the Spirit. When we abide in Christ, He will give us the discipline that leads to Christ-likeness. To have self-control is to have mastery of ourselves, which translates to mastery over our sensual appetites and control of our minds.

Self-control is not about constantly denying ourselves. God gives us appropriate times and places to satisfy our desires. Restraint enables us to escape the evil desires and wrong timing of our flesh and makes us useful in God's Kingdom.

Ponder, Pray, and Pursue:

1. Timing is a big part of self-control. Are you content to work within God's timetable, or do your desires cause you to rebel and demand what you want now?

2. Many of us struggle with self-control and feel that we will never improve in anything because we lack this one thing. But do not forget that self-control is a fruit of the Spirit. God can give it to you, and train you to use it. You are not a hopeless case!

JOB'S SOVEREIGN GOD

Roy D. Hall   May 7

Recently, the Bible class I teach studied Job. Our discussion reminded me of the rich lessons contained there. Even though God spoke with Job at the end of the book, He never explained to him why he had suffered! He simply told Job that he must trust Him!

That may not sound right to us, but it explains the purpose of the book. Job didn't understand, but he trusted God anyway. If God had explained everything, that would have diluted one of this book's lessons for us: *God is ultimately sovereign in all things.* He is in charge and is going to work things out in His time, according to *His* purpose.

We do not and will not understand why certain things happen: Why do we get cancer? Why do accidents happen? Why do people die young? God's silence in those times can be overwhelming. But don't confuse silence with uncaring. He is an awesome, sovereign, all-knowing God. We can trust Him.

The Bible says, *"**You have heard of Job's perseverance and have seen what the Lord <u>finally brought about.</u> The Lord is full of compassion and mercy.**"* James 5:11 (NIV) Job didn't see the outcome – but we did! We see God's sovereignty in Job's life. We must learn that He is sovereign in ours, too. When we cannot see the cause or the outcome of our struggles, we can still trust the God who does.

HIS GRACE IS SUFFICIENT

Debbie Carpenter   May 8

Read 2 Corinthians 12:7-10

*"**My grace is sufficient for you, for my strength is made perfect in weakness.**"* 2 Corinthians 12:9 (NIV)

When I am hurting, my first impulse is to go to God and ask Him to lessen or remove the pain. However, He doesn't always choose to remove the pain immediately in answer to my petitions. In fact, sometimes things get worse before they get better!

God never fails to answer me, just not always in the way I desire, or on my time schedule! Paul, in 2 Corinthians 12, speaks of pleading with the Lord three times to take away a "thorn in his side" some type of infirmity. The Lord answered, but did not take away the affliction. He left Paul weak so that He Himself could be Paul's strength.

Throughout my lifetime, God has provided strength sufficient to meet all needs. Another thing I have noticed is that whenever He brings me through a trying time, I emerge without some of the baggage I carried into the trial. It's as though the fire of testing burns away burdensome loads I would have been content to bear rather than battle.

Dear Father God, Thank You for providing Your strength that is ample for each day's needs. In the name of Jesus, Amen

TIME TRAVEL

Helene Burgess   May 9

*"**There's an opportune time to do things, a right time for everything on the earth.**"*
Ecclesiastes 3:1 (The Message)

During warm days when windows are kept open to let in a cool breeze, outside sounds often drift in. The house where I now live is just a few blocks from where I spent my growing up years, not far from a busy highway. One sultry May morning, the hum of trucks and cars whizzing by on that road reached my ears.

In a fleeting moment I was transported back to my girlhood – a bridge of time linking the young years of my life to the present golden ones. Where had the time gone? Looking back over those years, I realized what a gift God has given us that we could re-live them in our memories at will!

Truly, God has made us wonderfully!

Thank You, Lord, for all our senses and the memories they bring of times past. Amen

PROVERBS 31 – REVISITED

Pan Sankey   May 10

Listen, my children, and you shall hear of the daily life of each mother dear. She fills many a role – wears many a hat, and they ALL are important – imagine that!

When her children are small and need so much care…No more eight-hour-days – she's ALWAYS there! It's not "9 to 5," now it's 24-7, and with no days off, Boy! her motor's revvin'!

She's a Wife and a Mother, and the CEO of all household matters – just watch her go!

She's now the Chief Cook *and* the Bottle Washer, the Laundress and Seamstress and "Crisis Squasher"!

As her children grow up, she's a Coach/Referee, and Chauffeur as well with a Counselor's degree. She's the Financial Advisor and Budget Director, and in her spare time, the Home Decorator.

And what if the health of her family gets worse? She's not only the Doctor, but the full-time Nurse! But with all these positions and the hats she must own, the loveliest of all is her invisible crown.

For she is a Princess, a child of the King, and she's trained in her role by what the years bring. With each year that passes, as she grows in His love, she begins to look more like her Father above:

With eyes of compassion that come from her Father, and ears that can listen to the heart of another, with a hand that creates, and yet willingly serves, and lips that respond with Wisdom's kind words.

She is praised by her husband, by her children she's blessed, but in her Father, the King, her confidence rests. Let her works bring her praise at that time of reward when she joyfully praises her King and her Lord.

Behold, all these hats that she wears with finesse; such grace, and rejoice in her worth – she's a *real* Princess!

MOTHER'S DAY

Walter Stadler   May 11

**"Honor your father and your mother, so that you may
live long in the land the Lord God is giving you."**
Exodus 20:12 (NIV)

My first day of school was scary. I thank God that my mom walked with me up that five mile hill. On that cool pre-fall morning as we strolled along, she talked about my big day ahead. Mom reminded me that I was her big boy now and her little man. When we came close to the door of what appeared a humongous building, she fixed my collar and, with a tear in her eye, said, "Behave, make friends and learn something new."

"I will, Mama." I said. Then we hugged and I ran up the steps. I turned and waved and called back, "I love you, Mama!"

"And I love you!" she replied with a smile. Then into my new world I stepped – one foot in front of the other.

Looking back, it was one of the best times I ever spent with my mom. I never thanked her for walking with me up that awful hill; but I know she knew what was in my heart, because I had turned to say "I love you."

Gracious Father, thank You for the gift of mothers. Help children to learn Your words in Exodus and to remember to honor both parents, even when they are not perfect. You are a gracious God and a giver of undeserved gifts. Thank You. Amen

BE MADE CLEAN!

Judy Barron   May 12

"I am willing, He told him. Be made clean!" Mark 1:41b (CSB)

This verse is about being transformed – changed to a new shape; being set free from what binds us, be it illness, fear, sin, or death. Everyone will face all of these sometime. The only way to get through them whole and healed is through God and His desire to make us clean. He heals our broken spirits, our broken relationships, our broken bodies, our broken lives.

In the story of the leper, Jesus reached out and touched him – physically touched someone who had not been touched in years! I know people who have not been touched in a long time – either because they shrink back from an offered hand, or because they seem too strange or different for us to want to reach out to them. There are those who want only an acknowledgement that they exist! Maybe even that little can be a transforming event.

Guide me, Holy Spirit, to reach out and embrace the unembraceable – the "unclean" in our society. And transform me. Make me loveable and patient, understanding and forgiving, slow to anger and judgment of others. How can I be Your witness if I won't reach out in love? Please show me how in Jesus' name. Amen

SEEDS AND SINS

Jana Carman   May 13

"Being born again, not of corruptible seed, but of incorruptible, by the word of God, which liveth and abideth for ever." 1 Peter 1:23 (KJV)

Most gardening is done either bent over or kneeling, the perfect position for prayer and reflection. As I poke holes in the soft moist earth for the peas, I reflect that the seeds I drop into the earth look nothing like the plant that will spring from it. Just like sin.

Like seeds, sin starts small, as a mere thought. When it is planted in the fertile soil of the mind and nurtured, a dreadful harvest may be reaped. Impure thoughts grow into lust, and can mature into rape, adultery, or child abuse. Anger may sprout, develop into hatred, and even bear the bitter fruit of murder.

The weed-seeds of sin sprout from within because we are naturally wicked people. We tend to take these little thought-sins lightly and neglect weeding, instead of identifying and rooting them out. How easily they are pulled when they first poke their heads up, but when allowed to grow, their roots go deep.

A weed-free garden brings praise to its Creator. A harvest of shame and heartache is a big price to pay for neglecting our weeding.

"LORD, USE ME...."

Evelyn Minshull   May 14

Isaiah 6:8; Luke 5:11

Speak to us, Lord, we invite, *as You spoke to David, to Elijah,* although the hum and blare of traffic exceed the bleating of a psalmist's flock ... and a still, small voice might well be lost in the shrill command of cell phones.

Use us, Lord, we implore, although the press of work and family drains our daily energies. Still, we'd willingly reserve a tithe of our time for some small project You might choose.

But building an ark is simply not an option.

Equip us, Lord, we pray. Still, You know our limitations: a zeal unequal to Nehemiah's; a threshold of pain inferior to Job's; an aversion to verbal conflict, long desert marches and lions' dens.

Send us, Lord, we plead ... though not too far. We speak one language only; our roots are deep, our obligations many. A mission to Ninevah would be hugely inconvenient ... and please do recruit another to lead Your people out of bondage.

O, Lord, quiet our arguments, soothe our fears, and level the hurdles that restrict our serving You. Amen

PSALM 62:1-2 (NIV)

Esther Bordwell   May 15

"For God alone my soul waits in silence; from God comes my salvation. God only is my rock and salvation, my fortress; I shall not be greatly moved." Psalm 62:1-2 (NIV)

(An acrostic, written while my granddaughter was critically ill.)

E   Every time trouble comes my way,
S   Something tells me God is still there,
T   Taking charge of my problems,
H   Helping me by answering prayer.
E   Even if some doubts creep in,
R   Revealing that my faith is small

B   Bountiful love flows to cover
O   Over all
R   Reminding me of God's call.
D   Doubts can then be put in their place,
W   Where I will feel them no more,
E   Every day will bring new hope –
L   Lifting my spirits,
L   Letting them soar!

Thank You, God, for being my rock and fortress, and for Stephanie's recovery. Amen

DO YOU HAVE PEACE IN YOUR DECISIONS?

Annettee Budzban   May 16

"And let peace (soul harmony which comes) from Christ rule (act as umpire continually) in your hearts (deciding and settling with

finality all questions that arise in your minds in that peaceful state)...." Colossians 3:13 (AMP)

Batter up! It's that season again, when baseball enthusiasts grab their mitts and start swinging their bats.

A man stands behind the batter's mound wearing a uniform that identifies him as the umpire. All ears are attentive as he shouts, "Strike!" "Ball!" "Safe!" His call wrings glad shouts or hisses from the crowd. But regardless of disgruntled fans, the umpire has the final say. Without his wise discernment, the score may not be settled, and foul play may abound.

Every sport has an umpire who settles the score between teams. Although not everyone is happy with his call, he is the peace-keeper. Without his final decision, the game could not go on.

Daily we struggle to make decisions. Big or small, each one could be critical. A wrong move could destroy us. Like our sports, we need an umpire – someone who can help us settle the score.

God tells us that *peace* should be our final umpire. Inner peace is the prompting of God's Holy Spirit to lead us to blessing. God may have given us earthly umpires as an example to let *Peace* be our umpire in the Game of Life.

GOD'S GIFTS

Barbara Vath Dawson   May 17

"We have different gifts according to the Grace given us. If a man's gift is prophesying, let him use it in proportion to his faith." Romans12: 6 (NIV)

My husband loves flea markets. I try to be interested, and occasionally I find something I can use. One summer day we stopped at a tiny flea market. At one table I saw a set of etched glasses in a box, brown with age. The glasses were in perfect condition and I decided to buy them.

I wondered about the original owner. The glasses appeared to have been a gift, received years ago. They reminded me of presents I'd found when my grandmother died. She'd tucked them away, unused.

I vowed then that I would use those I received, and take pleasure in them, as the giver had intended. But what about the gifts I've received from God?

They are called by many names. There are spiritual gifts such as discernment. There is the gift of hospitality. Some gifts are called talents. We see these in various artistic abilities.

There's another gift. It's called opportunity. I wonder how many times we ignore an opportunity to use our talents to enhance life, and reflect God's love?

Maybe we are like my grandmother and the previous owner of my glasses. We know that we have gifts, but we don't use them. Instead, we choose to keep them tucked away.

Father, grant me wisdom to use my gifts when You give me opportunity. Amen

FRIENDSHIP

Joy Bradford   May 18

"Whoever claims to live in Him must walk as Jesus did."
I John 1:6 (NIV)

During the greiving process after Karla's husband died, she found it difficult to return to the church they had attended as a couple. After some time had passed, she sold their home and moved to a community closer to her daughter. One day she met up with an old friend, Jane – also widowed – who had relocated to the same new area. They talked for awhile, then Jane invited Karla to visit her church.

Karla thought Jane was just being nice and making conversation so she didn't give much thought to the invitation. But soon she listened to a message on her answering machine from Jane, following up on their earlier conversation and once again inviting Karla to church.

Jane was very specific with the invitation. She said, "Come, and I will meet you at the entrance at 9:30, and we will sit together in church."

Karla joined Jane and returned the next week on her own. Within a few weeks she walked down the aisle to join a new church family! The invitation and a follow-up phone call from Jane was just what Karla needed.

Father, help us to be more aware of the needs of others. Sometimes it is a simple thing or minor inconvenience. We want to be more like You by reaching out in caring love that goes beyond our good intentions. Amen

"PRAISE THE LORD ANYHOW!"

Joseph M. Hopkins   May 19

On a wall above the bed of polio victim Corinne Shott were the words "Praise the Lord Anyhow!" Her twisted body was confined to bed and wheelchair throughout her entire life. However, she was compensated by her Creator with an alert mind and an indomitable spirit, both abundantly evident in the beautiful poems she composed. I was privileged to set two of them to music, including one of the loveliest. Let me share it with you....

SUNSET
Corinne Caroline Shot
The sun is sinking in the west, and God is calling us to rest.
The veil of night is drawing nigh, but, oh, the beauty of the sky!
When all the loveliness is gone, the memory will linger on:
The sky with all its golden glow.
none but our God could make it so.

Dear Heavenly Father, thank You for Corinne's life. May her example remind all of us to be grateful for bodies that are able to walk, skip, run, and jump as children; and at least to walk as mature adults. Forgive us, Lord, for taking for granted your precious gifts of sound minds in healthy bodies; but also – and most important of all – spirits attuned to the beauty of Your creation and to the indwelling presence of Your Son Jesus. And if we lack, or have lost, any of our cherished physical or material advantages, help us to know that You will never leave us or forsake us, and to exclaim with Corinne, "Praise the Lord anyhow!" Amen

THE POWER OF LOVE
Charles Harrel   May 20
Read: Romans 9:1-5

Years ago, as I walked home from Montrose Elementary School, two sixth-grade bullies leaped from behind a sycamore tree and tried to scare me. Their plan worked well! I was terrified. They had badgered me all week and on Friday they decided to carry out their threat to thrash me. Before the first blow landed, however, someone rushed across the street and stepped in to take my place. It was my cousin, Dalton Ray.

Many individuals have strong family ties and are willing to put their lives in jeopardy for one of their relatives. Some will do the same for citizens from their own nation. But would they risk separation from God for the sake of others? The Apostle Paul pondered that very thought: ***"For their sake I could wish that I myself were under God's curse and separated from Christ."*** Romans 9:3 (GNT)

We know that God would never ask us to do such a thing. Still, Paul's concern for the salvation of his brethren ran deep. So did his love. Paul felt kinship to his own race, just as God does for all the families of the world.

I often wonder, how far would I go to help others in need? Maybe someday I will find out. In the meantime, I will keep my eyes on the Cross.

Dear Lord, show me the best way to express love and affinity to all Your people. Amen

CHOREOGRAPHED FLIGHT

Barbara Major Bryden   May 21

**"Those who hope in the Lord will renew their strength.
They will soar on wings like eagles"** Isaiah 40: 31 (NIV)

My daughter, Liz, and I stopped to smell the roses spilling over the top of the arbor by my driveway. Suddenly, Liz pointed to the sky. "Look! Are those hawks or eagles?"

"Eagles," I said. "They're flying too high to be hawks."

The birds soared overhead without moving their wings as they rode invisible currents of air. Gracefully, they glided in two overlapping circles. As though arranged by a choreographer, large circles alternated with smaller ones as the eagles flew over and under each other. Then, they caught an updraft, and, with no apparent effort, quickly rose in an upward spiral.

I ran for the binoculars. When I returned, the birds were pinpoints of black. Confidence in the strength of the air current allowed them to soar out of sight.

Though invisible, the wind supporting the eagles was real. They spread their wings and trusted the currents.

God's invisible too, but His loving support is real. To soar, we must trust the Lord. When we pray and ask God to take care of a problem we can't handle, that doesn't mean we do nothing. It means we give our worries to God and ask Him to show us what to do. Then we trust Him to guide us.

Like the eagles that ride the air currents, we can soar with confidence when we trust the Master Choreographer. Our problems may not be gone, but we can live joyously knowing He is in control!

TELL ME

Paul E. Vander Wege   May 22

Why is my heart broken by cruel words spoken?
Why should I care when others do not share
The love Jesus has for me?
Why does Satan bother with my faith? Oh, Father,

Why does he attack and try to set me back?
Is he afraid of me?
I know You love me, in life Your hand I see,
This makes me stronger so I can serve You longer.
Praise Your Holy Name!
Father, I thank Thee for counting me worthy
To bear the temptation of Satan's contemplation!
May You be glorified!

A LESSON FROM LIFE
Debbie Carpenter   May 23
*"...You were slain, and have redeemed us to God by your blood,
out of every tribe and tongue and people and nation."*
Revelation 5:9 (NKJV)

When my oldest daughter, Suzanne, was in high school, she had a favorite pair of shorts for her physical education class. They were dark blue, stretchy, and comfortable – nothing fancy or out of the ordinary. But Suzanne was frustrated when they disappeared from her locker one day.

Not long after that, Suzanne, her sister, Kristi, and I were comb-ing through clothing at our favorite resale boutique when I heard the words, *"My shorts!* These are my shorts!" Suzanne held out her find for my examination. Yes indeed, they did look like the genuine article!

We headed for the cash register with Suzanne clutching the old gym shorts that were of so much value to her. The clerk rang them up, and we were soon in the car, laughing about the irony of having to pay for shorts that already belonged to us.

Then from the back seat we heard Kristi say, "Isn't that just what Jesus did for us? God made us to belong to Him, but we sinned. Christ had to die on the cross to buy us back."

Thank You, Father, for using this little episode in our lives to paint for us a clear picture of what the Bible calls "redemption." Thank You for redeeming all who come to You through Jesus. Amen

MY GARDEN WEEDS
Deborah J. Tune   May 24

After facing bankruptcy, health problems, and my teenage daughter's rebellion, my faith was cracking from all the heartache. I prayed and sought comfort from God's Word, yet felt alone and be-trayed. Finances put a strain on my marriage and home life, but I tried to work and carry on a normal existence.

Someone would ask, "How are you?" I'd smile and say, "Fine."

One day, out in my garden with a hoe in my hand, I began to weed my plants and weep. I cried, "God, why me? How much more would you put on one of your children? What have I done to deserve all this?"

Little did I know, God was weeding ME! A loud, thunderous voice came from the clouds**: "Be still and <u>know</u> that I am God!"**

Trembling and shaking inside, I threw that hoe down, ran into my kitchen, and locked the door. Tight! (As though I could lock God out!) That was many years ago. I no longer question God as I did that day. He's restored our family both spiritually and financially. Through a speaking and music ministry, my family encourages many people of all walks of life in several states.

I am thankful for the weeding that took place in my life that year. He's weeded my spiritual garden many times since then, and has shaped me into the shining plant that now blooms for His Kingdom!

LIFE IN THE WORD

Charlotte H. Burkholder   May 25
"Blessed are those who mourn for they shall be comforted."
Matthew 5:4 (NIV)

The post-Christmas blues smacked Zachary hard. His favorite cousins, his "PaPaw" and "MeMee" were all traveling to their faraway homes. When I said "good-bye" to my eleven-year-old grandson, I asked Zachary to pick a theme verse for the New Year. "Take your time," I said, "and ask God which one it should be."

The next morning Zachary's e-mail appeared on my computer screen.

"Hi MeMee, I just wanted to let you know that I have picked out my Bible verse for this year. All of you guys had just left our house and we were not happy. Me and Mitch were in bed and we both missed everyone so much I couldn't get to sleep so I got out my Bible and looked up the word, 'Mourn.' I was hoping to find something like, 'he who mourns shall find courage in the Lord and stoppeth his mourning,' (or something like that). But instead, I found Matthew 5:4 which says: *'He who mourns shall be comforted.'* That message did comfort me, and so I picked it to be my verse for this year."

O Lord, give me a heart of obedience that I might faithfully apply Your Word to my life as quickly as my grandson! What a difference there is between just reading Your Word and actually letting it affect my life! Amen

"WAIT A MINUTE"

Valerie J. Chambers   May 26

I reach up as far as I can.
I grip your pant leg, I pull and tug.
I call Your name – "ABBA!"
"Wait a minute."
I stand on tiptoe; I jump a few times.
I fall at Your feet.
I cry out Your name – "ABBA!"
"Wait a minute."
I get frustrated, I whimper and cry.
I get up, I try again – "ABBA!"
"Wait a minute."
I crawl away in anger thinking
I just wanted You to pick me up!
I glance back, I see Your outstretched arms – "ABBA!"
I wish that I had obeyed You when You told me to "Wait a minute!"

TOOLS

Rose Goble   May 27

"What is that in your hand?" Exodus 4:2 (NIV)

God gave Moses a rod, a miraculous tool. Thrown on the ground, it became a crawling viper. Raised high above the Red Sea, it parted the waters. Later, Moses struck the rock at Mt. Horeb and water gushed out.

Gideon had a torch in a pitcher.

David used a sling and a stone.

The prophets used various tools. All glorified God.

In the New Testament, the hem of Jesus' garment healed the malady of the woman who touched it.

Peter's net caught a fish whose mouth contained the coin to pay his tax. His shadow had healing power.

What is the tool in your hand? It's a pen for me. I may not part a sea or flatten a mountain, but I'm determined to use it for His glory. I challenge you to part the sea and flatten mountains with the tool God has given you, but remember – **it's for God's glory!**

KEEP ASKING, SEEKING, KNOCKING

Joan Clayton   May 28

"And shall not God avenge his own elect, which cry day and

night unto him, though he bear long with them?
I tell you that he will avenge them speedily...."
Luke 18:7-8 (KJV)

Do you sometimes feel that your prayer has gone unanswered? Do you even feel that maybe your prayer has not been heard? Rest assured it has! Daniel's prayer was heard when he first offered it – but it took 21 days for the answer!

God is God and He arranges all circumstances to "work for good in our behalf." (Romans 8:28) It could possibly be that sometimes it is to our advantage not to have an immediate answer! Other times it is! The key is to trust and have the faith that our prayers have been heard and the answer is on the way.

If we hear our children's petitions and are eager to give good gifts to them, how much more is our loving Heavenly Father willing to answer our prayers. (Matthew 7:11)

Thank You dear Father, for hearing and granting our petitions. As we love our earthly children, so much more do You love us. We return that love to You, giving You all glory and honor. Amen

MEMORIAL DAY

Evelyn Quinby   May 29

2 Chronicles 7:14 (AMP)

When my children were little, at night they'd kneel and say a little prayer. One night Donnie, 6, told me he'd learned a new one in school that day. I thought he must have a great teacher and said he could use it as his bedtime prayer.

Dutifully, he folded his hands and prayed, "I pledge allegiance to the flag of the United States of America and to the Republic for which it stands, one nation, under God, indivisible, with liberty and justice for all. Amen."

I smiled and kissed him goodnight. Over the years I've thought of that "prayer" and that there might be a lesson I'd missed. The dictionary told me that "a *pledge* is a binding promise" and that "*allegiance* is loyalty."

We promise loyalty to the USA. But I realized that *God pledged allegiance to us when He sent Jesus.* To pledge is to promise. He promised He'd never forsake us. He is loyal, too. We can claim His loyalty and every promise in His Book! We fall short since we don't believe these promises are for us. Let's rise up in the Name of Jesus and exercise our faith!

On Memorial Day it would behoove us to remember another promise: *"If My people who are called by My name shall humble themselves, pray, seek, crave and require of necessity My face, and turn from their wicked ways, then will I hear from Heaven, forgive their sin, and heal their land."* (AMP)

Now that's a prayer!

THE LIVING AMONG THE DEAD

Lorena M. Estep   May 30
"Why do you look for the living among the dead? He is not here; He has risen!" Luke 24:5-6 (NIV)

I leaned against the trunk of a large oak tree. It reigned majestically on the bank of a river that bordered one side of a cemetery. The moist air was cool as it rose from the surface of the placid, flowing water.

I pulled away from the tree and began my trek around the cemetery. I sometimes found it comforting to walk among the tombstones, reading the engraved data and pondering what might have transpired in the lives of people who once had dreams of good futures.

This day, I had come seeking peace after I'd exchanged hurtful words with someone about whom I cared.

"Why do you look for the living among the dead?" The words popped into my thoughts, and I was taken in my mind to the empty tomb that had no longer held Jesus. The women who'd gone to the tomb had been frightened when two men there greeted them with these words.

I realized too that my comfort wouldn't be found among the dead, but in my living Lord and Savior. I spoke to Him about the quarrelsome exchange I had experienced. He eased my heart and gave me peace and a renewed love and understanding for the one with whom I had clashed.

Renewed in spirit, I returned home to heal a breached relationship – thanking the Lord for the loved ones in my life who *still lived* to share a life with me.

SOLDIERS OF CHRIST

Annie Bruening   May 31
Ephesians 6: 11-18 (NKJV)

Ephesians 6 tells us to be soldiers of Christ. Our battle is spiritual, against Satan and his demons as he works through the evil people in this world.

Verses 17 and 18 tell us, *"And take the helmet of salvation, and the sword of the Spirit, which is the Word of God: praying always with all prayer and supplication in the Spirit, being watchful to this end with all perseverance and supplication for all the saints."* Our two weapons of offense are God's Word and prayer. Christ gave us an example by quoting Scripture to defeat Satan during His time of temptation; and we are to do the same.

Secondly, we are to pray in the Spirit on every occasion when a brother or sister in Christ brings us a need.

Paul tells young Timothy, *"You therefore must endure hardship as a good soldier of Jesus Christ."* Here we are told to walk worthy of the vocation with which God has blessed us. So, we are called to be a soldier of Christ in our everyday lives – with our family, friends, and those in the workplace.

Dear God, we thank You for letting Your Spirit shine through us to every friend and stranger we meet today. Amen

IN SICKNESS AND IN HEALTH....

Jana Carman   June 1

*"Thy shoes shall be iron and brass;
and as thy days, so shall thy strength be."*
Deuteronomy 33:25 (KJV)

The bride looked startled as she opened my shower gift. Tucked in a plastic box was a thermometer, box of bandages, tube of burn ointment, aspirin, a sickroom bell, and several medicine cabinet items that every household needs sooner or later.

"Love is not always glamorous, but it will help you get to the bathroom when you're sick," Helen Woodhall wrote in an open letter to her granddaughter (*Guideposts*). It also helps you mop up when someone doesn't make it there in time, or go out in the middle of the night for cough medicine, or change sheets again and again.

Most of us, going into marriage, have had little experience with serious illness or injury. That happens to other people. Or so we like to think. It was during one of my crisis times that I leaned against my father and cried, "Daddy, I don't know how I can take any more."

And he said what I needed. "Take it one day at a time."

Someone has said that none of us can carry a lifetime's burden, but we can each carry this hour's worth. *"Your strength will equal your days."* Deuteronomy 33:25 (NIV)

O Lord, You alone are my strength. Pick me up when I collapse. Comfort me in pain, carry me in weakness. Infuse me with Your power to go on. Thank You for staying close. Amen.

REVIVAL

Helene Burgess   June 2

***"You'll be like a well-watered garden, a gurgling spring that never
runs dry."*** Isaiah 58:11 (The Message)

Did you see the drooped, parched plant?
The stooped, burdened man?
I did!
Both so shriveled!
Both so sad!
Oh, my!
Have you seen the plant revived by water?
The man revived by the Living Water?
I have!
Both so vibrant!
Both so glad!
Oh, so thankful and full of new life!

GOD HEARS KIDS, TOO!

Ruth Baldwin   June 3

Glady, my Shetland pony, was a feisty little animal. I tried to catch
her, since I needed her to ride to a neighbor's party. But, as soon as I
walked near her, she tossed her head, and ran off. This happened
several times. If I didn't catch her soon, I'd be too late for the festivities.
I was ten, and parties were pretty rare!

Then I remembered our minister recently saying that if we had
enough faith, we could move a mountain. (Matthew 17:20) Glady was
my mountain for sure, so I knelt behind a large tree and prayed, "God, I
have faith that You will help me catch Glady. I need her today. Please
help me!"

When I walked toward her, she stood still, as though someone was
holding her. I bridled her, and rode to the party. She remained docile
that whole day. This was the first time I had asked God for something
and been answered so quickly. What a thrill! God heard and answered
me! It surprised me that He listens to all of us – kids as well as
grownups!

I sang, "Thank You, Lord, thank You, Lord, thank You, Lord" in time
to my pony's gallop all the way to the party and all the way home. I was
grateful, not just for His catching my pony, but that He would help a kid!
He cared for me, and showed it.

He will hear you, too!

WHEN DISASTER STRIKES

Joy Bradford   June 4

***"Do not forsake your friend and the friend of your father,
and do not go to your brother's house when disaster strikes you
– better a neighbor nearby than a brother far away."***
Proverbs 27:10 (NIV)

Suzanne called and asked that my husband and I both get on the phone. What she told us was chilling. *My childhood friend has invasive ovarian cancer. How can it be? We plan to grow old together and someday live in the same assisted living place.*

Our lives have intertwined over many years and we've shared many good and some painful experiences. We ended up living in the same area far away from our families of origin. I have gone to her many times with my troubles, and she has always been my trusted friend.

Now Suzanne shows me how to live with cancer. She is optimistic and upbeat. We have already experienced answered prayers!

We have reconnected with her adult children and happily recalled the family times we shared. During her surgery, long-lost mutual friends gathered at the hospital and we caught up on our lives. Suzanne and I are closer than ever as we share another life experience with God's help.

Father, You have walked with Suzanne before in troubled waters. As she witnesses for You, thank You for Your continued presence in her life. I pray for healing and more years of her service in this life. Amen

INSTRUCTIONS

Helen Kammerdiener   June 5

Read Psalm 119:105-112

"Thy word is a lamp unto my feet, and a light unto my path."
Psalm 119:105 (KJV)

"First, throw away the instructions." That ironic statement became a byword in one family.

The valve in the toilet tank needed to be replaced. As Jim worked on it, his wife opened the package and took out the new valve. When she mentioned the directions, Jim snapped, "Throw 'em away; I know how to do this!"

He removed the old valve and began to install the new one. He worked; he struggled; he tried everything he knew. One hour passed. A second hour was almost gone when Jim finally retrieved the instructions. Fifteen minutes later, the valve was installed – a new improved type that didn't work like the ones Jim had installed in the past.

I've met people who act that same way toward our Instruction Book for Life. They think they've studied the Bible enough. They've read it through a number of times; they know what they're doing; they don't need the directions.

But we do. God's word doesn't change; we won't find it different today from what it was last year – but we will find the situations we face aren't quite the same. When we read God's instructions in the midst of new circumstances, we may see a deeper meaning than we had found before.

Dear Lord, please help me to follow Your instructions in my life. Amen

HIS SONG

Basle Cox   (A Word Picture)   June 6

Imagine a heavenly voice from above raised in song. The high, strong voice, sweet with vibrancy, would echo around the world. No words – just notes – high and clear.

Picture the earth standing still while those looking up listened to the powerful peal of the voice which was rich and true, full of authority and passion. No one would dare move for it was God's will that Jesus die on Calvary's hill. The song would rise and swoop as the flight of an eagle. Some of the tones would bring sadness to the world – a sadness so deep the people would cry and forget to wipe away the tears.

The sadness it would carry would be more than grief at the death of men. It would be anguish at the death of *HIM*. Those who heard the rising, dipping notes would remember their hopes and dreams that had died without being realized.

No one would be able to stop crying while the song was sung. Then, like light at eventide, the song would end and release the world from its grasp. The angel would withdraw to Heaven. The song of all songs would never be heard again.

Then, imagine how the people rejoiced for the life of *HIM* who came and died for all our sins – and who is alive forevermore!

Again, I say, ***Rejoice!***

STEWARDSHIP

Carey Ann Meyer-LaSor   June 7

Read Malachi Chapter 3

"Bring all the tithes ... into the storehouse – and prove Me now by it, says the Lord of hosts, if I will not open the windows of Heaven for you...." Malachi 3:10 (Amp)

Growing up as a PK (preacher's kid), stewardship in our house was an important concept. Many pastors dread it, because "it's all about the money." It's *not* all about the money! It's about you – under-standing Whose you are! It's about faith – not to be brave enough to give money – but brave enough to really allow Christ to be your Lord – of every-thing!

I had it all, then my whole life fell apart and I learned the truth of stewardship. Truly, there's nothing I had or have that meets the needs of Jesus, except what's in my heart. I've lost the trappings, and no thing, no one, is mine. Parents, children, siblings, friends, house, car, *stuff?* Not mine. Skills, voice, music? Not mine! Even prayers, love, and concern for the mission of the Church – not mine! All I have is a gift from God.

Money? Right now, money is a concern. So I choose to give as much as I can, plus all of the other "stuff" – everything God's given me (that isn't mine!) to glorify Him.

One caution: If anything in you balks at the word "stewardship," you may need to have a long conversation in the mirror. I trust you find someone there who is 100% sold on a radical cause. I hope His name is Jesus!

SEEK GOD'S FACE INSTEAD OF HIS FAVOR

Violet Herlocker   June 8

"God will bring me out of my darkness into the light, and I will see his goodness." Micah 7:9 (TLB)

My mother was to be obeyed. Submission is certainly a good thing, and biblical – we are charged with obeying our parents and with obey-ing God. My mother took this further, though, I was not only to do as I was told, but I was never to question her.

If my mother were living today, I know that she would say her love was unconditional; but in my childish understanding, her mood (if not her love) was totally conditional. I felt that I earned her love and favor by my behavior. I grew up expecting God to be like my mother: existing to be pleased or appeased.

I lived in fear of punishment in a world of darkness. I imagined a God whose wrath was directly controlled by my behavior; whose favor was conditional, and given only if I was the perfect and faultless child. Over the years, I learned the true character of God – He *does* love me unconditionally, and when I seek His face instead of His favor, I see the goodness of His love.

Dear Father, help me to seek Your face instead of Your favor. For when my eyes are on Your face, then my heart and my actions meet Your favor. Amen

MESSY KITCHENS

Leigh DeLozier   June 9
"But you – who are you to judge your neighbor?"
James 4:12b (NIV)

I'm a work-from-home mom, so our family needed to make some adjustments when my husband also began working from home two days a week. Although he didn't ask, I'm sure he wondered why I left the kitchen in a mess most days.

The answer was simple and made sense to him once I explained. When our son got home from school, he usually settled at the kitchen table to do homework. I wanted to hear about his day and be nearby in case he needed help (or a little prodding to keep on track).

So I left dirty dishes in the sink or grocery bags on the counter until he arrived. Then I puttered in the kitchen, putting things away or starting dinner while he tackled homework.

On the surface, it looked like I was a terrible housekeeper who wasn't taking care of her family or carrying her share of the load. In reality, I was using every minute the best way I could by focusing on work things during the school day and mom things once our son got home.

How easy it is for us to make a snap judgment based on what we see rather than scratch the surface to discover what's really happening! Let's try to look beyond the messes to the underlying reasons before jumping to conclusions – and leave the real judgments to God!

THANKING JESUS FOR THE SUN

Stefanie Smith   June 10
"Through Him then, let us continually offer up a sacrifice of praise to God, that is, the fruit of lips that give thanks to His name." Hebrews 13:15 (NASB)

One day while teaching a Sunday school class of preschoolers I had begun, "Dear Jesus, thank You for the Bible—" when two-year-old Timmy whispered, "And for the sun!" So, I thanked God for the sun. "And the flowers!" Molly piped in excitedly. Smiling, I praised God for the flowers as well.

The preschoolers in my class are learning to say "thank you," and they love to thank God for the little things. Their prayers made me wonder how long it had been since I had acknowledged God for the simple blessings in my life, like a pretty day, falling leaves, or a good night's sleep?

As the Lord's children, shouldn't we all be this way? The Lord taught me from the simple prayers of toddlers to be grateful to God for everything I can think of. Now when I see a pretty sky, or hear the song of a bird, I'm learning – like the kids – to say, "thank You" to a loving God who showers blessings on His children.

Lord, thank You for the blessings that You give us every day. Thank You for using children to teach us how to love and serve You more. Amen.

BETTER THAN ARTESIAN?

Evelyn Minshull   June 11

Read Luke 13:1-9

When God stood by Moses, water flowed from rock. It was water fit for drinking, and for a time it quenched the grumbling of Israel's flock. But only for a time. It satisfied, after all, only a physical thirst.

The Psalmist spoke of a different thirsting – the soul-thirst for God's presence, God's leading, God's love.

Often, it seemed, the children of Israel were concerned only with *physical* hungering and thirsting. Too often, it seems, so are we. Jesus spoke to this short-sightedness when he met the Samaritan woman at the well. He told her of "Living Water" and promised that anyone who receives it will never thirst again – not that she would never again carry water from the well for cooking, washing and drinking.

Not that we will never again have to turn on a spigot, or bend to a drinking fountain, but that our souls will be spotless. The cisterns of our spirits will be filled. Life's desert places will become oases. Dryness will soften and blossom. Even the withered fig tree will bear fruit.

O Lord, even Satan is awed by Your power; the angels declare You worthy of unending praise; each day – in our own sight – creation attests to Your majesty; every dawn proves Your mercy. Lord, accept us and accept our worship. May we bloom and bear much fruit for You. Amen

YOU DON'T WEIGH ENOUGH!
Janelle Leonard   June 12

The day begins with screaming children, a stubborn husband, a broken glass, and a leaky toilet. But suppose you know that, at five o'clock, you get to go to your favorite bookstore, slowly sip a cup of coffee, and be alone. It would sure make the trials of the day seem small compared to the joy of the peace and quiet to come!

It's like Paul said in Romans 8:18, *"For I consider that the sufferings of this present time are not worthy* (the word *worthy* here, in Greek, suggests the idea of weights and balances, or "weighs the same as") *to be compared with the glory that is to be revealed to us."* (NAS)

Paul kept the trials of everyday living in perspective, knowing that on one side of the scale he had God and Eternity. On the other side, he had only the trials of everyday living. He knew that the problems of today weigh nothing compared to the thought that, at any moment, he could be in the presence of God!

So, with confidence, you can look at your spouse, your kids, or any problem you face, and weigh it against the privilege of seeing God at any moment. Then you can say, "You don't weigh enough to make me grumpy or ruin my day!"

THROUGH A MAZE
Lorena Estep   June 13
"'Come, follow me,' Jesus said....'" Matthew 4:19a (NIV)

Traveling through Virginia, my daughter and I decided to attempt the maze outside the Luray Caverns. Our tickets showed that they were to be stamped at each stage we reached.

We soon realized it was not going to be the breeze-through we had anticipated. Over and over again we would come to a dead end, or find ourselves back where we had started. We finally stumbled upon the first station and stamped our cards.

Several times in our wanderings the man in charge came through with tools or plants and would ask if we wanted him to show us the way out. We stubbornly insisted we would do it ourselves. At last we made it, pleased to have accomplished our goal.

Later, during difficult circumstances, I thought how life is much like that maze. We wander around thinking we're going in the right direction, only to come up against dead ends or back where we started.

How often does Jesus say, "Follow Me!"? But we stubbornly ignore

His help, insisting on doing it ourselves. In the "maze of life," how much simpler it would be to follow Jesus, saving ourselves from many dead ends and much unnecessary stress.

Lord Jesus, help me to follow You every step of the way. Amen

THANK YOU, FATHER

Chris Snow   June 14

Alone in the dark I walked – a lost, frightened child.
Satan crept up on me, and urged me to run wild.
Always partying and living in the fast lane, little by little,
I lost what I loved. I was full of sin and living with shame.
The man in the mirror I could not bear,
for it was hard to cope with the hurtful stares.
It was clear to see, the rock star within me
had to die; the pain and sin smothered my soul.
So, I hit my knees and wept toward the sky,
"Lord, this isn't me, this isn't who I want to be!
Please show me the way with Your love-filled light.
Forgive me of my sins and make me Your man."
Since I repented, a man in Christ is now who I am
And to sin I am forever dead.

I love You, Father, for rescuing me. You knew who I wanted to be, even before I was a lost, frightened child. Praise and thanks forever be to You, because with You my dreams and prayers come true. Amen

THE IMPORTANCE OF DAD

Jennifer Kanode   *(Father's Day)*   June 15

**"Fathers, do not embitter your children,
or they will become discouraged."**
Colossians 3:21 (NIV)

In today's society, it seems like fathers are becoming more and more obsolete. There are more single-family homes where the mother takes care of the children, and Dad is nowhere to be found. I'm so thankful that my dad was always around when I was young. He was the strong, silent type. Growing up, it appeared that Mom ran the house. But Dad was the final decision-maker.

In the Bible, God calls the man to be the spiritual leader of the family, and I can honestly say that my dad did that. Now that I'm older, married, and starting a family of my own, I realize more and more how important that was. And I see the value of having Dad still close by. I hope that my baby boy grows up to be just like his grandfather.

"Thanks, Dad!"

Lord, thank You that there are still Godly fathers around. Thank You that I am blessed to have one who is the spiritual leader of the house. May You raise up more men who will carry the torch and be the leader at home and church. Amen

THE GREATEST CALL

Paul Soderberg   June 16

"But when this priest had offered for all time one sacrifice for sins, he sat down at the right hand of God."
Hebrews 10:12 (NIV)

Being an umpire can be a trying experience. You have to be open-minded, impartial and show no prejudice or bias. Having been an umpire, I've had to make some close calls. I have to admit that some were probably not correct.

During a close game, the wrong call can change the course or direction of the outcome. Also, in life, we – by our own choices – can ruin our lives by making the wrong calls. But there is hope!

The greatest call of all was a death on the Cross, by Christ, who is the resurrected Mediator of all. The choice to accept Jesus' sacrifice and be cleansed by His blood is to insure that I win the game and will be with God forever in Heaven!

Let us rejoice for the greatest call of all!

Thank you, Jesus, for Your sacrifice. And, thank You for being my Mentor, Mediator, Master and Manifester of light. Help me make the right calls in life, so I can also be a radiant light for others. In Your most precious, potent, and powerful name I pray. Amen

A ROAD MAP FOR THE CHRISTIAN LIFE

Lanette Kissel   June 17

On vacation, my husband drives while I read the map. I enjoy studying our route since the map gives us detailed directions.

When it comes to our Christian life, we also have a Road Map we can follow as we make our journey through life. Christ has given us the Way by setting the perfect example with the life He led, documented in the Bible. Jesus invites us to follow in His footsteps for our journey on this earth. None of us could fill His sandals, yet He urges us to emulate His example.

On a superhighway, we're tempted by signs which beckon us to exit. If we take the bait, these attractions delay us in reaching our destination.

So, in life, many distractions lead us astray and take our focus away from a Christ-centered life. Although detours may detain us, it's important that we quickly find our way back to the highway we are traveling with Christ. We must always keep our focus forward on His Way, instead of constantly checking our rearview mirror to see what we've left behind.

With Christ's example as our Road Map, we can follow His lead. We can walk in His footsteps as the Holy Spirit shines His light on our map. With Him as our Guide, we can embark on life's journey, beginning at our starting point here on earth, and ending at our final destination – our eternal home in Heaven!

WASHED UP?

Rick Leland   June 18

Bill grinned, saying, "Jesus is washed up." We looked at the unsigned, untitled painting at the art gallery. His comment touched off indignation in me. But I was silent.

The splashy watercolor depicted a Laundromat scene. In the painting, a mom and son were standing inches away from an array of front-loading, glass-doored washers. Mom focused on her laundering duties at the upper level while her son stood at eye-level to the lower set.

The scene had one peculiarity. The son stared intently at one of the glass-faced washers as if he were looking into a mirror. Instead of his reflection, however, there was an image of Jesus – and He appeared to be inside the washer!

Even though mom and son were standing close, they seemed to be in different worlds.

Just like them, my companion and I stood close; yet we were a million miles apart in our spiritual worlds. I follow Jesus. He does not.

The Bible talks about this great gulf: ***"An unspiritual man does not accept the spiritual things, things of God, for they are foolishness to him; and he cannot understand them."*** 1 Corinthians 2:14 (NASB)

My good friend's mind doesn't comprehend the part of my world which gives my life substance and meaning. Without Jesus in my life, I would be washed-up.

I turned to Bill and offered my appraisal of the painting: "Jesus washes away sins." Oh, that he would listen!

"LONDON GRACE"

Robert McCreight   June 19

Read Isaiah 26:1-4, 8-9, 12-13,19-21

"Thou wilt keep him in perfect peace whose mind is stayed on thee: because he trusteth in thee." Isaiah 26:3 (KJV)

The people of Isaiah's day were living under constant threat of Assyrian oppression. Isaiah gave them the dream of a "city of refuge" – a city with walls strong enough to withstand attackers, giving the people victory (verse 1). With victory comes peace (verses 3, 12) as well as a *new life* (verse 19). Isaiah called them into God's "safe city" to live in peace.

John Newton – slave trader – who gave us "Amazing Grace," later became a parish priest in the Church of England. At one point he was called from the village of Olney to pastor a congregation in London. When he faced a new life in the bustling city of London, he prayed for "London grace," or "grace to enable him to live as a Christian, even in London."

Newton's prayer is identical to Isaiah's hope for his contemporaries, and for Christians today. The challenge to escape oppression and receive God's gifts of victory, peace, and rebirth invite us to come into a "New Jerusalem," and live with our Lord.

Lord, please give me "London grace" to live in this new place, for, If not today, some enemy will bump me off the path. I know that enemies will challenge my faith in You. Give me Your hope of victory, and a vision of peace. Guide me into a place where I can experience the gift of new life in closer relationship with You. Amen

AN ANGEL ENCAMPED ON THE VISOR

Betty King   June 20

"The angel of the LORD encamps around those who fear him, and he delivers them." Psalm 34:7 (NIV)

I recently found some angels made for car visors. Each package included a prayer for protection for the driver. I purchased one for my son who drives a lot on his job. I had often cautioned him to be careful when he left on work-related excursions. I hoped that the angel on the visor would remind him to be cautious and remember that his mother was praying for him.

One day he told me that he always reaches up and touches the angel while praying, as he begins another trip on the road.

Of course, that angel is only an ornament. But it reminds him to ask

God to go with him and surround him with His guardian angels.

Even so, I continue to pray for my son's protection, too. We need to stand in reverence of God, asking Him for His divine preservation of our loved ones. We all need reminders that God and His angels are always available to help, protect and guide us through this life, if we only ask.

If you need a sticky note, an angel ornament, or some other sign, then use it to nudge you into remembering to ask God for His safe-keeping.

KITTY GARDENING

Rose Goble   June 21

"Every plant that my heavenly Father has not planted will be pulled up by the roots," Matthew 15:13 (NIV)

I have two cats that believe they are gardeners. My older cat removes my cuttings from their water glasses. Each morning I replace them, snipping off the ends, and hoping the stems haven't dried beyond resuscitation.

The kitten enjoys the coolness of the soil and lies on top of my plants, suffocating those not broken beyond repair.

Their gardening is more like killing than cultivating.

I wonder if God looks down on how I disciple in the same manner as I observe the cats' help? He has those in the church growing tender new roots. They don't need to be yanked out of the living water or smothered by my interference. He alone knows exactly how to fertilize and encourage their growth.

I think I'll leave well enough alone and watch for the blossoms and fruit instead.

TIMING IS EVERYTHING

Carol J. Lee   June 22

"Then you will know that I am the Lord; those who hope in me will not be disappointed." Isaiah 49:23b (NIV)
"Wait for the Lord; be strong and let your heart take courage...." Psalm 27:14 (NASB)

Several years ago, my husband and I sold an office building. Like most people, we had our moments of anxiety like most people; we wanted it sold right away. However, it took about five months before we got an offer. All went well, and, in a few days, an agreement was reached and papers signed.

What was so special about the timing of the signing is that we did it on our way out of town! We were going on a two-week camping adventure to the Northwest Territories which we had wanted to do for years!

God could have helped us sell that building at anytime – but He seemed to want the right moment to be a special one! To sign the papers on our way out of town increased the joy of our trip, knowing the office was sold and we need not worry about it anymore. What a great start to our Northwest Territories adventure!

Father, let this experience be a reminder to me in other situations when I need to wait. While waiting, I'll put my hope in You, knowing that You have the best for me. Your special timing comes from Your love. Amen

JESUS WILL BREAK MY FALL

Pat Collins   June 23

"Fear not, for I am with you; be not dismayed, for I am your God. I will strengthen you, yes, I will help you, I will uphold you with my righteous right hand." Isaiah 41:10 (NKJV)

As I slip and slide along life's way,
Always in a hurry, not stopping to pray,
I sometimes wonder if I'll make it through.
My heart cries out to God, "What should I do?"
Then that comforting voice from within tells me,
All will be fine if I listen to Him.
I may stumble and bend, but will not break,
For Jesus forgives each mistake I make.
Jesus is always there to break my fall,
I need never worry – He will handle it all!

STANDING IN JOY AND STRENGTH

Lydia Harris   June 24

Read: Nehemiah 8:1-10

"The joy of the Lord is your strength." Nehemiah 8:10 (NIV)

"Let's all stand in honor of the reading of God's Word," the visiting pastor told our congregation. This sign of respect during Bible reading was new to us, but not to the Israelites. When Ezra stood to read, everyone stood. And the Scripture wasn't short; it lasted all morning. As the Israelites heard God's Word, they fell on their faces, weeping in repentance.

But Nehemiah told them not to grieve. The Feast of Trumpets was to be a celebration of joy. The people were marking the rebuilding of the walls of Jerusalem. The joy of the Lord, Nehemiah said, was to be their strength (verse 10).

Years after our children graduated, I returned to their public school for a recital. A student stood and said, "I'm singing this song for my family and friends. But mostly, I'm singing it for my Lord." Her song expressed her Christian faith.

When she finished, I jumped to my feet and applauded. But I stood alone. The woman beside me said, "She was good, but not *that* good."

The student's joy in the Lord gave her courage to witness before peers in a secular school. And my joy in the Lord provided strength for me to stand alone without embarrassment to honor her Lord and mine.

Lord, we honor You for Your Word. You alone are our source of joy. Today, whatever we face, may our joy in You provide the strength we need. Amen

THE CELLO

Gloria Hillman   June 25

Recently, during worship at our church, a tall gentleman played the violoncello (a mid-size instrument larger than a violin and smaller than a bass viol) not for *us*, but for God.

We listened as he played from Bach, Saint-Saens, and many others – the melodies rolling like beach waves onto the shore. This, a gift from God, was given back to the Giver.

We shared in the celebration, knowing that such beauty, such depth, is not of earthly origin. How could we ever doubt the goodness of the Giver? Pain and grief were not intended for us; music and art remind us of His Love. It's there! See it, hear it, and be glad!

When tears of joy come to my eyes, I ask, "Why am I crying, Lord? I'm full of joy!"

I hear, *"Listen to the music, see the sunset, be in awe at the grandeur of the trees, and know that I am there! I treasure your tears of joy!"*

ARE YOU OVERDRAWN?

Joan Clayton   June 26

Read Matthew 20

"But he that is greatest among you shall be your servant."

Matthew 23:11 (KJV)

Life is like a bank account. If you continually withdraw from it and never make a deposit, you will soon be overdrawn and heading for bankruptcy. I believe we have been given an abundant life and God expects us to put something back into it.

Maybe you can't repay someone who has sacrificed for you, but you *can* make sacrifices for others. I know a first grade teacher who had a crippled student whom she had to carry everywhere.

Other teachers asked, "Why do you do that? Why not just leave him in his seat as much as you can?"

She replied, "How can I better show my gratitude for my own healthy children than by helping someone less fortunate?"

How does your bank statement read today? Are you putting something back into life? A card, a visit, or food for a sick neighbor are ways to make deposits into your life's "bank account."

Father, forgive our self-centeredness. May our thoughts be so full of others that we lose ourselves in Your service. Amen

THIS IS THE WAY, WALK IN IT
Donna J. Howard   June 27

"O people of Zion, who live in Jerusalem, you will weep no more. How gracious He will be when you cry for help! As soon as He hears, He will answer you. Although the Lord gives you the bread of adversity and the water of affliction, your teachers will be hidden no more; with your own eyes you will see them. Whether you turn to the right or to the left, your ears will hear a voice behind you, saying, "This is the way; walk in it."
Isaiah 30:19-25 (NIV)

Life isn't always easy. Sometimes the Lord gives us "the bread of adversity and the water of affliction," but He will never leave us to walk through those times alone.

He will show us the way out.

"Whether you turn to the right or to the left, your ears will hear a voice behind you, saying: 'This is the way, walk in it.'" Isaiah 30:25 (NIV)

That promise makes me feel much more secure. I hope it does you, too!

I SEE MORE FRUIT ... WHEN I'M ON MY KNEES

Glenda Joy Race   June 28

"I picked all the blackberries yesterday," my mom told me. At first glance that seemed to be true. As I looked straight ahead, I saw that all the remaining berries appeared to be green. But as I peered down into the bush, I saw a cluster of ripe ones I could not reach unless I stooped to their level.

"Mom, could you get me a plastic bag?" I asked, as I knelt down. She came back in a minute and found that I had a handful of ripe blackberries already picked. Within ten minutes we had a pint of them to add to Mom's previous harvest.

Being able to find more berries when I got on my knees made me think of how often I overlook the harvest that the Lord has prepared. In Matthew 9:37, Jesus tells us *"The harvest truly is plentiful, but the workers are few."* (NIV) As a laborer for Christ, am I just reaching the easy fruit, or am I getting on my knees to reach those others may not see?

Lord, give me the humility and opportunity to look for the harvest that You have prepared everywhere. Amen

PROVISIONS

Kathy Johnson   June 29

"Look at the birds of the air; they do not sow or reap or store away in barns, and yet your heavenly Father feeds them. Are you not much more valuable than they?" Matthew 6:26 (NIV)

Walking through the San Diego Zoo, we spotted elephants eating their food, and polar bears playing with their toys in the water, while koalas and pandas relaxed during the heat of the day. None of them paid much attention to the visitors.

The animals at the zoo were well-cared for and didn't worry about how they would acquire their next meal or toy!

Sometimes our lives seem out of control. We worry about the payment due or the surgery scheduled. It's at times such as these we need the Lord to come and remind us once again that *He is in control!* Has He not always cared for us, and supplied our needs? We're certainly of more worth than the birds and all the animals in the zoo!

Thank You, Lord, for all You have provided for us – our homes, families, clothing, food, jobs, and good neighbors. Keep us in Your care. Amen

TRUST

Valerie J. Chambers   June 30

Don't be afraid, My little one, your Daddy's always near.
I will never leave you; let your heart be full of cheer.
Your troubles have been many, but I've had My eyes on you.
Set your heart upon Me. I will always bring you through.
Although it seems this valley is deeper than the rest,
Place your heart within My hands and you'll be truly blessed.
For I am your Redeemer, your Lover and your Friend;
You can trust My love for you because it has no end.
I know the end from the beginning; your times are in My hands
Your flower will not wither as those in desert sands.
Set your roots down deeper; drink solely from My well
At the end of this new trial you'll have more truth to tell
Of My faithfulness and goodness, and of My love for you,
How I nurtured and cared for you and how I brought you through!

JULY
WARS

Evelyn Quinby   July 1

*"And you will be hearing of wars and rumors of wars; see that
you are not frightened, for those things must take place...."*
Matthew 24:6 (NASB)

My paternal grandmother was a little girl during the Civil War, or the
"War between the States," as she called it. Her mother went onto the
battlefield in Virginia where they lived in search of loved ones. She
identified one relative from a piece of clothing she had made from cloth
she had woven! Grandmother said that the children would climb onto
the roof of the chicken house and lie there, listening to the sounds of
war. I don't know how many men in our lineage died, paying the price
so that we could live in freedom.

We can go all the way back to the Declaration of Independence
and remember those loved ones who gave their lives for our country.
The list is long for all of us.

Freedom is a rare commodity in this world, and we need to be
grateful to God for giving us this country, and to those who paid the
price for it. Jesus also paid to set us free, not only in this life, but in the
life to come. We were liberated from sin by His sacrifice. He deserves
the highest praise and honor due His name!

Father, we thank You that the grave could not hold Jesus – and that

110

He lives forever, making intercession for us. We thank You, too, for the promise that the grave cannot hold us, either, because we are free in Jesus, our Savior! Amen

"OLD GLORY"

Albert S. Hickey   July 2

> Behold "Old Glory," flying free – symbol of our liberty –
> Like the eagle, soaring high, the emblem of American pride.
> We the people of the USA,
> together give thanks for our freedom today.
> So fly "Old Glory!" Salute it with pride
> and grateful thanks to those who died.
> Freedom costs. It's never been free.
> Let the stars and stripes wave to remind you and me.
> Be ever thankful that "In God we trust,"
> Who provided Another Who died for us.
> Let us serve our great country wherever we can,
> and pledge our allegiance to our own homeland.
> I salute you, "Old Glory," flying free,
> And forever bless God for our liberty.

"WASTE NOT"

Jason Carpenter   July 3

"When they all had enough to eat He (Jesus) said to his disciples, 'Gather the pieces that are left over. Let nothing be wasted.'" John 6:12 (NIV)

Being a Korean War veteran, my dad wasn't big on the noise surrounding Fourth of July celebrations. It also bothered him that people in our area spent hard-earned money on fireworks that popped and wasted away in thin air. Also, someone might get hurt.

Once, to get his point across, he took out ten $5 bills and raised a box of matches to symbolize how easily the money could be burned in the same wasteful way as purchasing firecrackers. He saw no difference.

As affluent Americans, we often spend money on things that pop, fizzle, and disappear. We individually have some sort of "fireworks" in our lives that we unwisely choose to spend our money on. Scripture calls us to be good stewards of our resources. Jesus taught us in the book of John to waste nothing. When I was a child, I didn't understand my earthly father's teaching, but now I do.

Dear Father in Heaven, help me to take Your Word and apply it to my life. You taught us not to waste anything. How careless it is to use money unwisely. Mid-year, let us see the needs of those around us and act in Your behalf. Amen

PERFECT LIBERTY

Joseph M. Hopkins   July 4

"You will know the truth, and the truth will set you free."
John 8:32 (KJV)

On a rock outside the log-cabin home of my sister and brother-in-law in a wooded rural area of North Carolina are inscribed these words: "Perfect liberty is perfect obedience to perfect law." It was the theme of Laurence Cooper's high school valedictory. Everybody wants emancipation. The USA is "the land of the free and the home of the brave." But the release after which most people lust is "imperfect liberty." The freedom to do as *they* please, not as God pleases.

A railroad train is free to roll – as long as it stays on the rails! To leave the rails is to court disaster. The Ten Commandments, as explained by Jesus in the Sermon on the Mount (Matthew 5-7), are our rails. They define the good life: the life of love, joy, peace, and goodness. Yes, and freedom! Freedom from guilt, heartache, pain, alienation, and evil. "Perfect liberty is perfect obedience to perfect law." How true!

*Lord, help us to exclaim with the Psalmist, **"Oh, how love I Your law! It is my meditation all the day!"** (Psalm 119:97) By Your indwelling Spirit help us to love and obey the rules for living You have provided for our welfare, happiness, and usefulness in serving You and others. In Jesus' name and to His glory. Amen*

ARMING MYSELF FOR THE DAY

Gloria Clover   July 5

*Father God, I put on the **full armor** You have provided so that I may take my stand against the devil's schemes. If today is a day of evil, I pray that I will be able to stand my ground.*

*I buckle the **belt of Truth** – the Lord Jesus Christ – around my waist. I acknowledge that You are Creator, Giver and Sustainer of all life, the one God, the only God, the Master of mankind. All wisdom begins in You. All generosity and compassion flow from You. The truth is that we are nothing without You.*

*Father, I latch into place the **breastplate of righteousness**, mine*

112

because Jesus is righteous, because He did not sin, because He was obedient to death, and lives. I praise You for my righteousness, purchased by His blood.

So, I plant my feet with the readiness to share **the Gospel of peace**. I pray not to miss opportunities. Please raise up workers for the harvest. Bless your missionaries, preachers, teachers, and prophets. I ask for the Truth to be spoken in basements and from rooftops for those who have ears to hear and believe. I ask it in Jesus' name.

Lord, I take up my **shield**, my very faith that You provide, that You strengthen, that You test for imperfections and weaknesses, and that You restore. I hold it against the flaming lies and accusations of the evil one. I trust You with the outcome because I know the war has been won.

ARMING MYSELF FOR THE DAY
Gloria Clover   (Continued)   July 6

I fasten the **helmet of salvation** upon my head, and stand firm in the knowledge that nothing can separate me from Christ's love found in You. I know that You have arranged salvation for Your glory and our need. I acknowledge that I must take my thoughts captive to the obedience and authority of Christ. I confess my sins of rebellion and pride that have opened me to deception. I confess I have not resisted temptation even though You provide a way out. I'm sorry.

And, Lord God, I take up my **Sword of the Spirit**, Your Holy Word, the Lord Jesus Christ, in whom I live and breathe and have life. I carry Him before me, opening doors, ripping through webs of deceit, shining light on all the dark lies of this world. I hold the Truth high in my life so that I might see and others might see You.

I pray in the mighty Name of Jesus for Truth to reign in my heart, my marriage, my church, and in my community. I pray for Truth to reign in this country, Lord Jesus, for You to take Your rightful place as Master and Lord.

ARMING MYSELF FOR THE DAY
Gloria Clover   (Continued)   July 7

I pray for all lies to be exposed in the Name of Jesus.
I pray for all captives to be set free in the Name of Jesus.
I pray for the broken and the wounded to be healed in the Name of Jesus.
I pray for the lost to be found and restored in the Name of Jesus.

Jesus, I trust You to bring about Your Holy Will. I trust You to do exactly what You came to do. I thank You for the promise that You will return in power. I thank You for the promise that You have not abandoned us, but have left us in the mighty arms of the Comforter. I thank You for Your faithfulness.

You do all things with compassion and grace, with justice and mercy, in time and out of time. You are Lord, the Holy God. You are the great I AM. You are not shocked, dismayed, or frustrated.

Your will is perfect. Bring Your perfect will into my life and the lives of my loved ones and Yours, the Church armed for this day. This I ask in Jesus' name. Amen

HOW DO YOU MEASURE A LIFE?
Norm MacDonald   July 8

How do you measure a life
Through days lived, or lives touched?
Is it what you do or who you are?
Can I measure it in dollars and cents
Or will any one know that I cared?
Is it what I didn't do that causes me grief
Or what I did for selfish reasons?
Will the days I wasted be gathered somehow
Or will the harvest be shortened for lack of planting?
Can you pick up where you left off
Or leave off where you picked up?
Can I bounce my life against another's for meaning
Or will it simply bounce back as "nonsufficient funds"?
What can I say that hasn't been said
When I try to say what needs to be said?
What is it about losing your life to gain it?
Oh … that's right –
That is how you measure a life!

SYMBOL
Mary A. Koepke   July 9
"Thy word is a lamp to my feet and a light to my path."
Psalm 119:105 (RSV)

Someday, if I were to paint a very special still life, I would arrange a group of well-known symbols on a sapphire cloth draping an altar-like form.

Its composition would include a rugged, brown cross with an Easter lily lying at the base. Beside it, a pure, white, ceramic dove would be poised near a broken loaf of bread and a golden chalice. In a numinous background, a muted image of Jesus would be moving forward. Below Him, there would be a yellow, pink-tipped, Peace rose in a milk glass vase to honor His mother. The center of interest in the foreground would be my old, open Bible, illuminated by a glowing shaft of light, inviting all to take and read.

Although I chose only a few of many symbols (probably in the composing and rendering process I could include many, many more) but my old Bible will always shine as my Guiding Light.

AMAZING GRACE

Shirley Stevens   July 10

I met my pew mate Louise at The Christian Church where we became friends. After she went into assisted living at age 99, I often visited her. I even attended her 100th birthday party where a bagpiper in full tartan plaid played "Amazing Grace."

One day she told me about how she had left Scotland and had celebrated her 16th birthday at Ellis Island. Afterward, I had lunch with my friend Patty and mentioned Louise's hometown.

Her mouth dropped open. "What town did you say?"

I said, "Kirkintillich."

"Why, my grandfather is from Kirkintillich, too!" she gasped, "And I have a painting of the town which I will lend you to share with Louise."

The next week I took the watercolor to the nursing home. As I described the street scene in the picture, Louise pointed to the foundry building in the foreground. She said, "My father lost his leg in an accident there."

She told me stories about growing up in Scotland and coming to America – alone – to earn money so that she could send some home to help her parents. Louise, who married and reared three sons, never returned to her native country. With a tear in her eye, she sang a verse from the hymn "Amazing Grace":

"The Lord has promised good to me,
His word my hope secures.
He will my shield and portion be,
As long as life endures."

Dear Lord, help us to remember the courage of our ancestors who came to this country trusting You and working hard to build a better life. Amen

BELIEVE

Janice May Harris   July 11

"If you believe, you will receive whatever you ask for in prayer."
Matthew 21:22 (NIV)

Kathleen was appalled when she found her grandson's goldfish floating belly-up in the fish tank! She remembered how much pleasure this pet had given Kailo! Even though the fish appeared dead and beyond hope, she didn't hesitate to pray.

It wasn't a long prayer. "Jesus, please heal Kailo's fish."

Before leaving the house to do errands, Kathleen glanced back at the tank. The fish was still lying motionless and upside down in the water. Her faith, however, was not shaken by this.

Kathleen arrived home later, and to her delight, found that the goldfish was frolicking in the fish tank as if nothing had ever happened! That small, answered prayer gave her courage to pray bigger prayers, remembering that ***"All things are possible if you believe and do not doubt when you pray."***

Thank You, Jesus, for Your faithfulness in answering our prayers – even when we pray for a "dead" goldfish! Amen

GETTING EXPERT HELP

Dee Hartman   July 12

"Ask and it shall be given you...." Matthew 7:7 (KJV)

My long-haired Chihuahua enjoys frolicking through our yard. Unfortunately this summer, fleas shared the yard, too. Unknown to me, they jumped onto my little "Pokey," making themselves right at home in her jungle of hair. Soon, however, I noticed Pokey scratching incessantly. I spied one of the little black critters on her and tried to get rid of them, using anti-flea shampoo and a flea collar.

Pokey was, however, still constantly scratching. My poor dog was miserable, exhausted from the constant irritation of her allergic reaction to the fleas. I tried using various over-the-counter medications, but nothing seemed to help. After a few days, I took her to the vet. This doctor gave her a steroid/allergy shot.

Finally my little dog found welcomed rest. I put on the "full armor" against that army of fleas by going to an expert to take care of the problem.

As I thought about this situation, I compared it to my relationship with God. I sometimes attempt to handle problems myself, instead of "putting on the whole armor of God" and immediately seeking His help.

116

I often become desperate before going to Him. How much better it is, when I put God in charge right away. I need to remember He is always available and I should ask His help as soon as problems surface.

Lord, may I quickly turn to You at all times, rather than trying to address problems on my own. Amen

CREATOR OF MY SOUL

Debbie Carpenter																			July 13

"Jesus answered, "But whoever drinks the water I give him will never thirst. Indeed the water I give him will become in him a spring of water welling up to eternal life." John 4:14 (NIV)

Creator of my soul,
the One whom I adore,
With every breath I breathe You give new life to me.
As I walked the desert sand You took me by the hand.
I was parched, my heart was dry.
You wiped away the tears I cried.
Then the river came and washed me whole again.
Streams of living water refreshed me and brought renewal.
Creator of my soul, the One whom I adore.
With every breath I breathe,
You give new life to me!

LOOKING YOUR SPIRITUAL BEST

Brad Nelson																			July 14

"… ye are like unto whited sepulchers, which indeed appear beautiful outward, but are within full of dead men's bones, and of all uncleanness … ye also outwardly appear righteous unto men, but within ye are full of hypocrisy and iniquity."
Matthew 23:27-28 (KJV)

How much time do you spend getting yourself ready in the morning? We all like to look just right, and we devote a considerable amount of time in choosing the proper outfit to wear.

How much time do you spend daily getting your soul ready? Many of us devote far more time to primping and prepping our exterior than we do our interior! It's okay to look good. However, we need to make sure we are giving equal – if not greater – attention to *being* good.

In this passage, Jesus harshly chastises a group of religious leaders for focusing more on the exterior than the interior. We would be wise to learn from their poor example and take care to prepare our souls each day. Spend time asking Jesus to cleanse your soul (1 John 1:9). Bathe in the waters of God's Word (Ephesians 5:26). Make sure you've put on the sweet aroma of Jesus (2 Corinthians 2:15). Clothe yourself in the "new man" (Ephesians 4:14) and God's armor (Ephesians 6:11). Strive to look your spiritual best as you go out into the world.

Father, forgive me for focusing on my external appearance. Help me to prepare my interior diligently as I enter each day. Amen

A GLOWING COMPLEXION

Evelyn Minshull   July 15
Read Exodus 34:29-35; Luke 9:28-43

Whenever Moses had been apart with God, his countenance glowed. The people shielded their eyes from its brightness, as we protect our sight when sunlight glances across glazed snow, as we cringe from sudden floodlights, and view eclipses of the sun only obliquely.

And so Moses wore a veil when he moved among the people. But when he reentered God's presence, he laid aside the veil.

When Moses and Elijah appeared with Jesus on the Mount of Transfiguration, the face of Jesus shone; the whiteness of His clothing dazzled His disciples. Their awe was tinged with terror, as a cloud engulfed them and the voice of God acknowledged Jesus as His Son.

Light is a necessity. It illuminates; it warms; it fosters growth. And the greatest of all lights is Jesus – Who came to banish darkness of the spirit; to warm the hearts of both the sorrowing and the stolid; to encourage spiritual growth.

When the veil of sin falls from our eyes, His Light embraces us. Not to frighten us, never to blind us, but to fill and complete us.

O, God, flood us with Your Light so that our faces glow and our lives reflect Your Glory. Amen

IS THIS THE ABUNDANT LIFE?

D. Jonean Walton   July 16
"The thief comes only to steal and kill and destroy, I came that you may have life, and have it more abundantly."
John 10:10 (NRSV)

Christ can use any situation you experience to make your life more abundant.

Being a "word nerd," I used Logos Bible software to further investigate "abundant life." The closest translation to the original Greek is the word "excess." Interestingly, "excess" is only a measure-ment and has neither good nor bad connotation as some suggest. However, the part of the translation which caught my eye for "life" is, "***It is experienced both now and eternally.***"

A multitude of believers have lived long, dedicated spans of incessant struggle. Some constantly battle with health problems or barely make it from paycheck to paycheck. Is this the "abundant life" Christ came to give His children? Do you think….

The abundant life is suddenly gaining a financial windfall?

Is it living with a disability or a debilitating illness?

Is it loved ones who are left behind to grieve?

Is it riding on the joys of marriage or relying on God's loving grace to survive a bitter divorce?

Is it surviving on the street, living from hand to mouth, while knowing you have a mansion waiting for you, thanks to your Father?

Since life is experienced ***both now and eternally***, the answer to all of those questions is "yes." So when life feels excessive and is turning you every which way but loose, don't panic.

Christ can use any situation you experience to make your life more abundant!

A FOOL FOR CHRIST

Derrick K. Osorio   July 17

In the morning, when I awake, I fall down to my knees
Unto the Lord I take all my cries and pleas.
In His tender, loving care is my faith and trust
As I unearth the devil's lair – which is this world's lust –
I walk along His path with His Word in my hand
As I endure the evil wrath of the ungodly band.
I sing praises to His name and proclaim His holy message
As the heathen defame and mar His visage.
Spiritual sacrifices I make as I bear my cross
I suffer and give up all things for His sake –
but count it all but loss.
He makes me to heal the lame and cast out evil spirits
As I spread the love of His name and live as a "Fool for Christ."

KEEPER, EATER, OR TROPHY?

Kathy Johnson   July 18

*"'Come, follow me,' Jesus said, 'and I will
make you fishers of men.'"* Matthew 4:19 (NIV)

My brother-in-law went through a phase when he fished often.
However, it was difficult to cast a hook with him and hope to have a
meal of walleye – since, according to him, most of the scaly creatures
were not "keepers." I think he would have released even a "trophy" fish!
Once you have a fish on your line, you have three possible outcomes:
Either it will shake free, you will release it, or you will catch and kill it.

Our Lord makes us fishermen, women, and children, but with a
different result. Our "catch" for the Lord is neither *dead* nor *gone*, but
rather "alive in Christ Jesus."

Dear Lord, grant guidance to my fishing abilities for You. Amen

THE BUMPER STICKER

Bill Batcher   July 19

The traffic ambles along the expressway at half the posted limit. I
begin to observe other drivers. I notice the crews waiting to set out the
cones for the day's construction. I consider whether the sky confirms
the forecast. I turn off the Christian radio station, but hymns from long
ago keep echoing in my head.

Then I notice a bumper sticker. "God Loves You," the blue Volvo
blares. I've seen it on a hundred cars before; sometimes with the
impudent addendum, "and so do I." God loves me? What arrogance!
Can we really read the mind of the Almighty? After all, He is *"immortal,
invisible, God only wise, in heights inaccessible, hid from our eyes."* We
cannot know a thing about Him, let alone His love, unless he declares it
– but He *has* declared it by saving me!

*"Amazing Grace, how sweet the sound, that saved a wretch like
me."* Some hymn books write it, "a worm like me." Me, so sinful, so
pathetic, so worthless and yet He saved me. Isn't that love?

How easily the pious respond with John 3:16. God loved us so
much that He gave His Son! What a price! The answer comes from a
verse of another obscure hymn out of the deep recesses of my brain:

*"If it were in my power to save the world from sin
and from the grave,
I would not give my only son, but that is what the Lord has done."*

DO YOU FEEL ALONE IN YOUR PAIN?

Betty King   July 20

*"You've kept track of my every toss and turn through the
sleepless nights, each tear entered in your ledger, each ache
written in your book." Psalm 56:8 (The Message)*

Do you sometimes feel alone in pain? We all have physical, mental
or emotional pain the world knows nothing about. People cry privately in
the confines of their homes, in the dark of night, feeling hurt and alone.
They feel no one understands the hurt and distress they're going
through.

It is in pain, fear and worry that we feel alone. We wonder if we are
the only one to feel such distress. We think no one knows about our
situation or even cares if they do. But the Bible tells us God is keeping
count of every time we toss and turn! He has recorded every tear we
have shed. He knows every ache.

The next time you toss and turn in the middle of the night, when
sleep will not come, and you wet your pillow with tears, let the Scripture
above comfort you. Alone in the dark of night, or standing in the middle
of a crowd when you are hiding your pain, know God knows how you
feel. He knows what you are going through.

Also remember what the Scriptures say, *"...Never will I leave you;
never will I forsake you."* Hebrews 13:5 (NIV)

"THIRD SHIFT"

Valerie J. Chambers   July 21

It is dark. I am alone and afraid.
Every noise I hear shatters the silence.
I am drawn into the clutches of the unknown.
My sinking heart is captured.
I see fleeting dark shadows.
The hairs on my arms rise up.
I fantasize about what might be out there.
I recall every horror story from the news.
My breaths are short and labored.
My ears are attuned to every tick of the clock.
It sounds like a dripping faucet.
I long for morning.
I speak Your Words; out loud:
*"Fear thou not; for I am with thee:
Be not dismayed; for I am thy God:*

I will strengthen thee; yea, I will help thee;
Yea, I will uphold thee with the right hand
of my righteousness."
(Isaiah 41:10 KJV)
I am thankful that God never sleeps!

FAITH

Deborah J. Tune   July 22

That chilly winter day, gloom hovered over me. My husband, our sole provider, had been in a horrible truck accident. After exhausting all our finances, I was trying to keep the faith. But I needed a miracle that day – or our electricity would be turned off!

A rare knock came at the door. Opening it, I was surprised to behold a neighbor I hadn't seen in a while. She reached out her hand and placed something in mine. I put it in my pocket, thanked her, and she left.

As I went back to my laundry, I looked in my pocket. In her poverty, she had given me a generous offering! I thanked the Lord, but still had to trust Him for more to cover the bill.

Lo and behold! I heard another knock. How strange to have visitors twice in one day! Again, I opened the door. The same little lady stood on the porch.

"The Lord told me to bring you that offering this morning. But on my way to town, He told me I had given you the wrong amount."

She opened my hand and I took what she offered me. I was shocked, knowing she was quite poor.

"Oh, my dear, thank you! The Lord will surely bless you," I said as she left.

I counted the money she had given me this time – and, when added to the rest, it was *exactly* how much I required! Thank God! He was faithful to supply my need.

PHYSICAL AILMENTS

Nancy Dearborn   July 23
Read Philippians 1:19-26
"Is any one of you sick? He should call the elders
of the church to pray over him and anoint him with oil
in the name of the Lord." James 5:14 (NIV)

I left the doctor's office a little discouraged. Besides my long-term illness of 25 years, other physical ailments were stacking up. I had strep throat, a kidney infection, hot flashes, hypothyroidism, and my bones were deteriorating. (Thank God we get new bodies when we get to Heaven!)

After obtaining medicine for some of my ailments, I made an appointment to speak to a pastor. He and I agreed that – after church Wednesday night – I would have the deacons lay hands on me, pray over me, and anoint me with oil. They did this in the back of the sanctuary near the prayer room.

An acquaintance from the church called me the next day. "I saw you last night being anointed. I know you're struggling with some physical challenges, but it was a witness and testimony to me that you had the deacons anoint you and pray over you. What tremendous faith you must have!"

I was surprised at my friend's words. I'd had the anointing because I desired healing, yet God had used my health concerns to be a witness to another believer!

Lord, thank You for using us, even in our illnesses, to be a witness and testimony to You. Amen

FOOTPRINTS IN THE SAND

Dave Evans   July 24
**"And it came to pass … he entered into one of the boats …
and taught the people out of the boat."** Luke 5:1-2 (Webster's)

Down from the hills, one lone set of footprints
Leads through the sand to the water's edge.
Soon the crowd gathers,
And multitudes of footprints wrap around the
Curve of the shoreline, covering the beach.
Stepping into a boat, the Master
Begins to teach as the crowd listens and learns.
Around a sea of glass, the Heavenly host sings,
Elders cast down their golden crowns,
Legions of angels utter praise;
And multitudes, gathered from throughout the ages,
Fill the shoreline, their footprints covering the sand.
Seated on the throne, the Master
Listens and receives the honor due Him.
**"And before the throne …four and twenty elders fall down before
him … and worship him … saying, Thou art worthy, O Lord, to
receive glory, and honor, and power…."**
Revelation 4:6-11 (Websters)

IN TIMES OF ADVERSITY

Lanette Kissel   July 25

**"...the Lord gave and the Lord has taken away;
may the name of the Lord be praised."** Job 1:21 (NIV)

Job enjoyed the good life and had accumulated much wealth. God had richly blessed him. Yet God allowed Satan to take away those material blessings, and others as well.

The wise Job realized that none of the riches and possessions he had accumulated were of importance. His relationship with God the Father was what really mattered to him.

Though the walls of Job's existence were crumbling around him, this steadfast servant did not lose his focus upon God or his faith. In the face of terrible adversity, Job still honored and praised God!

In times of adversity, we are extremely vulnerable. At those times, we seem to need God more than ever. Many of us are quick to turn to Him when things get rough. However, are we able to praise God during those times? It is far from easy to give thanks when things seem to be crumbling around us. Yet, that is exactly what Job did.

All-knowing Father, please help us to be able to praise You in all things, the good and the bad. Amen

BLOOM WHERE PLANTED

Janet R. Sady   July 26

**"...And he said, He that showed mercy on him.
Then said Jesus unto him, Go, and do thou likewise."**
Luke 10:37 (KJV)

Someone gave me a bookmarker with a rosebud that reads: "Bloom Where You Are Planted." What does that mean to us as Christians?

I think it means that in every circumstance, wherever we find opportunity to help those in need or serve, we should respond in a positive way. Jesus gave us the parable of the Good Samaritan, which illustrates that we are to help persons we don't even know. God sent the Samaritan down that road for the purpose of helping a person in need. The Samaritan did indeed "Bloom Where He Was Planted."

We can remain in the bud of our relationship with Christ, or we can strive to be like Him, and bloom as a rose in His garden of service and sacrifice for others.

Father, help me to show Your love to those around me that are in need of help. May my life send up a sweet smelling fragrance in service for You. Amen

PLANS FOR YOU

Elouise H. Hults   July 27

"For I know the plans I have for you, says the Lord. They are plans for good and not for evil, To give you a future and a hope."
Jeremiah 29:11 (TLB)

You have no choice about:

When, where, or by whom you were born.
Your inherited shape: is it apple or pear?
Your family: your mom, dad, siblings and all.
Your natural talents and personal whims.
Whether you're hyper, strong-willed, or not.
Because you are a gift from God, planned by Him a long time ago.

But you *can* choose:

What your body does or where it goes.
Your attitude: Does it stink or shine?
If you care or if you share.
What you reflect: good or ill.
What you see, hear, or consume.
What you will do with God.
Your ancestry you cannot choose,
Genes, or your birth design.
But what you do with what you got
Is up to you.

"Choose ... this day whom you will serve...."
Joshua 24:15b (NIV)

THE WORK OF AN EVANGELIST

Debbie Carpenter   July 28

"...Be watchful in all things, endure afflictions, do the work of an evangelist, fulfill your ministry." 2 Timothy 4:5 (NKJ)

Doing the work of an evangelist is exactly what led our friend, Dave, to be a bush pilot in a third world country. Sometimes his mission work is filled with adventure.

One day Dave received an urgent plea on behalf of a man I'll call Ramon who lived in a remote mountain village. A fight had erupted at a rowdy drinking party and Ramon had been stabbed and lay struggling for life. The closest regional hospital was a six-hour drive away. There was no way the wounded man could survive such a trip.

Dave knew that he could fly Ramon from his village to medical help in a matter of 18 minutes. Convinced that God was sending him on this mission, Dave made the flight, and Ramon's life was saved. Several years later, the rescued man accepted Christ's forgiveness for his sins and was saved from spiritual death as well!

God has not called each of His children to witness to dying men in remote villages in a far off part of the world. But He has called us all to spread the gospel wherever we are – which is an exciting and adventurous job! – no matter where we live.

Lord, please equip us to take Your life-giving Word to others. Amen

GOD'S TRUTH – PLAIN AND SIMPLE

Lydia Harris   July 29

Read: 1 Corinthians 2:1-5

"My message and my preaching were not with wise and persuasive words, but with a demonstration of the Spirit's power." 1 Corinthians 2:4 (NIV)

"How old is Jesus?" my daughter asked when she was a little girl of five.

"He always was."

"But he *was* born," she insisted. "How old is he?"

To answer, I talked about the three parts of the Trinity.

"There are four parts," my three-year-old son corrected.

"What are they?" I asked.

"God, Jesus, the Holy Spirit, and the Heavenly Father."

I chuckled to myself, but explained that God and the Heavenly Father are the same.

Paul also had to explain spiritual truths. He spoke to the Corinthians in simple words. His goal was not to appear eloquent, but to proclaim his message with clarity and humility.

Paul is an example of meeting people where they are. If those around us are new in their faith, we can share in simple terms, offering them "milk." If they're mature in Christ, they'll understand deeper truths and be ready for "meat." (1 Corinthians 3:2)

When my children were preschoolers, my answers were at their level. Now that they're adults with children of their own, we share deeper truths. But I also share God's love simply with my grandchildren.

Heavenly Father, thank You for Your Spirit Who gives us the right words to share. Enable us to speak Your truths with power so others will understand and respond to You. Amen

A SUBSTITUTE FOR SIN

Donna J. Howard   July 30

Read: 2 Samuel 19:31-38

After the death of his son, Absalom, King David returned to Jerusalem. He invited Barzillai the Gileadite to go with him, but Barzillai was very old, and he felt unworthy to go. He preferred to die in his own home town, so he offered his servant Chimham to go as a substitute for him.

Do you see a picture of the Cross there? God invites all of us to go to Heaven to be with Him. But because we have sinned, we are unworthy to go and be in God's presence. So God not only offered – but provided – a substitute for us in His own Son, Jesus Christ, who died on the cross in our place. Now, to those who will accept Jesus as their Savior, the invitation is given to live in Heaven with the King of kings!

"For God so loved the world that he gave his one and only son, that whoever believes in him shall not perish but have eternal life. For God did not send his Son into the world to condemn the world, but to save the world through him. Whoever believes in him is not condemned, but whoever does not believe stands condemned already because he has not believed in the name of God's one and only Son." John 3: 17-18 (NIV)

I encourage you to accept Jesus as your Savior today!

IN SEEKING HEAVEN

Neil C. Fitzgerald   July 31

In the passage of life to death, flower and tree and animal,
Never cognizant of the fact, follow a selected pattern.
The human, created by God in His image,
always aware of His presence,
Finds in life the eternal truth that sustains both belief and actions.
Thus, prayer becomes the light of life, the hope of all understanding,
The means that to reach out to Jesus is to be lifted up beyond time.

AUGUST
THE PERSON IN THE PEW

Valerie J. Chambers   August 1

The person in the pew waits and listens intently for God to speak,
Forgetting that the One Who said, "Hear my Word" said also, "Go ye into all the world...."

The person in the pew waits patiently, longing for a fresh touch from His Spirit, Forgetting that the One Who said, "I am with you always," said also, "Follow Me."

The person in the pew searches for meaning and purpose, Forgetting that the One Who said, "I am your God," said also, "You are My child."

The person in the pew tries to comprehend how awesome God is, Forgetting that the One Who said, "Be still and know that I am God," said also, "Work while it is day."

The person in the pew is exhilarated by the music and worship, Forgetting that the One Who said, "Praise," said also, "Pray."

The person in the pew fellowships with Him, sharing thoughts and dreams, Forgetting that the One Who said, "Abide in Me," said also, "Bear fruit."

The person in the pew wants to be drawn to Him – to stay with Him – Forgetting that the One Who said, "Come unto Me," said also, "Go unto them."

The person in the pew realizes that, although I can't do every-thing, I can and must do something!

SO THAT WE DO NOT DRIFT AWAY

Barbara Peer   August 2

The other day my husband took me out to lunch at a restaurant overlooking the water. Dozens of yachts lined the pier, some large enough to contain luxuriously furnished multi-bedroom apartments! As we ate our salad, a spectacularly beautiful boat pulled up. We held our breath as the captain gently nudged the yacht against the pier. Then two men came out on deck and busied themselves tying several lines to the pilings. They made sure all was secure before they disembarked because they did not want this valuable possession to drift away and be lost!

It brought to mind Hebrews 2:1 ***"We must pay more careful attention, therefore, to what we have heard, so that we do not drift away."*** (NIV)

God has promised us eternal life through His son, Jesus Christ. It is our continued attention to Him through reading the Word, praise, worship and fellowship that ties us to the pier and keeps us from drifting away. We are, after all, His precious possessions!

"LORD, GRANT US FAITH LIKE ABRAHAM'S"

Evelyn Minshull   August 3

God grant us faith like Abram's: to exchange the glitter of civilized life for the softened glow of spanning stars; to resign to memory the flagrant music of cymbals and trumpets, welcoming instead mellow strains of breeze and the gentle, hollow sounds of solitary footfalls. May we relinquish wealth – its welter of goods, refinement, luxury – and willingly embrace a wandering through hostile desert reaches. Perhaps it required small courage to abandon lifeless gods and follow One who spoke and led. But it took mammoth faith to wait past decades for fulfillment of a promise that seemed at times more distant than the dimmer galaxies, less tangible than cloud.
God grant us faith like Abraham's.

GODLINESS WITH CONTENTMENT

Janet R. Sady   August 4

"But godliness with contentment is great gain; for we brought nothing into this world, and it is certain we can carry nothing out." 1Timothy 6:6-7 (KJV)

There once was a wealthy woman. Oh, she was so rich! No, not in worldly goods and treasures. On the contrary, she had very little in the material way.

On a sparse income, she scrimped and saved to give to mission projects and her church. For over 30 years, she wore the same clothes. The amazing thing was that they didn't seem to wear out! (Just like the Children of Israel's sandals as they wandered in the desert.)

What my friend considered of great value was not her bank account; it was spreading the message of the Gospel to the lost.

She chose what was best, and set an excellent example of what it means to be "rich in good deeds."

Father, may I strive to be like my friend, and to be known for sharing my worldly goods with the less fortunate. Most of all, Father, may I be known for sharing Your message with the lost. Amen

GIVING THANKS IN ALL CIRCUMSTANCES

Shirley S. Stevens   August 5

"Therefore I will give thanks unto thee, O Lord, and sing praises unto thy name." II Samuel 22:50 (KJV)

Recently on NPR, an 80-year-old former city clerk from Greensburg, Kansas, talked about her experience when a tornado demolished her hometown.

During the storm, with winds registering over 200 miles an hour, she was trapped in a corner of her house where she kept her collection of 12 china angels. She held one of the angels in her hands as she promised God that, if He spared her life, she would not become a whiner. Four days later as she searched through the rubble for two diamond rings – one a gift from her mother and the second, a gift from her husband – she did not complain about her loss. Instead she said, "I am thankful to be alive!"

Dear Lord, help me to maintain a thankful heart in all circumstances. May I remember that even though I may lose possessions, I can hold on to Your promise that You are with me in all of the trials of life. Let me be more Job-like, holding onto my faith in You. Amen

BE THANKFUL FOR MERCY
Christy Stenger   August 6
Read Psalm 118

God is so good to us, because His mercy lasts forever. We don't deserve such grace. It was mercy that put Jesus on the cross. He could have come down from it at any time – but compassion kept Him there!

We do all kinds of things every day to give God reasons not to forgive us, but He continues to do so anyway.

When I'm in trouble and pray for a way of escape, because of His mercy, God sends help. Did you ever think that He doesn't have to answer our prayers? He doesn't have to bless us!

Mercy means "unmerited favor." He gives me favor that I haven't earned. The reason we can't out-give God is because we don't deserve anything He bestows on us.

I'm thankful for His mercy, because I now have hope. I now have an opportunity to be saved and to tell others about Him. I can now give back to Him the only thing He really requires – and that is my love and *obedience.*

Let's be thankful for mercy, because it provides a way for you and me to make it to Heaven.

GOD'S GRACE
Carol Cleal   August 7
"He Himself has said, 'I will never desert you, nor will I ever forsake you ...' so that we confidently say, 'The Lord is my Helper, I will not be afraid....'" Hebrews 13:5-6 (NASB)

As I face the challenges of life, I need to stay focused on God. I expect Him to pull me through, to find the perfect solutions to my problems, and to acknowledge my desires.

What if God's answer is "No, My grace is enough?" Will I still keep Him in the center of my life? Will I continue to believe that He can do anything? I need to submit to the will of God. He is all-knowing. He is in control and extends His love to me. He is God of the Universe and He is my God.

How, then, can I fear? In times of trial my Lord is near.
He gives peace, comfort, strength within.
Mountains become molehills, challenges are conquered
Because my Lord is near To guide and shield.
He is a light that shines to give hope
I know my Lord is near – His love is ever present.

THE SMELL OF THE HEIR
Jana Carman   August 8

The nose knows. The navy raincoat looked exactly like mine, but the owner's perfume permeated the fabric, and I don't use perfume. Isaac's nose fooled him, however.

Isaac planned to give the traditional blessing to his favorite son, Esau, the older twin. But Jacob – determined to get the blessing by means fair or foul – deceived his blind father by wearing his brother's outdoorsy-smelling clothing. *When Isaac caught the smell of those clothes, he blessed Jacob, and said,* **"Ah, the smell of my son is like the smell of a field that the Lord has blessed."** Genesis 27:27 (NIV)

Nothing we do, say, or wear can ever fool our Heavenly Father. Yet when we enter God's presence wrapped in the righteousness of God's beloved Son, our earthly smell is covered by the "smell of the Heir," that Lily of the Valley/Rose of Sharon fragrance. We are accepted in the Beloved. More than merely accepted, we have been made co-heirs with the Beloved of God, to share in everything He, the Firstborn, is entitled to. Talk about blessings!

How greatly You have blessed me, Lord. May my life waft the fragrance of Christ to those around me. Amen

RABBIT-RIDDLED OR SPIRIT-FILLED?
Margaret Steinacker   August 9
"But the wisdom from above is first pure, then peaceable, gentle, reasonable, full of mercy and good fruits, unwavering, without

hypocrisy. And the seed whose fruit is righteousness is sown in
peace by those who make peace."
James 3:17-18 (NASB)

Rabbits have damaged a variety of plants around the parsonage for years and this one was no different. The gnarled old McIntosh tree has suffered the most permanent damage. The rabbits have eaten the bark around the base of the tree, barring passage of the rich nutrients and moisture it needs for proper growth. Year after year, the apples continue to emerge as small, bug-ridden, worm-infested balls. All of Pastor Todd's visions of Rhonda's Dutch apple pie and apple strudel made from their own fresh fruit are fading into oblivion.

Like rabbit-riddled bark around the base of the apple tree, sin in our lives can wreak havoc with the flow of God's grace. As sin zaps our spiritual growth, the production of fruit seems almost impossible. However, unlike the gnawed apple tree which has slight hope of ever regaining its full potential, we can begin anew with Christ in our lives. We may come to Him at any moment. If we ask for forgiveness, He will cleanse our hearts and replenish our spirits.

Father, help us to bring our gnarled and gnawed souls to You for refreshing. Then as we give You control of our lives, let Your life-giving grace flow through us. Help us to serve You and produce fruit for Your Kingdom. Amen

THE PRINCESS, THE PEA, AND THE "LITTLE" ISSUE OF SIN
Eunice Tan   August 10
"So, as the Holy Spirit says: "Today, if you hear his voice,
do not harden your hearts...." Hebrews 3:7-8 (NIV)

Remember the Hans Christian Andersen story of *The Princess and the Pea*? Did you know it was also called *The Real Princess* or *How to Tell a True Princess*? One stormy night, a girl takes shelter in a castle, claiming to be a real princess. To see if she really is who she claims to be, the queen places a pea under 20 mattresses and eider-downs. In the morning, she asks the girl how she slept. "Very badly," the girl replies. She is black and blue all over from lying on something hard. This confirmed to the queen that the girl is genuine royalty, because nobody but a real princess could be as sensitive as that!

As true daughters and sons of the King, are we as sensitive to the presence of sin in our lives, no matter how inconsequential and "pea-sized" it seems – or how many layers of reason, excuse, or denial we use to cover it up?

Hebrews reminds us that, if we keep listening to the Spirit's voice and responding to it, our hearts will remain sensitive to the things that cause us to stumble. And we'll prove, like that princess, that we're who we claim to be – children of the King!

PATIENCE IN MOTION

Janice May Harris   August 11

Read Hebrews 12:1-13

It was a lovely summer's day in August when I left the super-market and headed to my car. I was stopped in my tracks by an elderly couple entering the crosswalk in front of me. As vehicles and pedestrians waited, all eyes were on this precious pair. Watching them pass was like viewing a movie in slow motion. Not a sound was heard; it was as though we were silently cheering them on.

Both were severely hunched over, heads bowed to their waists. The husband carefully held his wife's hand, fearful of falling down. Each step she took was difficult, requiring her to concentrate on the place-ment of her quivering foot.

This elderly couple's pluck spoke volumes to all who witnessed their crossing that day. What an inspiration to us all. As they reached the curb, I was reminded of Paul's words: ***"Let us run with patience the race that is set before us."*** Hebrews 12:1 (KJV)

Although this pair was not running, they still made it to their destina-tion because they never gave up.

Dear Lord, help us during times of weakness and discourage-ment. Please give us patience to finish the race well. Amen

IT ONLY TAKES A SPARK

Dave Evans   August 12

For a week thick, gray smoke billowed from the Cleveland National Forest in California as flames leaped above the Santiago Canyon. Television news reports kept viewers informed of the Sierra fire and the progress the firefighters were making. Thankfully, no lives or houses were lost. By the time it was completely under control, nearly 11,000 acres had burned; over 2,000 firefighters had toiled many hours, and the estimated cost totaled nearly $6.9 million. The cause of the fire? Smoldering embers from a controlled burn.

Just so, it takes only a little spark from the tongue to ignite a fire that can torch a whole forest. In James, Chapter 3, we are informed that the tongue is a fire, a world of iniquity. It defiles us and sets our lives ablaze with the flames of hell. *"In the multitude of words sin is not lacking, but he who restrains his lips is wise."* Proverbs 10:19 (NKJV) The tongue cannot be tamed by human efforts – it is only with the power and help of the Holy Spirit that we use it for good. *"The lips of the righteous feed many...."* Proverbs 10:21a (NKJV)

Gracious Father, please forgive me for lighting fires that have caused much destruction. Please heal those injured by my words, both intentional and/or merely careless ones. Let my tongue be controlled by Your Holy Spirit to bless and uplift others. Amen

LEAVE IT!

Jane Miller   August 13

"Cast all your anxiety on him because he cares for you."
1 Peter 5:7 (NIV)

Our Sadie is a therapy dog, trained to visit nursing homes. She had to pass a rigorous obedience test of ten criteria to be certified through *Therapy Dog International*. Beyond the basics of "sit," "down," "stay," and "come," she had to learn "leave it." It is important for a dog's safety that he or she not eat anything on a nursing home floor.

Sadie, a 90-pound *Bouvier des Flandres* we adopted from a no-kill shelter, had to turn away from a dog treat dropped directly in front of her. To teach her this restraint, the trainer at Animal Friends instructed me to hold out both hands with a visible treat in one, and command "leave it." As soon as Sadie turned away, I was to offer a better reward from the other hand!

One morning, walking with my dog and my husband, I saw a person who had hurt me in the past. I felt anger rise up in me.

Just then, my husband barked, "Leave it!" I was startled at the words until I saw that Sadie was about to snatch food from the side-walk. She turned immediately to her master. Then I realized it was an obedience lesson for *me*. I didn't need to pick up anger.

"Leave it!" I now say to such thoughts. I know that we can leave whatever it is with our Master.

Dear Lord, thank You for taking our hurts. Help us to trust You, knowing Your rewards are far greater.

WHAT ARE WE HERE FOR?

Joseph M. Hopkins   August 14

"By this My Father is glorified, that you bear much fruit; And so prove to be My disciples. John 15:8 (NASB)

134

Jesus wants us to "bear much fruit." Just what does this mean? Immediately there comes to mind Galatians 5:22-23: **"The fruit of the Spirit is love, joy, peace, patience, kindness, goodness, faithful- ness, gentleness, self-control."** But these virtues are not ends in themselves. They are means to the end of winning souls for Christ's Kingdom. Is not this what St. Francis of Assisi implied when he said Christians are called to "Preach the gospel. If necessary, use words." The most effective witness is a Christ-like life.

But is this all? Words <u>are</u> necessary. In Romans 10:9, Paul wrote, **"...if you <u>confess with your mouth</u> 'Jesus is Lord,' and believe in your heart that God raised Him from the dead, you will be saved."** (NIV)

We heard at a prayer breakfast recently that 50% of the churches in a denomination – well-known for its emphasis on evangelism and missions – did not add a *single convert* to their rolls last year. What a sad indictment! But come to think of it, did I share the good news of Jesus Christ with even one person last year? Or the year before that? Or … have I ever?

Lord, I want to be a fruit-bearing Christian. Help me to share Jesus' message of love, mercy, and joyful hope with at least one other person today. Amen

TREAD SOFTLY

Charlotte Burkholder   August 15

Read: James 3:17 (NKJ)

"But the wisdom that is from above is first pure, then peaceable, gentle, willing to yield, full of mercy and good fruit, without partiality." James 3:17 (NKJ)

Springtime announces its arrival gloriously. Buds burst forth; tender shoots of new growth spring up. Glistening from the recent rain, all nature worships its Creator. Glancing down, I notice that I am stepping on tiny, delicate flowers. Fragile and new, they don't have a chance beneath my heavy boots, but lie wilted and crushed.

Are new believers treated the same? Their life in Christ may be so fragile it is in danger of being crushed, either from thoughtlessness, or even worse, unacceptance.

The country song, *"Wounded Baby," describes a teen in long hair and faded jeans giving his life to the Lord at the altar. But it isn't long before religion tells him that he must cut his hair and dress and look like everyone else. The refrain of the song goes, "Babies always cry before they talk, and they fall down a lot before they walk."

Lord God, may we never be guilty of discouraging those who are young in the faith. Help seasoned believers to be sensitive and walk in wisdom beside them as they grow.

*"Wounded Baby" by Tina Sadler

COME THIRSTY!

Lydia Harris   August 16

Read John 7:37-41
"Let anyone who is thirsty come to me, and let the one who believes in me drink." John 7:37-38 (NIV)

Several years ago I taught a class in my home on how to prepare and serve a three-course tea. Although the women who attended didn't know me or each other, our hearts blended while sipping tea. Before the women left, I shared that although tea was physically satisfying, it couldn't slake spiritual thirst. "Only Jesus," I said, "can give us living water to quench our spiritual dryness."

In John 7, Jesus offered "living water." It was the last day of the Feast of Tabernacles. The people had gathered to commemorate God's faithful provision during the 40 years the Israelites wandered in the wilderness while living in tents, eating manna from Heaven, and drinking water from the rock.

After a week of celebration, Jesus stood before the crowd and announced: "Let anyone who is thirsty come to me." I wonder how many understood His incredible invitation? Did they realize he could satisfy their spiritual thirst? Did they come?

Some in the crowd called him a "prophet" and "the Messiah." But others were skeptical and weren't ready to believe. As we hear Jesus' invitation, are we spiritually thirsty? Will we drink of the life Jesus offers?

Lord Jesus, You are the living water who quenches spiritual thirst. Today I come longing for Your righteousness. Let Your living water satisfy me and flow out to others. Amen

YOU NEED ONLY TO BE STILL

Joanna Ronalds   August 17

Read Exodus 13:17 – 14:31
"The Lord will fight for you; you need only to be still."
Exodus 14:14 (NIV)

This must have been hard advice for the Israelites to take, what with the Egyptians bearing down upon them, intent on recapturing them and returning them to slavery!

Sometimes God calls for us to stand and fight, and other times He calls for us to be still and allow *Him* to do the fighting in our stead.

If your effort and striving seems only to be pulling you backward, then find a quiet spot and take the time to ask God if perhaps your hard work is not what He wants. Maybe He is waiting for you to be still so that He can fight for you!

Remember Psalm 46:10a tells us, *"Be **still**, and know that I am God...."* So we have our orders from the Lord Himself!

OUR USE OF GOD'S GIFTS

Daisy Townsend   August 18

Read I Samuel 26

"Now to each one the manifestation of the Spirit is given for the common good." I Corinthians 12:7 (NIV)

Have you ever stopped to consider that the gifts and abilities God has given you can be used either to bless or to curse others? When David and Abishai found Saul lying asleep with his spear stuck in the ground near his head (the same spear that Saul had used repeatedly to try to take David's own life!) David resisted the temptation to use his God-given talent as a warrior to get revenge. I am amazed when I think of such self-restraint.

Considering my own life and the verbal skills God has given me, both in speaking and writing, I wish I could say that I've used these abilities only in ways that would be beneficial to others. Instead, there have been times when my temper and my desire to get even have taken the lead, and I've used my talents in ways that I regret.

As I study David's example, I am challenged to surrender all of my abilities to God, asking that through the power of His Spirit, I would use them only to build up the Body rather than tearing it down.

Father, purify our hearts so that we will use our gifts in ways that bless the heart of the Giver. Amen

LORD, MY SHEPERD

Christian Lagow   August 19

My Father and best Friend,
You guide me through my everyday life.
You deliver me when I'm in strife.
You work the many miracles that I ask
And answer my prayers – it seems not a task.
Waking up each morning from a peaceful sleep,

I'm protected by angels so Satan can't creep.
Yea, though I walk my daily life in the flesh,
I know I'm a Christian, and I fear not death.
Lord, You are with me,
Your living Word and Your love, they guide me.
You prepare my heart and mind and help me defeat the enemy,
You bless my spirit with Your love.
My heart confesses that
Surely blessings and miracles will follow me
Every day of my Christian life,
And, I will dwell in Your Word
And Your House forever!

THE LESSON OF THE BIRD

Ruth M. Baldwin   August 20

The sky was cloudy and cold as my daughter pulled into a store's parking lot. I waited in the car as she went in to shop. Two almost identical cumulous clouds were merging high above the trees. Pilots of small aircraft are advised to avoid such clouds because of the intense turbulence within them.

Suddenly I saw a raven flying, no – *soaring,* circling underneath the billows! Its wings were outstretched, leaning into the wind as it was being carried higher into the sky, then into the clouds. That adventurous little bird was soaring just for the joy of soaring! I perceived its exhilaration and its joy permeated my being.

I remembered how after each phase of His creation, God had paused, and said, *"It is good!"* Genesis 1:10, 12, 18, 21, 25, 31 (KJV). God felt joy then, and cared about His creation. He watched it then, and He still watches over it. I went home filled with my own joy and the wonder that God would be so faithful all those years. No matter what happens, He is with us, turbulent clouds notwithstanding!

Oh, Father, I am so thankful for the raven which brought these thoughts to mind. What happened to it later? Why, it got the ride of its life! And it brought me a lesson I'll never forget.

VARIETY OF LOVING WAYS

Carol J. Lee   August 21
"...the earth is full of his unfailing love." Psalm 33: 5b (NIV)

"The Lord must really love you!" my husband said one morning as I sat down for breakfast.

"Why'd you say that?" I responded.

"Read Psalm 127:2," he replied.

So I did and found *"... for he grants sleep to those he loves."* I saw what my husband meant. I sure do sleep well!

God shows His love in a variety of ways, but getting good, sound sleep was a blessing for me after several years of less than adequate rest, due to some physical and emotional issues. The first retirement years provided a change in this area. Getting deep, healing sleep was now a nightly blessing.

I thanked God for bringing this to my attention. It was another sign of His love that is always available to me. Then I wondered how many other acts of His love I overlooked each day. I will need His help to be more aware in future.

Open the eyes of my heart daily, Lord, to see more of the incidents in life which reveal Your love for me. Amen

NAVIGATING BY THE MORNING STAR

Barbara Major Bryden   August 22

"I (Jesus) am the Root and the Offspring of David, and the bright Morning Star." Revelation 22:16 (NIV)

For centuries, sailors used the stars to navigate. In 1955, when my husband, Ken, joined the Navy, ships still used celestial guidance.

Ken talks of the awe he felt when he stood with the navigator on the bridge of the ship waiting for first light. That moment came when they could distinguish the sky from the sea. Then they used the first visible star – the morning star – to fix the ship's position. The navigator had only seconds after first light to take his readings.

In the evening, they waited for the first star to appear to set the ship's course for the night. The sailors depended on the navigator's quickness and accuracy to reach their destination in the time allowed. At noon, he used the sun to confirm their course.

As Christians, we want to be "on course" as well. To navigate successfully through life we must set our eyes on Jesus, the bright Morning Star. Many Christians pray morning and evening, even if their prayers are short. But I find it's helpful to stop a few minutes at noon to check my direction, too. It's a time to focus on God, thank Him for the morning, and ask for continued protection and guidance.

ALONG LIFE'S ROAD

Debbie Rempel   August 23

I'm on a prayer journey down a narrow road
carrying a heavy load.
I need to give those burdens to Him to keep within His care.
I can share with my Lord as I walk along the path
and talk with Him.
I can leave my load safely with Him as I walk this road,
For I know He will bear my burdens
so I don't have to carry them anywhere.
Heaven-bound, I'm going to my new Home,
to a place where I don't have to carry any load.
And I know when it's my time to go,
I'll meet my Lord at Heaven's golden gate!
"O, Lord, this poem prayer – these words –
came from somewhere within my heart.
May they encourage those who read them to pray
what's on their hearts – words that are from You.
When I spend time alone with You,
thoughts like these come out of the blue."

IT'S HERE SOMEWHERE!

Lisa Christine   August 24

Read: Psalm 91:1-2

"Trust in the LORD forever, for the LORD, the LORD,
is the Rock eternal." (Isaiah 26:4, NIV)

Recently, I admitted something I've suspected all along: I'm unorganized. Really, I try to put things in a "good place" – but then I don't remember where that place is. Storage bins, folders, and organizers don't help much.

Today I misplaced my keys. You probably know exactly how I felt. You've looked and looked; you retraced your steps, only to fail.

At last, when I couldn't think of any other places to check, I asked, "Please, God, pinpoint exactly where the keys are. You know where I placed them. I can't waste any more time searching. The keys are probably staring up at me right now, having fun at my expense."

After more failed attempts of hunting in cabinet drawers, laundry piles, and jacket pockets, at long last I found my keys! There they were, wedged behind a sofa cushion! *What a relief!* I thought as I hugged them to my breast.

"Oh, thank You, Lord, for helping me! I'm truly thankful and glad I didn't give up."

I'll know I've reached the pinnacle of organization when I no longer find pens and pennies in my car's crevices, or when I open the glove compartment, an array of papers does not fly out at me. In the meantime, I am going to work on my method of arranging, knowing God will be there when something else is misplaced and I need a search party.

There are areas in life where I'd like to improve. Lord, I rely on You to help me. Amen

POLARIZED

Rick Leland   August 25

"Are they polarized?" I asked the optometrist who was helping me select new sunglasses. (Good, that's what I want.)

Later I ran a dictionary word search through my brain. *What does polarized mean?* I really didn't know, yet in my good-better-best conquest, I instinctively knew I wanted *polarized* sunglasses. The word "polarized" stimulated my "desire" glands to salivate. From trinkets to 20-year-mortgage purchases, I'm vulnerable. (So are you.)

Rich, wise Solomon who lived thousands of years before the mall experience, understood. His words: ***"As goods increase so do those who consume them, and what benefit are they to the owner except to feast his eyes on them."*** Ecclesiastes 5:11 (NIV)

(I bought the sunglasses. They're great!) But I know I need to guard what I feast my eyes on. I need to remove my polarized "I-want-it" sunglasses and see the light of the truth. I need to under-stand what's really important – today, tomorrow, and for eternity.

What do I need to keep my eyes on? What does my life really stand for? Solomon had the prescription when he said, ***"Stand in awe of God."***

(Stand with me.)

EDEN

Gloria Hillman   August 26
"And he showed me a river of the water of life, clear as crystal, coming from the throne of God and of the Lamb, in the middle of its street. And on either side of the river was the tree of life...."
Revelation 22:1-2a (NASB)

Recently, I was on a tour of some summer gardens with a group from our church. These lovely, scented, floral landscapes were created by some of my friends. Such beauty! Such reverence for nature! We were awed by their splendor. Before long, I felt peace begin to bloom within my soul. I wondered how the gardens could flourish in this sanctuary, paying no attention to the hustle-bustle of a nearby highway!

Tall shade trees shielded us from the sun as we entered into a hidden world of greens, yellows, scented reds and pinks. Oh! And an ornate fountain splashing water onto cold, gray rocks! Along with birdsong we heard piped-in dulcet cello music. Farther on, weeping willows gently beckoned us to "rest here."

I wondered, *Was Eden like this?*

Thank You, Father, for the beauty of Your earth. How generous You are! We give You praise and look forward to Your Heavenly gardens! Amen

MY PRAYER

Ray Kantowski   August 27

"The Spirit of the Sovereign Lord is on me, because the Lord has anointed me to preach good news to the poor. He has sent me to bind up the brokenhearted, to proclaim freedom for the captives and to release from darkness the prisoners." Isaiah wrote in 61:1 (NIV)

Have you ever asked God what your anointing is? Do you think He might want *you* to "preach the good news to the poor?" Would you like to "bind up the broken hearted?" Wouldn't it be exciting to pro-claim "freedom for captives and release prisoners from darkness" – especially if you could witness it? Jesus did – and His desire is for us to do the same! Remember His instructions to the disciples, **"Heal the sick, cleanse the lepers, raise the dead, cast out devils; freely ye have received, freely give."** Matthew 10:8 (KJV)

In order to do this you'll need to be able to walk in the power of the Holy Spirit which He has made available to us! All we have to do is ask! Then step out in faith, on the Word, and make a difference in this sin-filled world!

My prayer is to walk closely with the Lord,
Till the ways of sin and strife and a meaningless life
Are extracted from me by the Spirit's sword!
Give me this day, O Lord, my daily bread,
And, above all, let not Thy Holy Spirit forsake me.
Draw me close to those You have chosen from above,
That I might share Your precious Word and truth
And, above all, Your everlasting love! Amen!

142

PROMISES

Jennifer Kanode   August 28

"And we know that in all things God works for the good of those who love him, who have been called according to his purpose."
Romans 8:28 (NIV)

When my husband and I were told we had to move out of the house we were renting, we panicked. I was pregnant, and we had a foreign exchange student living with us at the time. She had only two more months of school left – and we had only two months to find a place to live. We had no idea how God was going to work everything out.

With God's help, we were able to find another host family for our exchange student so she could continue to go to the same school. We were also able to find a place to live in a decent neighborhood, not far from my husband's work. There was even a daycare close by for our newborn baby!

The Lord says in His Word not to worry about tomorrow for "nothing is impossible for Him." Sometimes I believe He has to test us to remind His children of this promise. Isn't it a comfort to know that God is in control?

Lord, thank You that you take care of Your children. Forgive us when we doubt and worry. May we cling to Your promises in Your Word each day. Amen

THE HEDGES

Janet R. Sady   August 29

"Also I heard the voice of the Lord saying, Whom shall I send and who will go for us? Then said I, here am I; send me." Isaiah 6:8
(KJV)

In Bible times, hedges of thorns and brambles were placed around a flock of sheep to keep them from straying. There was a gap in the hedge where the shepherd slept to protect his charges. No one or no animal could get to the sheep without stepping over the shepherd. It was a dangerous place, but he risked his life for them.

Today, who will be willing to stand in the gap to block the destruction of America's reverence for God? Will we continue to allow the minority to dictate our policies? Our nation was founded on the principles of God's laws. Now, however, non-believers want to eliminate any trace of Him from history. If we allow this, then it is no longer history, but a fairy tale.

We need to hedge America in prayer – and then be willing to speak out for God!
Lord, help me to be among those who stand in the gap for You. Amen

LOST IN MY MIND....
Darryl Sherlock   August 30

> Lost in my mind, Oh! What can I say?
> Lost in my mind, Oh, where is the way?
> Lost in my mind, I'm empty and cold.
> Lost in my mind, with no one to hold.
> Lost in my mind, how long will this last?
> Lost in my mind, I'm stuck in the past.
> Lost in my mind, with no place to go.
> Lost in my mind, does anyone know?
> Lost in my mind with nothing to gain.
> Lord, touch my mind and keep me sane!

"Come unto Me, all who are weary and heavy-laden and I will give you rest. Take My yoke upon you, and learn from Me, for I am gentle and humble in heart; and you shall find rest for your souls." Matthew 11:28-29 (NASB)

Dear Father in Heaven, I come to You for rest for my soul. Thank You that You welcome me, even in the depths of my despair. You alone can help me. Let me crawl up into your lap and rest. Amen

ALARMING STATISTICS!
Joseph M. Hopkins   August 31

World Magazine (March 17, 2007) reported that when a Barna poll asked Republicans and Democrats about their faith, 51% of Republicans and 38% of Democrats said they were "born again."

Asked if "good works can earn salvation," 65% of Republicans and 77% of Democrats said yes. In other words, a vast majority of those polled deny the basic Christian teaching that salvation is by grace alone through faith alone, *"not by works, lest anyone should boast."* (Ephesians 2:9 KJV)

Even more shocking is the disclosure that only 75% of Republicans and 65% of Democrats believe that "God is the all-knowing, perfect creator of the universe."

God's Word tell us, *"Blessed is that nation whose God is the Lord, the people He has chosen as His own inheritance."* (Psalm 33:12 NASB) In these days of secularism and apostasy, when even the

144

mention of Intelligent Design evokes scorn and anger from the "politically correct," we need to pray for the spiritual renewal of our beloved country. *"If My people who are called by My name will humble themselves, and pray and seek My face, and turn from their wicked ways, then I will hear from heaven, and will forgive their sin and heal their land."* (2 Chronicles 7:14 NASB)

Oswald Chambers in *My Utmost for His Highest* tells us that "The key is prayer. *'Pray ye therefore the Lord of the harvest.' ...* And He will engineer circumstances and thrust you out."

Let's pray before it's too late!

SEPTEMBER
FOUR STEPS TO FRET-FREE LIVING

Jana Carman   September 1
"Do not fret - it leads only to evil." Psalm 37:8b (NIV)

"Don't fret." Easy to say, not so easy to do. One meaning of fret is to chafe, fray or wear away. That vividly pictures what happens to a fretful mind, as we mentally chafe at a situation we can't control. It rubs our spirits raw. But how can we become fret-free? Three thousand years ago, David learned how – the hard way. In Psalm 37, he shares his hard-learned lessons, and they work equally well for us today.

The first step, he says, is to <u>trust in the Lord </u>(verse 3). Recognize that God knows the situation, has it well in hand, and can be trusted to do what is best for us.

Second: <u>delight yourself in the Lord</u> (verse 4). Notice the promise in this verse: He will give you the desires of your heart. When you delight in the Lord, He delights in giving you what will delight you!

The next step is to <u>commit it to the Lord </u>(verse 5). Hand it over. *"It's all Yours, God. Handle it as You please, when You please. It's no longer my concern."* This step may need repeating a few times until you can learn to walk away from it and leave it with Him.

And finally, <u>wait for the Lord </u>(verse 7). Patiently. Now you have switched your focus from the problem to the Problem-Solver. And while you wait, do not fret (verses 1,7,8)

Peace will come. He has promised. (check out verse 11)

ASK THE LORD TO KEEP SOMEONE

Joan Clayton   September 2
"Now unto him that is able to keep you from falling,
and to present you faultless before the presence of his glory
with exceeding joy." Jude 24 (KJV)

Can you imagine what a blessing I experienced when one of my second graders walked into my classroom and said, "Teacher, I prayed for you last night."

"And what did you ask the Lord to do for me?" I inquired, brushing back the tears. "I asked him to keep you," he said.

My mom's death was a sweet release for her, but it had still saddened me. My student had asked the Lord to "keep me" and His peace did comfort me. Our youngest son had recently gone through very painful surgery. I had prayed earnestly for him. My student's prayer was answered again. I had peace. The Lord indeed kept me and the sincere faith of a little child kept me in the care of my Creator. Is there someone in your life today that you need the Lord to "keep?" Only eternity will reveal the results of our prayers for others.

I'm so thankful for that student's prayers for me. I asked the Lord to keep him too, along with my other students.

Why not ask the Lord to "keep" someone in your life today?

Dear Lord, thank You for children and their childlike trust. Help us to recapture that wonderful childhood of faith. Amen

"FATHER, FORGIVE US"

Evelyn Minshull							September 3

"And just as Moses lifted up the snake in the desert, so the Son of Man must be lifted up, that everyone believes in Him may have eternal life." John 3:14-15 (NIV)

Just like the ungrateful grumblers in the wilderness to whom God sent poisonous serpents ... like the soul-blind in Jerusalem who cried, "Crucify Him!" neither do we recognize the enormity of our offenses.

Father, forgive us...for we know not what we do. Amen

THREE PILLOWS

Mary A. Koepke							September 4

"So faith, hope, love, abide, these three; but the greatest of these is love." 1 Corinthians 13:13 (RSV)

While we were still struggling from shock over the diagnosis of my husband's multiple myeloma cancer, we received a package in the mail from a good friend. It was a soft, wine velvet pillow about six by eight inches, bound with gold cord. Embroidered in gold across the front was the word "Faith." It couldn't have come at a better time. Touched by our friend's generosity, we hung the pillow over the corner of the bed above Howard's head – a constant reminder of God's presence.

146

During the traumatic treatments, back surgery, and pain of the next year, another pillow arrived. It was smaller – but the same lovely, wine velvet and gold – and this time the letters spelled "Hope." We were encouraged to keep up our hope.

The third year, Howard's cancer progressed. Through prayer with our pastor, we chose to enroll in a hospice program. With the constant care of an angel nurse, Howard was mobile and active on a limited basis for 18 months. When the third pillow arrived, we were overcome by its velvet and gold beauty and the shining, embroidered word "Love."

The Lord had spoken to our friend's heart. Out of compassion he had sent these gifts at the perfect times of need. Now, they continue to comfort me as I live out my role as widow, and are a constant reminder of God's never-failing love.

COME
Christian Lagow   September 5
"Come to me, all you who are weary and burdened, and I will give you rest." Matthew 11:28 (NIV)

Have you ever come to Jesus? Watch the stubbornness of your heart and mind! You will find that you will do *anything* rather than the one simple child-like thing – **come**. I have learned that the attitude of coming is that the will resolutely lets go of everything and deliberately commits the whole thing to Jesus, who meets our sins, our sorrows, and our difficulties with one word – **come**.

Dear Lord, in the bright light of morning I come sometimes with face beaming and heart bursting with joy and contentment. But often, Lord, I'm stumbling, dragging, my cheeks wet with tears on mornings that bring no joy or contentment. And yet You are there. Thank You for receiving me whether I am walking on winged feet or crawling. You hear and help. Hold me close. Amen

HAVING DAYS LIKE A CHILD
Leigh DeLozier   September 6
"Even a child is known by his actions, by whether his conduct is pure and right." Proverbs 20:11 (NIV)

The bus stopped at our home at 7:12 a.m., regular as clockwork. The driver, Ms. Carla, once pointed to my kindergartner climbing on behind her big brother. The school year was young, and my daughter's perpetual grin over kindergarten was still in place.

"Does she always smile?" Ms. Carla asked with a smile of her own.

"She's the happiest thing."

I laughed and answered that she – like all of us – has her not-so-good moments, but that most of them are okay.

Later I thought of how happy our daughter is to go to school, no matter how bad the morning might have been. She's quick to forgive and quick to move on – and always excited about the day ahead.

Can I say the same thing about myself? Am I quick to forgive disagreements or hurt feelings, or do I nurse the injury so it festers instead of healing? Do I let one bad thing ruin the morning, or do I stop and ask God for new focus and a clean start? Am I happy to face the day because I know God is in control, or am I anxious or stressed because I didn't hand each moment to Him?

Now I try to ask myself these questions more often, thanks to our daughter's attitude. Sometimes the youngest among us teach us the most important lessons!

THE LAST GATE

Annie Bruening   September 7

Read Nehemiah 3

Nehemiah had been commissioned by King Artaxerxes to rebuild the wall around Jerusalem, and the Miphkad Gate was the last one in the wall. "Miphkad" means "register or review." Strangers had to come through this gate and register before entering Jerusalem. It was also the gate through which David reviewed his soldiers when they returned from war. He would reward and thank them for their courage and faithfulness.

2 Corinthians 5:10 tells us, *"For we must all appear before the judgment seat of Christ; that each one may receive the things done in his body, according to what he has done, whether good or bad."*

How have we served God with the gifts He has given us? Could we have done more? Been more obedient? Done our jobs with more compassion? Praised and worshiped God more? We will have to account for 24/7 when we come to this gate! If we offer up each day to God and serve Him to the best of our ability, thanking Him for all our blessings – especially Christ Jesus – and praise God for all He is, we won't dread meeting Him.

Dear Father, when it comes time for us to meet You at this gate, we want to hear You say, "Well done, good and faithful servant." Thank You for helping us reach this goal in the precious name of Jesus. Amen

BECAUSE OF YOUR GREAT MERCY

Joanna Ronalds   September 8

Read Daniel 9:1-19

"We do not make requests of you because we are righteous,
but because of your great mercy." Daniel 9:18 (NIV)

We need to remember that we must not ever make requests of God
because of who we are, or because of what we've done…. Such as –
   because we forgave someone...
   because we read our Bibles today...
   because we prayed for hours...
   because it really is what needs to happen...
   because everyone else agrees...
   because we're righteous...

   Let us make requests of God only because of what God is – great,
awesome, faithful (Daniel 9:4), righteous (Daniel 9:7), and forgiving
(Daniel 9:9).

GOD'S NAME FOR YOU

Janet R. Sady   September 9

"He that hath an ear, let him hear what the Spirit saith unto the
churches: To him, that overcometh, will I give to eat of the hidden
manna, and will give him a white stone, and in the stone, a new
name written, which no man knoweth except he that received it."
Revelation 2:17 (KJV)

   What's your Internet name? No! Don't tell me. That's between you
and your computer. It protects your privacy, and allows you to access
your e-mail.

   Having a secret name is not a new concept, as we see in the above
passage. Jesus sent an angel to the Isle of Patmos, where John had
been exiled. The things the apostle recounted were written in an
apocalyptic genre. Some of the events were to be forthcoming in the
near future, while others are to take place prior to the time when Christ
returns to set up His earthly Kingdom.

   Some of the letters to the churches list their parishioners' lack of
action or misdeeds; while other congregations are commended for their
faithfulness. The ones who heed the warnings, repent, and overcome,
will receive a name engraved on a white stone.

   Jesus said, *"I give them eternal life, and they shall never*
perish, neither shall any man pluck them out of my hand." John
10:28 (KJV)

What name would you prefer God give to you?
"Beloved" would be nice!

THE GOSPEL REVISITED

Gloria Clover   September 10

"Jesus replied to them, 'What about those 18 people who died when the tower at Siloam fell on them? Do you think that they were more sinful than other people living in Jerusalem? No! I can guarantee that they weren't. But if you don't turn to God and change the way you think and act, then you, too, will all die.'"
Luke 13:4-5 (God's Word Translation)

I cannot read of a tower falling without thinking of the day the Twin Towers crashed under attack. Following, many stories reached us of how certain Christians had been kept from arriving at their offices on that day. Other stories circulated of Christians in the Towers being in positions to do noble and heroic acts. Equal stories abounded of nonbelievers.

Jesus' Word tells us that people who die in disasters aren't more sinful than others. *"But if you don't turn to God and change the way you think and act, then you, too, will all die."*

Turn to God – confess Jesus as Lord and believe He died as a substitute for you. Repent of your independent living from God. Be baptized to receive the gift of the Holy Spirit. And with the Holy Spirit living in you, take your thoughts captive to the obedience of Christ and choose to believe Truth, not every lie that pops into your head. Then, your actions will change as you live in the Spirit and obey the Word – and you will not die, but have eternal life!

If you've never made a resolution to submit to Christ, today is a good day. Tomorrow ... a tower may fall in your life, figuratively or literally. Then, "you, too, will die."

HOLOCAUST: SEPTEMBER 11, 2001

Pan Sankey   September 11

"Surely the day is coming; it will burn like a furnace. All the arrogant and every evildoer will be stubble, and that day that is coming will set them on fire." says the LORD Almighty.
Malachi 4:1 (NIV)

We watched it happen – the fiery blast…and then another…and *another*. We heard the screams of those who ran in fear, and saw a flaming holocaust consume 3,000 lives within a city's heart.

150

We watched the aftermath – the rising smoke, the sifting ash; we saw the anguished eyes of those who did escape, reflecting anguished hearts. We heard the pleas on television; we read the posters. "My loved one hasn't come home – did he escape? Is he alive or dead? I need to know, though nothing heals a broken heart."

These same questions were asked 60 years ago by multiplied millions, whispered from German concentration camps of horror. But then, no one was watching. It seemed that no one cared. Now, the scene was eerily the same: the rising smoke, the sifting ash, the anguished eyes, the desperate quest by those who did survive to find out what happened to the rest, as hatred tried its worst to decimate a people's heart.

The enemy is the same: Evil is its name. It spawns a hatred, which then acts beyond reason, and rends a nation's heart.

Let us never forget that the final day of accountability is in the hand of the LORD alone, as recorded in Malachi 3:16-4:2.

WHERE IS YOUR FAITH?

Pat Collins   September 12
"All that the Father giveth me shall come to me; and him that cometh to me I will in no wise cast out." John 6:37 (KJV)

We talk about "believing" and "having faith,"
All the faith in the world. Wait! Faith in what?
Should we be putting our faith in a world
Where people can and do deceive us?
Put all your faith and belief in God.
He will never disappoint or deceive you.
He wants your faith and trust in Him to
Come from your heart. Talk to Him.
God wants to hear from you at all times,
Not just in times of trouble.
Put your faith in the One who deserves it,
And will never betray you.

DEBT

Paul E. Vander Wege   September 13
"I owe a great debt to you and to everyone else...."
Romans 1:14a (Life Application Bible)

As a child I was taught not to owe money. Later, when my wife and I wanted to purchase a home, we had to borrow. To keep the debt low we went without some things and made extra payments to reduce the amount we owed faster.

But, oh! The debt we owe God! He gave His Son to die on the cross so that we could be justified in His sight and live with Him after we die. The Apostle Paul gave his entire life from that point on the Damascus Road to tell others about Jesus.

What about me? What am I doing to give back to God for what He has done for me? What am I doing to tell others about Jesus? Could I do more?

I owe everything I am, ever hope to be, or possess to God. It is all a gift from Him. I am only a caretaker of what God has permitted me to have or be.

Dear Father, since all I have or hope to be is a gift from You, help me glorify You by how I live my life and use what You have given to me. Help me return it all to You. Amen

THE VISION

Florence W. Biros   September 14

At the Soldiers and Sailors Museum in Pittsburgh, Pennsylvania, a portrait of a dog caught my attention. Why would a mongrel-looking mutt be displayed in a museum honoring America's war heroes?

Upon investigation, I learned that the dog had gone to the Civil War with men from a Pittsburgh Volunteer Fire Department. The dog, Jack, had become the regiment's beloved mascot. Further research through their chaplain's memoirs made the heroics of the men and the dog so real to me that I could envision them in my mind. I prayed that someday **Dog Jack's** story would come alive on the screen.

That was 38 years ago. Seeing the dog, the chaplain and those brave men come alive in a Christian Family Feature Film became almost an obsession. I felt the Lord had given me the vision, so I continued to strive toward that goal.

Even though the novel I later wrote received a warm reception, I determined to see the story on film. Did I have setbacks and disappointments? Oh, yes! Too many – but I "kept on keeping on."

Miracles still happen! Next month the film will be released. It's up to the Lord whether it makes it to the theaters, but I will leave it in His capable hands.

I write this to urge you to fulfill whatever vision the Lord has put on your heart. "Never fear, just persevere."

Remember: *"No man, having put his hand to the plough, and looking back, is fit for the kingdom of God."* Luke 9:62 (KJV)

MISJUDGING OTHERS

Neil C. Fitzgerald   September 15

On my first day of teaching I entered an 8th grade classroom as a substitute and looked for the lesson plans left by the regular teacher. Soon the bell rang and students filed in and took their seats. Then another bell signaled that all students were to be silent.

At the back of the room were two girls in an animated conversation! *Ah!* I thought. *Here's my chance to exert my authority! I must maintain good discipline.*

"You two in the back row! You know you're to be quiet. You'll both stay after school."

"But—" one of the girls protested.

"Not another word!"

Then the bell rang and the students filed out to their first period class.

Somehow I made it to the end of the day. Finally, the bell rang for the pupils to return to homerooms for dismissal. They all came, and at the final bell, they left. All, that is, except the two girls in the last row.

"Now tell me," I said, "what was so important that you had to talk during quiet time?"

One girl was quick to answer. "We were trying to decide whether to tell you that you're supposed to lead us in the Lord's Prayer as part of our morning exercises."

I'm sure the good Lord enjoyed my discomfort. He has a way of keeping us humble! Flustered, I mumbled something about raising your hand next time, and promptly dismissed the girls.

Fifty years have passed – 30 in the classroom and 20 in retirement. Still, that incident is vivid in my memory. I guess the Lord taught me a lesson that day.

DEPENDENCE ON GOD

Nancy Dearborn   September 16

Read Matthew 6:25-33

"And my God will meet all your needs according to his glorious riches in Christ Jesus." Philippians 4:19 (NIV)

Some time ago, I volunteered to watch a three-month-old baby named Ilee on Fridays. Since she was so young, she was totally dependent on others to meet all of her needs.

While she was in my care, it was my responsibility to feed her, change her, burp her, keep her warm and clean for the day. Then, too, I had to make sure she received enough rest so that her small body would stay healthy and strong.

I loved to hold Ilee, snuggling her tightly in the curve of my arm, amazed at how trusting she was in my care.

Then I thought about my relationship with God. Ilee's dependence on me was a type or picture of how God wants me to rely totally on Him to meet all of my necessities. We never outgrow our dependence upon our Heavenly Father.

Lord, just as young children rely on their parents and other caregivers in their lives, help me to rely on You to meet the needs I have in my life. Amen

I SANG MY WAY OUT

Michele L. Tune   September 17

"Sing and rejoice, O daughter of Zion: for, lo, I come, and I will dwell in the midst of thee, saith the LORD."
Zechariah 2:10 (KJV)

Gospel music filled the room where I lay confined to my bed. Excruciating pain ripped through my entire body. My mind couldn't handle the physical torture that plagued me. Consumed with weak-ness from the pain, the very essence of life begin to leave me.

Desperately trying to concentrate on the message of the lyrics, I struggled to sing along, losing the words to the big gulp in my throat as hot tears made their way down my face. They burned to the depths of my heart and soul.

As I was unable to care for myself, Mother tended me – sacrificing her time so I wouldn't have to go to a nursing home. Many times, the darkest of thoughts flashed through my mind.

The world would be better off without me. I'm just a burden; my life is going nowhere. Lord, why don't You just take me home?

One day, my mother brought a karaoke to where I lay in my bed. "Michele, why not sing while you lie there?"

So, equipped with her old soundtracks, I did just that. I believe it changed my life. In my weakened state, I could barely make it through a song. But with time and persistence, my voice and spirit grew stronger. I'm no longer in that bed; I now travel and sing. I give my testimony that – thanks to God and my momma – I sang my way out!

NO LONGER FOREIGNERS

Charles A. Waugaman   September 18

"Consequently, you are no longer foreigners and aliens, but fellow citizens with God's people and members of God's household." Ephesians 2:19 (NIV)

"Morning has broken like the first morning
Morning has spoken like the first bird."
...Eleanor Farjeon 1881-1965

THE BLACKBIRD IS A THRUSH

I thought him so; although for a moment
I did not know but what some robin
Had followed from home to brightly mark
My stroll along St. James' Park.
Who else would hop with a pert, cocked head and a yellow bill?
But, when he turned my way with his ebony front,
I felt the chill of a lonely man on an alien shore,
The more deserted for imagining someone inquired
How his journey had transpired.
But when the blooming cherry caught his fluting,
energetic song, I realized
Even a stranger could belong.

THE CHERRY DINING SET

Judy Glyde   September 19

"Delight yourself in the LORD and he will give you the desires of your heart." Psalm 37:4 (NKJV)

My attention was drawn to an ad in the newspaper: "Estate sale, cherry dining set." I had wanted one for years. Perhaps it had the elegant, rich color I so enjoyed. I had gone to estate sales before, but the furniture was always too expensive or sold before I got there.

On the day of the sale, I arrived 45 minutes early. Eager shoppers lined the front sidewalk. The lady ahead of me was looking for antique dolls. The man behind me was an antique dealer who also had interest in the dining set. When the door opened, there was a major surge of people looking for their special bargains. I went straight for the dining room table, gave it a five-second look-over, and removed the sale sign. The price was reasonable and I was thrilled with my find.

At home, as I unloaded the chairs, I received a terrific surprise. The manufacture date was stamped on the bottom of the seats: 4-19-51.

That was the day I was born! My dining set and I were released from our "manufacturing plants" on the same date. What a wonderful surprise and confirmation that this set was just for me!

Thank You, Lord, for caring about things that are important to us and for Your surprises. Amen

TAKING TIME FOR GOD

Elizabeth Van Hook   September 20

"There is a time for everything, and a season for every activity under heaven." Ecclesiastes 3:1 (NIV)

At church last Sunday, Shirlee mentioned to me that when she doesn't take time for devotions in the morning, her day just doesn't go right! I paid little heed.

This morning I was scheduled to start work an hour late, so I had more time for my devotions. I picked up my Bible and then put it down saying, "Later."

Since I had extra time, I worked on a special project. Time passed, and I ran to the post office. But alas – I found the bus schedule had changed that day, too, and I was now an hour late for work. When I finally got there, I was stressed. I took my medicine. Then I remembered I had taken it at home! I worried all day how the extra dose would affect me.

Then I had to make up the lost hour by taking a short lunch and staying late. By the time I left, I had missed the last express bus. I ate supper late – and all my projects were put on hold.

The moral of the story is – don't put God aside! Have a conversation with Him in the morning, and – as my friend said – He'll make your day go right!

Today, Lord, each hour is Yours, not mine. Whatever happens, I trust You completely. Amen

CONSIDER THE ANT

Brad Nelson   September 21

"Go to the ant, thou sluggard; consider her ways, and be wise: Which having no guide, overseer, or ruler, Provideth her meat in the summer, and gathereth her food in the harvest."
Proverbs 6:6-8 (KJV)

Every believer in Christ should spend time observing ants. This may seem like a childish endeavor, but Proverbs tells us it is time well spent.

There is much we can learn from ants. They are *self-starters*. They don't require an overseer, guide or ruler. They know what needs to be done and they take initiative. Ants are also *prepared*. This more than anything describes an ant's life. They spend the summer making provision for winter. In life, we prepare for tough times during good times. Ants are cooperative. Each one has a task which it performs the best it can.

Those in the Body of Christ have jobs as well and should be doing them the best they can. Ants are also *community-minded* and function best in a colony. Believers function best when fellowshipping in the church.

Finally, ants are *weak*, yet unbelievably *strong*. Compared to humans, an ant is fragile. But it possesses unbelievable strength, carrying many times its body weight. Every believer possesses glaring weaknesses; however, we have within us the ultimate Power – God's Holy Spirit! Through Him, believers accomplish extraordinary feats.

Spend time at your next picnic checking out the ants and learn some valuable life lessons!

Father, make me like the ant as I diligently pursue Your will for my life. Amen

A LOVING GIFT

Shirley Stevens   September 22
"He that soweth sparingly shall reap also sparingly; and he which soweth bountifully shall reap also bountifully."
2 Corinthians 9:6 (KJV)

I recently heard about a doll collector who gives baby dolls to a local, long-term care facility. At the home where she leads a monthly Bible study group, she developed a relationship with the residents and noticed that many of them were lonely. After she lost her husband, she decided to donate dolls in his memory.

She has given away more than 50 dolls and has expanded to include a second nursing home. Patients with Alzheimer's often form an attachment with their new baby.

Although she has had a stroke and doesn't get around as well as she used to, JoAnn still feels the need to continue the giving program, which she feels has blessed her as well as the recipients of the dolls.

Dear Lord, help us to recognize a need and reach out to others to fulfill that need. Amen

SINNERS

Dave Evans   September 23

*"This is a faithful saying and worthy of all acceptance, that Christ
Jesus came into the world to save sinners,
of whom I am chief."* 1 Timothy 1:15 (NKJV)

The chief of sinners
The apostle Paul claimed to be;
Then surely I must rank second.
Paul's sins and mine brought forth sweat like blood
As Jesus agonized in the garden,
Soon to endure God's fury
In order to pay for Paul's sins and mine.
On the cross He finished the atonement,
He paid the debt;
His broken body and wounded spirit
Bearing the overwhelming burden,
Suffering such anguish
To save not only the chief of sinners and me,
but all sinners who will call upon His name.
"...for whoever calls on the name of the Lord shall be saved."
Romans 10:13 (NKJV)

HEAT WARNINGS AND RESULTS

Joy C. Bradford   September 24

Recently, North Texas has experienced serious drought. As a result, we are seeing beautiful, mature trees dying. The grass is brown and the ground is separating from homes – causing damage to foundations.

Last summer it was sizzling across the U.S. with temperatures soaring dangerously high. The National Weather Service issued warnings of excessive heat. In states like Illinois and Minnesota that are normally less sultry, the governors took action to provide cooling centers. Meteorologists in Colorado, South Dakota, and Washington State all reported record-breaking heat.

Prayer meetings petitioned God for relief, and I was reminded of David's words in Psalm 42. *"Why are you downcast, O my soul? Why so disturbed within me? Put your hope in God, for I will yet praise Him, my Savior and my God."* Psalm 42:5 (NIV)

What does it take for us to seek His attention? Are we guilty of just calling out to Him in our time of need? Do we praise Him for the gentle-

158

ness of spring or the beauty of winter? Do we put our hope in Him and remember our many blessings?

Dear Father, because I remember the joy of each season, I trust You for the future. Thank You for Your faithfulness. Amen

HOW DO I PRAISE YOU, LORD?
Pamela S. Thibodeaux   September 25
"Yet thou art holy, O Thou who art enthroned upon the praises of Israel...." Psalm 22:3 (NASB)

Lord, how many come to You out of a sense of obligation instead of love? Reach deep into our hearts and kindle a new fire within us, a fire of Your love. One that nothing can quench, no doubt or fear, failure or success – nothing will snuff it out to take Your place!

How do I praise You, Lord, when words seem so inadequate? Yet words are all that I have. Here is my praise to You....

You are everything to me, Jesus! You are my light and my salvation, my rock and my fortress. You are my life, my sweetness and my hope. You are my strength, my shield and my stronghold.

You are my delight and the lover of my soul. I love You more than words can express, more than doctrine can dictate; my desire is to seek Your face and to know You more intimately, to do Your will, to be used by You, and to be a blessing to others. You are everything to me, Jesus!

THE FRUIT OF GENTLENESS
Evelyn Minshull   September 26
"Consider the lilies of the field...they toil not, neither do the spin" Matthew 6:28b,d (KJV)

Jesus chided Peter for expressing an earthly perspective, rather than a heavenly view. Could not the same be said of us? When daily we deal with concerns of the world, is it surprising that they shape our speech?

We stand by the closet, considering. What to wear? What is most fitting for the occasion? What will put us in our best light?

But Jesus tells us not to be concerned. "Consider the lilies of the field," he said, "Solomon in all his glory was not arrayed like one of these."

We agnoize over finances. Will we have enough to cover current bills? Can we provide adequate shelter, food and healthcare for our families?

But Jesus pointed outh the Father's concern for even the lowly sparrow.

Martha of Bethany worked tirelessly for the comfort and pleasure of her guests. But Jesus reproached her zeal. Time spent with Him—learning—is more praiseworthy than perfect hostessing.

We shop, we acquire; we polish, protect and treasure our belongings. Yet they are temporal, breakable, depreciating and tarnishing. Jesus said, "Seek first the kingdom of God." What He offers us—the things of Heaven—are eternal.

O, Lord, far beyond your concern for the flowers of the field and the birds of the air, You care for us. Let us rest in that protection and focus on heavenly treasure. Amen.

STEP INTO THE REALM OF FAITH

Angelicia Roberts   September 27
"This hope we have as an anchor of the soul, a hope both sure and steadfast...." Hebrews 6:19a (NASB)

What does it mean to trust God? I believe that there is a peace that you can't fully explain or understand, but at the same time, it's real. It's as though He proves to us that He's in control of our circumstances which, to us, seem to be out of control. This peace may not provide the answers, but it does provide the strength to move forward in faith – or just wait and be still. We can rest in confidence, knowing who God is. We can also learn, perhaps for the first time, who we are in Christ.

Take the challenge, receive God's peace. When you choose to trust Him, you're choosing to step into the realm of faith. Remember this: that faith requires some sort of action! It comes back to the decision to either "stay or go" depending upon His guidance. Don't give up or give in because of "HOTMF" (heat-of the-moment feelings) or "OPP" (other people's perspectives). Make the decision to hold steadfast through God's Word in pursuit of His will, developing His character and receiving His promises.

LIGHTHOUSE OF THE SOUL

Risa L. Ulmer   September 28
"You are the light of the world ... let your light shine before men, that they may see your good deeds, and praise your Father in heaven." Matthew 5:14 (NIV)

A lighthouse stood on the rocky shore.
Its amber light shone out, bright with glee

As the darkness swept over the earth-bound sea.
And the ocean waves roared at the tiger eye
As it warned of the rocks near the shore.
The sea captain looked for the amber light
That was to him such a friend, since
The ships that cross ocean depths at night
Fear not the storms as the wild waves roll
For God is the Lighthouse of the Soul.

TOGETHER

LaDonne Weyman   September 29
*"The world and its desires pass away, but the man
who does the will of God lives forever."* 1 John 2:17 (NIV)

My husband Don and I spied the marinated artichoke hearts and
decided, "Yes, we want those." We headed home with a large jar. Once
there, Don gripped it with his large hands – twisting the lid full force.
Nothing! He tapped the lid. Tried again. Nothing.

I told him to stand back and let me tap it my way. I laughed to think
that I would be able to open it when he could not. Of course, I failed.
Tapping again, I asked Jesus to help me open the jar. That usually
works, but not this time. Now Don and I both laughed. Under my
husband's instruction, I held the bottom while he gripped the top. Still
laughing, and after much strain and working together – success!

The treasure was ours. Mine eaten with fresh veggies. Husband's,
as pizza topping. We sat at the table, happy with our individual choices,
enjoying the moment.

Marriage involves a common desire, hard work, laughter along the
way – and our realization that it works only when we bring Jesus into
the mix. Although we're "one" in the Lord, we're still individuals, and we
must allow each other to be who we are.

May the Lord bless you with love, companionship, warm hugs and
fresh ideas. May He open your eyes to the goodness around you, let
you enjoy your blessings, and renew your heart for Him and others in
the most unexpected ways!

THE SCRABBLE GAME

Elizabeth M. Van Hook   September 30
"A word aptly spoken is like apples of gold in settings of silver."
Proverbs 25:11 (NIV)

Since I have trouble sleeping, instead of reading a book to ease my restlessness, I play Scrabble on my bed. Words of life, love, sadness, joy, death, compassion, comfort, and understanding are easy to place on the board during the night.

However, in the daylight of the real world, such words are often difficult to say to friends and family. I need to call someone today to share my feelings. Have you tried calling just to offer words of comfort or joy?

Father, we thank You for speaking to us in the night, so that we can be a blessing to someone in the light of day. Amen

OCTOBER
"A CUP OF WATER IN HIS NAME"
WORLD COMMUNION SUNDAY

Evelyn Minshull   October 1
"I tell you the truth, anyone who gives you a cup of water in my name ... will certainly not lose his reward.'" Mark 9:41 (NIV)

Whether it is for a child coming hot and sweaty from play, a derelict – unwanted anywhere, his throat parched, his speech inaudible from long dryness – or one of our elderly in nursing homes, water is life-giving, life-preserving.

When this cup of cool refreshment is given with compassion that mirrors Christ's, the giver will be rewarded.

When a piece of fresh fruit, a morsel of meat, a slice of bread is given in His name, the giver will not lose the reward. The act of offering physical sustenance with Christlike caring is ministry.

How infinitely greater when the *Living* Water, the *Living* Bread, is offered to the soul-parched, the spirit-starved. Whoever gives knowledge of Christ to one who has not known Him, or who has wandered from earlier belief, will in no way lose his reward.

O God, help us to reach out to all who hunger and thirst – whether physically, emotionally, or spiritually. Amen

PUSHING AGAINST THE CURRENT

Charles A. Waugaman   October 2
"And we know that in all things God works for the good of those who love him, who have been called according to his purpose."
Romans 8:28 (NIV)

Geologists tell us that the Grand Canyon is not only the result of the cutting action of the Colorado River. It is equally the product of earth forces pushing up against the sawing power of water's seasonal surge and flow.

Our lives can gain beauty also, by resisting the common human ebb and flow of problems and dreams, advances and retreats.

Constant ease would never release the hidden beauties of potential that God has layered into His plan for our lives.

Lord, please help us push against the current and force adversity to burnish beauty into the contours and surface of our experience. In Jesus' Name, Amen

GREEN HOPE

Judy Barron   October 3

"May the God of green hope, fill you up with joy, fill you up with peace, so that your believing lives, filled with the life-giving energy of the Holy Spirit, will brim over with hope!"
Romans 15:13 (The Message)

What is Paul telling us in this Scripture verse? Our God is a God of hope and Paul prays that He may fill us with all joy and peace so that we may abound in hope.

Do we need to feel joy and peace to be hopeful? Whether our circumstances are positive or negative, we can be confident by the power of the Spirit.

I love *The Message* translation of this verse! Is "green hope" a living, growing, renewing, refreshing, life-giving expectation? I think so. And not only can we abound with hope, we will brim over with it so that we can spread this hope to all we meet!

Father, please fill me so full of joy, peace, and bountiful hope that I overflow to others. In Jesus' name, Amen

JESUS, BE MY PEACE

Angie K. Dilmore   October 4

Jesus, be my peace in a busy, bustling day.
Jesus, be my peace through the hurry-hustle hours.
Traffic tangling, horns a-honking,
Sales alluring, to-do list growing,
Jesus, be my peace
In a busy, bustling day.
Jesus, be our peace in a worried, wayward world.
Jesus, be our peace amidst the evil one's stronghold.
Wars are waging, bellies empty,
Storms are surging, illness spreading,
Jesus, be our peace

In a worried, wayward world.
Jesus, send Your peace to a lost and lonely land.
Jesus, send Your peace to the crying, grieving souls.
Lavish love and spread Your Sonshine,
Dry the tears, erase the heart pain.
Jesus, send Your peace
To a lost and lonely world.

TOUCHING CHRIST

Charles E. Harrel   October 5

Read: Luke 8:40-48

***"For he had healed many, so that those with diseases
were pushing forward to touch him"*** Mark 3:10 (NIV)

The hour was late when I answered the telephone. I wondered
what midnight crisis had occurred this time. Then I heard my daughter
sobbing, "Dad, can I come home?" Further inquiry seemed unnecessary. I knew her marriage had hit bottom. After hanging up the phone, I
knelt down to pray. Tears ran down my cheeks.

Often I have waited for answers from the Lord, but not that night.
My daughter's heartache ran deep, so I needed a different course of
action. Instead of biding my time for the Lord's response, I pressed
through the crowds of uncertainty and touched Heaven for my
daughter's welfare.

In Luke 8:43, a woman suffering with hemorrhages for twelve years
had waited long enough. As Jesus passed by, she pushed through the
crowds – past her fears – and grasped at Christ for her healing. Although Jesus asked His disciples who had touched Him, I wonder if He
already knew – but kept it to Himself? Nevertheless, the disciples
learned an important lesson that day: It doesn't matter if we touch Him,
or He touches us, the result is the same. Faith in action works both
ways.

*Lord, I hope You don't mind if my prayers seem a little pushy.
Sometimes the need requires that I reach out and touch You first. And
thank You for healing my daughter's wounded heart. Amen*

STANDING FIRM ON THE ROCK

Lorene M. Estep   October 6

". . . He set my feet on a rock and gave me a firm place to stand."
Psalm 40:2 (NIV)

I climbed steadily to the top of a huge rock and gazed across the

164

hills and valleys spread before me. The scene was etched in detail as only the Master Artist could paint it.

Breathing deeply of the cool refreshing air, I thought back over the trials of the past ten months, thanking the Lord for the way He had brought my husband and me through each one. I smiled as I reflected on the special blessings that had accompanied the changes He had made in our lives.

Times when I felt too distressed and exhausted to go on, He reminded me from His Word that He is always with me – a solid Rock that continues to hold me, giving me a firm place on which to stand.

So I held my arms toward Heaven and twirled around slowly, reveling in the firmness of the mass beneath my feet. I praised God as my spiritual Rock who will always be a firm place where I can stand, steady in Him, whatever changes are taking place in my life.

"The Lord is my rock, my fortress and my deliverer; my God is my rock in whom I take refuge." Psalm 18:2 (NIV)

HOPE IN GRIEF

Shirley Stevens   October 7
"Surely he hath borne our griefs and carried our sorrow."
Isaiah 53:4 (KJV)

Recently, I was impressed by Virginia Governor Tim Kaine, who reached out to parents, students, and faculty after the tragedy at Virginia Tech. When he was a law student at Harvard, he took a year off to volunteer with missionaries in Honduras. There, he served as the principal of a small Catholic school that taught teenagers basic carpentry and welding skills.

It is heartening to see such a person in a political position. Governor Kaine spoke about the trinity of lessons he learned from the Virginia Tech tragedy:

1)   the immense preciousness of human life
2)   the universality of human grief
3)   the universality of human hope

Dear Lord, help us to remember in our time of despair and grief that we can find hope. It has been so ever since the time of Your crucifixion. Amen.

I WRITE FOR HIM

Michele L. Tune   October 8

Since childhood I've written incessantly. It's my life's passion. But my dreams were lost in the confusion and despair of domestic violence. At last, I'm free from that dominating relationship. Now, perched high on a mountaintop, I look back into the valley realizing that with each step I took, Christ was guiding me all the way. At times He held my hand; when I was too weak, He carried me.

God can move mountains, although He doesn't choose to move every one. Sometimes He wants us to *climb* so His power can be revealed in our lives.

On my desk is a gift from Aunt Shirley. It's a writer's block of sticky notes decorated with springtime flowers and butterflies. Printed on them is the Scripture, ***"With God all things are possible."*** Matthew 19:26 (KJV) I've discovered firsthand that this is true.

It's taken several years to come full circle and pursue my passion of seeing my writing published. But at last I'm a "published author!" As such, I have the opportunity to share how real God has been in my life and how, with His grace, I have overcome adversity and risen above a painful past.

For a season, I danced with death. Today, I dance in victory! From a high place where eagles soar, I write to encourage, inspire, and shed light on a dark world. I write for His glory; *I write for Him!*

Lord, help me to always put You first in my writing and all aspects of my life. Let me shine for You!

This devotion also appeared in the Doniphan Prospect News, February 2007.

OUR MODERN GOD

Jean L. Croyle   October 9
"The Lord is my light and my salvation; whom shall I fear? The Lord is the strength of my life; of whom shall I be afraid?"
Psalm 27:1 (KJV)

Recently, I had a new computer built and installed. The serviceman was explaining the importance of the "firewall" to me, the consumer. He said, "Jean, you cannot be without it. It protects against turbulence, and keeps viruses from infecting your drive. Interference from unsolicited or unwanted individuals will be blocked. You can breathe easier, knowing that you won't be compromised by any kind of breakdown in your system. You wouldn't want to be without it."

I thought about this and a light went on in my mind: **God's my firewall!** He protects me every day from the unsteadiness of daily living; He certainly keeps viruses, the devil himself, away; He wards off unwanted and unsavory things from my life; and most significantly, He knows I rest in the fact that He is sovereign and omnipotent. I couldn't – and wouldn't – live without Him!

The words of the Bible, to some people, may sound like an ancient message, but the power of the Word is as timely now as it's always been. Receive Jesus today, and breathe more easily in your knowledge of His care for you. His peace, His devotion to those who follow Him, is forever. He is the "ultimate firewall!"

O, God from everlasting 'til today, shine the light of Your protection on my house. We may rest in the knowledge of Your love for us and in Your unwavering grace upon those who worship You. Amen

TORNADO!

Elizabeth M. Van Hook   October 10
"When I am afraid, I will trust in You." Psalm 56:3 (NIV)

I had tuned in to the weather channel that morning and learned that a tornado had ravaged Lady Lake, Florida at 3:00 a.m. while residents slept. Lives were taken, homes flattened, and buildings damaged. A new church, built to withstand wind, had been demolished!

I empathized. The previous year on a bus going home from work I had seen a black funnel cloud in the distance. As we rode through torrential rain, we watched the brilliant saw-toothed lightning, and heard reverberating thunder that sounded like a train. Hailstones pounded the roof of the bus.

Frightened and helpless, I looked around, noting passengers had bowed their heads in prayer. Then we felt the bus swerve! We were driving away – very fast – from the storm! Soon, I was home and the sun was peeking through the clouds. I was safe! Hailstones littered my lawn and my 200-year-old oak tree had split in half. It was leaning against my bedroom window. By some miracle the glass was not even broken!

Now, I thought about the Lady Lake church. While the building had been destroyed, the spirit of its members had not. They were planning a service of thanksgiving. Neighbors were showing up to help remove the debris and plan for Sunday. Praise God for His care!

Father, we thank You that through the storms of life You give us peace and protection. We are grateful for helping hands, too. Amen

IN THE GLOAMING

Mary A. Koepke   October 11
"And it shall come to pass in that day, that the light

shall not be clear, nor dark ... And it shall come to pass, that at evening time it shall be light." Zechariah 14:6-7 (KJV)

That supernatural time of day we call "twilight," the Scots call "gloaming." It is at dusk or nightfall that the world should stop, look, and listen!

When the tired sun creeps into bed over the horizon, the summer wind holds its breath for a brief interlude. A dimmer knob is turned, and reflected light from behind the hills takes on a soft glow. All nature is bathed in mystical fluorescence. Grass and leaves shine greener, Queen Anne's white lace dazzles, the Peace rose's pink-edged-petals deepen, their perfume sweetens. Even the robin hushes its burbled lullaby.

Then ethereal stillness embraces body and soul. Here is an invitation to halt our frenetic busyness, open our eyes, and listen for God's loving words.

CHOSEN
Valerie J. Chambers   October 12

Before God created the vast expanse
Before the stars began to dance
Before the sun began to shine
Before the moon shone on the pine
Before the earth came into view
Before the ground felt morning dew
Before the sea raced toward the shore
Before the summer rain did pour
Before the mountains raised their heads
Before the valleys formed their beds
Before the birds flew through the sky
Before the beasts' first sounds did cry
Before the man drew his first breath
Before his sin caused certain death
Before the cut of my umbilical cord –
"I want this one!" said the Lord.

RULER OF THE WIND
Dave Evans   October 13
"But as they were sailing along He fell asleep; and a fierce gale of wind descended on the lake, and they began to be swamped and to be in danger. They came to Jesus and woke Him up, saying,

*"Master, Master, we are perishing!" And He got up and rebuked
the wind and the surging waves, and they stopped, and it became
calm. And He said to them, "Where is your faith?" They were
fearful and amazed, saying to one another, "Who is this, that He
commands even the winds and the water, and they obey Him?"*
Luke 8:23-25- (NASB)

In the darkness, before the sun embraces the morning
Strong, fierce winds gust through the canyon:
Leaves whistle, trees groan under the strain,
Small branches snap, metal stall roofs rattle;
Horses, nerves on edge, alert to danger;
The chill paints a rosy flush on my cheeks and nose—
Then a momentary lull, and calm.
It's then the Ruler of the wind captures my thoughts.
Out on the sea, strong, fierce winds
Send waves crashing across the bow of the small ship;
Flushed with fear, anxious disciples awake the Master,
Who, with a word, stills the waves and wind.

COVERINGS – (A PARABLE)

Marion E. Gorman   October 14

*"Above all, love each other deeply, because love covers a
multitude of sins."* 1Peter 4:8 (NIV)

Mary's heart was heavy with hurt because of a situation with a
sister in Christ. Her judgmental, critical thoughts prevented her from
considering the possibility that she could be at fault for the breach of
friendship.

As sun streaked across the open Bible in her lap, her attention was
drawn to the barren landscape wrapped in a blanket of snow. Icicles
dripped tears in the sunshine, reflecting her weighty mood.

So pure, so clean, she thought. The snow transforming the desolate countryside reminded her of Christ's love that enveloped her in a
robe of righteousness. Her mood lightened. Christ was offering the love
she needed to heal the relationship with her friend.

As she accepted His love, her thoughts changed. She absorbed
His righteousness as the earth soaks up snow to provide what is
necessary for growth.

Mary's hurt was replaced with the desire to forgive and be forgiven
for the sin that had fractured the friendship. She now realized that our
relationships with others reflect our relationship with God.

Lord, help me confess my sin to my friend and heal our friendship, for I believe the effective, fervent prayer of the righteous avails much. Amen

SING YOUR PRAISES TO GOD

Annie Bruening   October 15
I Chronicles 16:1-36 (NKJV)

In the above Scripture, David has moved the Ark about eight miles to Jerusalem. It symbolized the presence of God with His people. David was so happy to have the Ark where it belonged, he gave a generous gift to every man and woman in his kingdom! Joy does that to you. It causes you to be generous!

"Glory in his holy name: let the hearts of those rejoice who seek the Lord!" gave hope to the ancient people – and to us modern people as well. We study the Old Testament today because it contains the roots of what we believe. By returning the Ark, David instilled a new faith in God's people. *"Sing to the Lord, all the earth; proclaim the good news of his salvation from day to day."* Did you catch that? Salvation was coming from the Lord! What an amazing statement for David to make!

Carl, one of our residents in the nursing home where I work, loves to sing and he often does so at our church services. And sometimes, during a meal in the dining room, he breaks into a hymn and a hush comes over us as we listen. Carl sings unselfishly, because the Holy Spirit has put a melody in his heart and it cannot be contained.

Thank You, Father, for the songs You put in our hearts. Amen

ARE YOU A CRACKED POT?

Joan Clayton   October 16
Read Jeremiah 18:1-6
**"Woe unto him that striveth with his Maker!
Let the potsherd strive with the potsherds of the earth.
Shall the clay say to him that fashioneth it, What makest thou?
Or thy work, He hath no hands?"** Isaiah 45:9 (KJV)

Archaeologists found a cracked water pot in a recent dig. Today, it is claimed to be of "inestimable worth!" In some ancient civilization it was of no value to them once cracked.

Our lives can be "cracked pots," too. We may begin with zeal and love for the Lord, yet somewhere along the way that fire can begin to cool. We must guard lest the cares of this world and the deceitfulness of riches "cracks our pots" and renders us of no use to God.

The enemy would have us believe our usefulness is over, once we are cracked. But God can fix anything. Bring your "cracked" vessel to the Master Potter. He will make it brand new – of "*inestimable* worth!"

"Is your life cracked, chipped, or broken?
Did you lower your standard for some small token?
Bring it to Jesus, repent and confess,
He'll make you brand new, He can fix any mess!"

Thank You, Father for not giving up on us. Thank You for loving us. May we go forth with a renewed commitment to love and serve You. Amen

SEARCHING FOR GOD

Pat Collins   October 17

*God, they say You are always there.
I know You are, but sometimes I can't find You.*
"My child, look and listen.
Do you not see Me, among My creations?
See the trees, how they grow.
The leaves, changing color.
Watch the softly falling snow.
Beautiful flowers in the Spring. Open your heart.
See Me.
Do you not hear the bubbling brook,
The rustle of leaves at the slightest breeze?
Open your heart.
Hear Me. I am here.
Block out the loud and harsh things of this
World, be quiet and open to the gentleness of
My ways, and know,
I am there."

THE PROMISE

Florence Biros   October 18
"He Himself has said, 'I will never desert you, nor will I ever forsake you.'" Hebrews 13:5 (NASB)

At worship with friends, I noticed a woman three rows ahead with sagging shoulders. Even though I couldn't see her face, I could tell by her stance that she was feeling desolate and abandoned.

Yes, she was a stranger, but as she stood alone, her despair was not a stranger to me. Thirty years before I had stood in a praise service feeling numb and worthless, imprisoned by the misery of my life, when God had someone seek me out and minister just to me.

I was certain the Holy Spirit had placed her on my heart, but the sense of urgency to go to her was too overwhelming to ignore. Making my way forward, I stepped into the empty space beside her and put my arm around her. Leaning over I whispered, "Jesus loves you. He will never forsake you."

In a swoop, she embraced me. I held her close, tears streaming down my own cheeks. With a few more words of comfort, I returned to my seat. At the end of the service I went to her, put my arm around her waist, and said, "Jesus loves you. Don't forget that – whatever happens!"

On the way out the door my friends asked, "Did you know her?"

No," I admitted, "I never saw her before. All I know is, she was hurting and the Lord wanted to tell her He cared."

If you, too, are hurting or know someone who is in need of feeling His love, remember that – regardless of your circumstances – Jesus loves *you!*

PRAYER OF CONTENTMENT

Connie Ansong   October 19

"But godliness with contentment is great gain. For we brought nothing into this world, and it is certain we can carry nothing out." 1Timothy 6:6-7 (KJV)

We need to recognize our dependency on the Lord for survival in this anxious world. He has made Christ a brother to us by teaching us all His ways so we can be near to our Creator. Jesus has been tempted in all areas of our human experience. Therefore, He knows His grace is sufficient for all our needs.

Because of this, our first line of action when trials of life and temptations come our way is to cast our cares upon Him (I Peter 5:7) We should also remember how we have been protected before, and are now being protected. Remember that He knows and that He understands and won't let us down.

Thank You, Lord, for the "Spirit of understanding" and the peace we receive in the midst of all the chaos. In Christ's name we pray with thanksgiving. Amen

WINDOWSILL PRAYERS

Lisa Hetzel   October 20

"But when you pray, go into your room, close the door
and pray to your father, who is unseen. Then your father,
who sees what is done in secret, will reward you."
Matthew 6:6 (NIV)

I have discovered an unexpected place for my own prayer room! After dinner is over and the dishes are cleared, my family escapes for awhile. It is then that I find myself gazing out the kitchen window at God's beauty in nature – flowers and birds – as I wash the dishes. So I scrub and pray silently.

Peace settles around me as I realize that many other women around the world are doing the same thing.

What prayers do they offer You, God? Do tears trickle down their cheeks as they beg for just one more day or one more chance? Do their hearts break as they plead for Your protection, Lord? Do some hearts break with regret for those things spoken and unspoken?

Will they feel Your forgiveness? What about their enemies, Lord? Do they even dare to pray for them? Are they allowing themselves to pause for just a moment in their busy lives to receive Your peace?

And – also, Lord of all – **will I?**

Dear Lord, thank You for reminding us that You will meet us wherever we are. Continue to nudge us to take the time to be alone with You. Thank You for hearing our hearts' cry. Teach us to lean less on ourselves and more on You. Amen

SELFISH AMBITION

Evelyn Minshull   October 21

"Truly I say to you, whoever does not receive the kingdom of God
like a child shall not enter it at all." Mark 10:15 (NASB)

James warned about selfish ambition: seeking the most prominent place; garnering personal recognition. This all-too-human flaw separates us from God's intentions. While we wrangle for position, how can our thoughts properly bend toward God? How can our spirits sing of His glory, when we are busy promoting our own?

Even Christ's disciples fell victim to this flaw. "Who will sit at His right hand?" they asked, vying for that honor.

But Jesus, dismayed, stressed that the first shall be last; the last shall be first. We should seek to serve, not to *be* served, as when He made Himself servant by washing their travel-stained feet.

Time and again He reinforced His example: serving the hurting and helpless; reaching out to the wretched; practicing compassion with humility. Then, He drew a little child before them and presented a model of how we must approach His Kingdom – without artifice or self-promotion.

This means to relinquish control; to embrace humility; to shun selfish ambition. In perfect childlike trust, we glorify only God.

O, Lord, shatter our self-importance that we may serve You with the artless innocence and bubbling joy of little children. Amen

CHRISTIANS TURN THE WORLD UPSIDE DOWN
Janet R. Sady   October 22

"But the Jews who believed not, moved with envy, took unto them certain lewd fellows of the baser sort, and gathered a company and set all the city in an uproar, and assaulted the house of Jason, and sought to bring them out to the people. And when they found them not, they drew Jason and certain brethren unto the rulers of the city, crying, these that have turned the world upside down are come here also."
Acts 17:5-6 (KJV)

What were the circumstances for this uproar in the city? The disciples and believers were going about seeking to spread the message of Jesus' sacrifice for the sins of the people. All were invited to accept Him as their Messiah. The disciples also performed miracles by healing the sick, and casting out demons.

The religious leaders reasoned that they were losing control over the people. Jealousy played a large part in their opposition to the disciples. They felt as if their world had been literally "turned upside down" by the response to this teaching.

What a tremendous impact these believers made on the lives of the people from that city!

Wouldn't it be a wonderful blessing if someone were able to say that about us today?

Our Heavenly Father, we confess that we have not done nearly enough for Your Kingdom. Forgive us, and empower us by Your Spirit to greater works for Your honor and glory. Amen

174

FROM THIS DAY FORTH

Jana Carman   October 23

"And the Lord God fashioned into a woman the rib which He had taken from the man, and brought her to the man. And the man said, "This is now bone of my bones, and flesh of my flesh ... for this cause a man shall leave his father and his mother, and shall cleave to his wife; and they shall become one flesh."
Genesis 2:22-24 (NASB)

Over the years, we have had several beagles. Hounds like to find the carcass of a dead animal (the riper the better) and roll in it. I hate to admit it, but sometimes I get a similar perverted pleasure from reliving details of how so-and-so mistreated me. When the "so-and-so" is my husband, this grubbing in the garbage of resentment proves unhealthy for me and my marriage.

Scarcely was the honeymoon over before I found I had married a flawed human being – just like myself. He had some habits that irritated me. (I had one or two that exasperated him, as well.) Although we had been engaged for eighteen months, there were many nice and not-so-nice surprises as we began to work at melding our lives.

The wedding promise, "from this day forth," looks in only one direction. In building a marriage, every day needs to be "from this day forth." Burying yesterday's "garbage" reduces my temptation to go rooting through it. And that makes me nicer to be around!

Thank You, Lord, that You put my trespasses out of mind, and You no longer hold them against me. Help me to be like You. Amen

SECURITY THROUGH FAITH

Delores Hartman   October 24

Since believing in Jesus, I have become secure. It doesn't mean things will be easy, but it does mean He will always be there to sustain me. I need to remember this when things go wrong.

Scripture tells of Jesus walking on water and of the disciples in a boat, a good distance from shore. A violent storm came up, its strong winds threatening to sink the boat. Through the din of this storm, they saw someone walking on the lake, and it terrified them.

They cried out in fear, *"It's a ghost!"* *"But Jesus immediately said to them, 'Take courage! It is I. Don't be afraid.'*

"'Lord, if it's you,' Peter replied, 'tell me to come to you on the water.'

"'Come,' he said. Then Peter climbed out of the boat, and walked on the water toward Jesus. But when he saw the wind, he feared and began to sink, crying out, 'Lord, save me!'"

"Immediately, Jesus reached out His hand and caught him. 'You of little faith, why did you doubt?' And when they climbed into the boat, the wind died down. Then those who were in the boat worshiped him, saying, 'Truly you are the Son of God!'"
Matthew 14:27-33 (NIV)

Yes, our security is in Christ. We are safe and empowered when we remain with Him.

The more we focus on a problem – the bad things – our lives sink like stones. When Peter looked at the waves (his circumstances) as he walked on the water, he started to sink. He needed to keep his eyes on Christ.

Lord, I look to You. Keep me from focusing on the negative, and teach me to embrace the good, which is only in You. Amen

FALL EASTER LILIES

Helen Kammerdeiner   October 25

"O death, where is thy sting? O grave, where is thy victory?"
I Corinthians 15:55 (KJV)

"Oh, take it home and put it in your garden. Really, it will bloom again this fall."

It was weeks after Easter. The plant I had bought for the church looked yellow and dead. I certainly didn't believe there was any reason to waste time planting it, but my friend was so insistent that I finally did as she asked.

In October, I noticed some beautiful white blooms in my garden! *That's odd,* I thought. *Those lilies belong to spring and Easter. They seem strange among the fall flowers.*

Then I realized that fall is a perfect time for Easter lilies! As we face the cold, bare darkness of winter, they repeat the message of the resurrection. Death has been vanquished! We can believe that winter will end, and spring will bring new life and beauty into our gardens. We can also know that Christ has brought new life into our cold, dead hearts.

His love took Him to the cross to pay the debt we owed for our sin. Now we, who were dead, can live again in Him. He who defeated death will freely give us life.

Thank You, Jesus, for the life You offer us. Thank You for letting us see reminders of Your love when we most need them. Amen

SACRIFICIAL LOVE

Lydia Harris   October 26

Read: Romans 5:1-11

"...When we were still powerless, Christ died for the ungodly."
Romans 5:6 (NIV)

"How are you doing?" I asked my pregnant daughter when she called after her seven-month checkup.

"Okay, I guess." Her voice sounded flat. "I'm on bed rest so the baby won't come early."

I sighed. We had prayed she would get through this pregnancy without complications. With a two-year-old to care for, how could she rest? Although barely recovered from my own lengthy illness, I offered to help her. Several days a week I made the hour-long drive to her home to help with meals, housework, and her toddler. One day as I left her home, I said, "I'm investing in the life of my unborn grandson. Otherwise, he might not have one."

As I reflected on this comment, I realized that's what Christ did for us! He invested in our lives before we were born (or born again) so we could have abundant life on earth and eternal life in Heaven. ***"You see, at just the right time, when we were still powerless, Christ died for the ungodly."*** Why did He die? To demonstrate His love. I made a small sacrifice to help my daughter, but Jesus made the supreme sacrifice by giving His life!

Thank You, Lord, for Your sacrificial love. While we were undeserving sinners, You died for us. Thank You for giving us life by giving up Your own. Amen

THE FAVOR OF THE KING

Jana Carman   October 27

Read Esther 4:12-5:2

The rule was: no one approached the throne of King Ahasuerus uninvited – not even the queen! But to rescue her people from annihilation, Esther was willing to risk her life. First, though, she asked her fellow Jews to join her in a three-day fast.

However, there is a throne room where we are always welcome! We don't have to fast three days – or even one – before we come! In fact, the great King invites us to ***"...approach the throne of grace with confidence, so that we may receive mercy and find grace to help us in our time of need."*** Hebrews 4:16 (NIV)

The door to the throne room is always open to one of the King's children. He really wants you and me to come and talk to Him!

Lord, help me to pray with Esther's unselfishness and the confidence of a beloved child. Amen

IN SEASON OR OUT

Teresa Wiedrick   October 28

"Give thanks to the Lord ... for His lovingkindness is everlasting ... who remembered us in our low estate."
Psalm 136:1, 22b, 23a (NASB)

These days, when rain sprinkles down to saturate the earth before a freeze, not much sunlight appears. I see no hint of blue sky, only blankets of mixed white and gray fluff rapidly moving eastward as the cloud cover continues to envelop the heavens. Trees maintain their leaves, but not their vibrant glossy greens; rather, muted greens and browned reds appear. It is not quite winter when the earth will be blanketed with snow, but the breezy carefree summer days are gone. It is autumn.

There are days like these in our hearts, too. The sunshiny gloss is absent, even though no palpable evil has overtaken us. Nothing has changed in our circumstances, but a haze dims our sight. Muted colors prevail.

He reminds us that His lovingkindness is present and active in the autumn, too. It endures through each season in our lives, including our low estate – even beyond the next generation of seasons.

Dear Father, in season or out, may we give thanks for Your lovingkindness which You so graciously offer. May we remember that it is extended to us even in our low days. Amen

NEVER FORSAKEN

Evelyn Minshull   October 29

Psalm 22:1-11

The Psalmist cried, **"My God, my God, why have You forsaken me?"** Even David – in whom God delighted – sensed this separation, this space, this temporary absence of the Presence of God. Miserable in sackcloth and ashes while running sores polluted his flesh, Job sought to confront God, to arbitrate with Him – but could not find Him to force the issue.

Do we, ever, feel that God is unreachable? Do we sometimes pray fervently, unceasingly, yet discern no response?

Has He forsaken us?

On the Cross, Jesus echoed David's anguish: *"My God, my God, why have You forsaken me?"* Jesus, the sinless One, accepted the burden of the world's sins – of *our* sins – at that desolate moment. Even He experienced that vacuum, that desperate aloneness.

It was our sin that formed the barrier between the sacrificial Christ and His Father. It is *always* Sin that denies us God's closeness.

O, God, we know that You have not abandoned us. Help us to recognize – and cast aside – our sins, that we might never lose the knowledge of Your Presence. Amen

A LAMP TO MY PATH

Christian Lagow   October 30

"The unfolding of your words gives light."
Psalm 119:130 (NIV)

In the woods I stand alone as encroaching darkness threatens to create fear around me. Tree limbs begin to sway as a strong breeze springs up. I'm aware of evil, yet none touches me. Since my Father's Word is a light – a "lamp unto my feet" – I am sure-footed and at peace as I dodge every root and tree limb in my path. I will never cease to thank Him for His daily guidance and protection.

Heavenly Father, Your ever-precious loving Word throws light on my darkened world. Lord, I have proved Your Scriptures again and again as I go through the trials and tribulations in my life. I dodge them every day by believing in Your promises. Lord, thank You for granting me grace and for loving me. Amen

MINISTRY WITHIN THE CHURCH

Janet R. Sady   October 31

**"For as the body is one, and has many members,
and all the members of that one body being many,
are one body, so also is Christ."** 1 Corinthians 12:12 (KJV)

Which part of your body is most important? Would you be willing to give up your ears? What about an arm or a leg? Don't be silly! We know they are all needed, and of great importance.

Why is it then, in the Church body, that there is competition among believers? We have many different types of people. God has given to each one a gift for service. Some members are given wisdom to discern the Word; some are teachers, encouragers, preachers, etc. The fact is, they are all important in the work of the Lord.

Even though we are diverse in our gifts, we are to use them for the same purpose: to glorify God. Pride in our gifts is sin. Let it not be said of us!

All praise to You, O, Lord, for the gifts within Your body of believers. Bless each one who faithfully serves You. Amen

NOVEMBER
SCRAGGLY BLACK CATS

Kay J. Clark   November 1

Recently, I entered a shop to buy birdseed. Inside, was a cat – wearing a large sweat sock!

"Is your cat cold?" I said to Scott, the proprietor.

"No, he replied, "she has a cancerous sore and we cover it to keep her from scratching it. We dearly love this cat!"

I told him I understood. I related how three years before, our son had picked up an abandoned black kitten along the road. The kitty, searching for food, warmth, and love, cuddled into his lap as he drove. "Ever since," I said, "that black scraggly cat has made our house his home."

"Really," Scott mused, "aren't we all black scraggly cats?"

His words haunted me. Aren't we all like that cat, searching for food, for warmth, for safety, for someone to love us? Aren't we all longing for a home?

Our Lord Jesus Christ fulfills all these desires. He said, *"I am the Bread of Life,"* so we need not hunger. Jesus invites us to *"Come unto me and I will give you rest."* Here is warmth and safety! *"Do not be afraid; I have overcome the world. As the Father has loved me, so have I loved you."* And He promises us a home! *"I go to prepare a place for you that where I am you may be also."* (KJV)

All we "black scraggly cats" can know peace and joy with our Savior since His house is our home!

DNA

Joseph M. Hopkins   November 2

"Then God said, 'Let us make man in our image, after our likeness ... So God created man in his image....'"
Genesis 1:26-27 (KJV)

Just what is DNA? (I know you're just dying to know, so I'll tell you.) It is *Deoxribonucleic acid.* But you are wondering what is *that?* "Deoxribonucleic acid (DNA) is a nucleic acid molecule that contains the genetic instructions used in the development and functioning of all known living organisms." Every living thing – and that includes humans – has its own identifying DNA. There are 6 billion people on the face of the earth, and it's predicted that there will be 9.3 billion by 2050.

How do those scientists – whose BP is elevated at the mere mention of Intelligent Design – explain this phenomenon? If the miracle of life were accomplished by the interaction of mindless atoms, spewed forth as it were by a giant machine, wouldn't we all be cookie-cutter look-alikes? Yet each of us is unique – not only in DNA and fingerprints, but in our physical features and personalities. Even "identical" twins are not totally identical.

A convincing proof of God's existence, I believe, is the fact that all 6 billion of us are different from one another. And this goes for the billions who have lived before us and the billions who will follow. Only the infinite Creator can account for this awesome miracle!

And to think that "He loves us each one as if there were only one to love!"

CABIN BUILT FOR TWO

Debbie Rempel   November 3

"Let not your heart be troubled: ye believe in God, believe also in me. In my Father's house are many mansions ... I go to prepare a place for you." John 14:1-2 (KJV)

Just outside a cabin built for two
Grandma and Grandpa walk,
hand in hand, down one of Heaven's golden roads,
to a garden of flowers that bloom
in all the colors you can imagine.
Roses of red, violets of blue.
I know you loved me,
but I miss you.

HOLY PAPARAZZI

Sandra McGarrity   November 4

"Joyful are those who listen to me, watching for me daily at my gates, waiting for me outside my home!" Proverbs 8:34 (NLT)
"Blessed is the man who listens to me, watching daily at my doors, waiting at my doorway." Proverbs 8:34 (NIV)

The film *LaDolce Vita* tells the story of a journalist named Marcello who covers sensational news about movie stars, religious visions, and the decadent aristocracy. He is accompanied by a photographer colleague, Papparazzo. From this film comes an often heard term in our society – *paparazzi*. Its definition is: "a newspaper photographer who follows famous people about in the hope of photographing them in unguarded moments. Paparazzi go to difficult and even extreme lengths to follow the stars. One of their chief tactics is lying in wait for them outside their homes."

Jesus says that blessings will be bestowed upon those who watch and wait outside His home just to hear a word from Him. We receive no rebuke – broken cameras or tabloid headlines – when we set ourselves to go to extreme lengths to seek Him as the paparazzi seek the stars – just blessing!

Maybe the paparazzi are searching for the wrong star?

Jesus says: ***"I am ... the bright and Morning Star."*** Revelation 22:16

Lord Jesus, make me to be Your ardent "paparazzi!" Amen

FLOURISHING WHERE WE'RE PLANTED
Shirley Stevens   November 5
"Those that be planted in the house of the Lord shall flourish in the courts of our God." Psalm 92:13 (KJV)

In early March, my friend Sonia picked a periwinkle crocus and brought it inside the house to keep it from freezing. The flower immediately closed up its petals and died.

She said she remembered what her father told her when she and her siblings were young and fussing because they couldn't go somewhere or move some place. "God means us to grow where we're planted." Sonia said that when you live to be 80, you can find lessons in everything!

Dear Lord, please help me to respect where plants and people grow and not try to remove them from their environment. Remind me that I am not in control. You are. And help me to sink my roots deeply into Your soil. Amen

BE A GOOD LISTENER
Annie Bruening   November 6
Read Job 32:11-12 (KJV)

Can God, through young Elihu, teach us how to be good listeners?

"I waited for your words." (Respectfully wait for the other person to speak.)

"I gave ear to your reasons." (Listen to all the person has to say.)

"Whilst ye searched out what to say." (Don't finish someone's sentence when he pauses, and don't interrupt. Give him a chance to gather his thoughts first.)

And lastly, "I attended unto you." (Try to understand the reason behind what is being said.)

God did, after all, give us two ears and one mouth! Listening *must* be more important.

Lord, please help us keep our mouths shut more often! And make us pay attention to what is being said. Amen

"WE'D BETTER PRAY, MOMMY!"

Marjorie K. Evans   November 7

For Veterans' Day I took my two sons to the San Bernardino Mountains. David, seven, was in the front with me, while Charles, five, slept in the back seat. The weather prediction was "cold, with a possibility of snow," which especially excited the boys. However, I was apprehensive. I'd never driven in the mountains. When we ran into dense fog at 5,500 feet, I was dismayed!

We could see only a few feet ahead. Fortunately, the centerline of the road was quite visible. We could see the edge, but nothing beyond except a thick blanket of fog. I knew we could plunge down the steep mountainside!

White-knuckled, I cried, "I'd better turn on the headlights so other drivers can see us!"

"Mommy, I think we'd better pray!" David urged.

"Yes, David! Pray!"

"Dear Jesus," he began, "please help Mommy see the white line in the middle of the road, and help her stay close to it so she won't go down over the mountain!"

Trembling, I, too, prayed as we inched our way up the winding road. The slow, tedious trip seemed to go on forever. Finally, we reached the village of Big Bear and safety! (And there was snow for the boys the next morning!)

Dear Lord, thank You for a young son who realized the importance of prayer. Help me to seek You always – not just when I go through dense fogs of uncertainty, problems, and dangers. Amen

SPIRITUAL QUEST FOR TRUTH

Connie Ansong   November 8

"That night the Lord stood beside Paul and said, 'Don't worry, Paul; just as you have told the people about me here in

Jerusalem, so you must also in Rome." Acts 23:11 (TLB)

There was a plan by some plotters to put Paul to death. However, the Lord had the master plan for Paul's life. We too know Who's in charge of our days! When we are in relationship with the Lord, we live and focus on Him alone for direction and guidance. Therefore, there is nothing to worry about.

This sounds too easy to the sophisticated mind. However, Matthew 11:30 states, *"My yoke is easy and My burden is light."* All we need to do is to believe the Word. Even when we lack faith we can also ask for believing prayer to accomplish the impossible in our lives. I believe Paul must have been calm, resting in the Lord, because the order was clear and precise to him. Paul had no fear because his mind was stayed on the Lord. *"You will keep in perfect peace him whose mind is steadfast, because he trusts in you."* (Isaiah 26:3)

Lord, teach us to lean on – and keep our mind's focus on – You alone. You have promised to be with us at all times, and You will never leave us alone. Nothing can separate us from Your everlasting Love. Thank You. Amen

DANGEROUS DREAM

Audrey Stallsmith   November 9

Read Genesis 37:5-11

"So you want to be our king, do you?" his brothers derided. And they hated him both for the dream and for his cocky attitude."
Genesis 37:5-7(TLB)

Imagine that you have to begin restraining your behavior when-ever your insufferable younger brother is around. Otherwise, you know the self-righteous little pipsqueak will tattle on you. Then, to add insult to injury, he relates a dream he's had in which you and all his other family members kowtow to him.

Was it really necessary for Joseph to report his vision to his brothers? There's no indication God told him to do so. But there's little doubt Joseph felt morally superior to his siblings and saw himself as his father's "good" son. To him, the dream seemed to put God's stamp of approval on that belief.

It's fatally easy to fall into this kind of moral one-upmanship. But, if we feel superior to the "sinners" around us, they aren't going to take our patronizing perceptions with good grace. Rather, they'll resent both us and the God we purport to preach. And our pride, the devil's sin, will make us worse than those we're condemning.

It's probably fortunate Joseph knew nothing of the depths to which he would have to plummet before he became worthy of the high position promised by his dream. It's part of God's mercy, though, that pride so frequently ends in a fall. If it weren't for the correcting effect of those plunges, who knows what monsters we might become?

FAMILY FURY

Audrey Stallsmith   November 10

Read Genesis 37:12-20

"Here comes that master-dreamer," they exclaimed. "Come on, let's kill him and toss him into a well and tell father that a wild animal has eaten him. Then we'll see what will become of all his dreams!" Genesis 37:19-20 (TLB)

It was probably the brightly-colored coat Joseph wore that allowed his brothers to recognize him from a distance. The coat that so loudly proclaimed their father's favoritism.

Joseph was apparently not aware of how much his brothers hated him. Otherwise, he wouldn't have gone so blithely to an isolated area in search of them. But a teenager would have seen this trip, all on his own, as a great adventure – proof that his father now considered him a man.

Favored young people can often be so naively self-centered that they really don't take seriously the negative reactions of those around them. But they aren't the only ones.

Many of us adults also treat those near to us worse than we would strangers, because we think other family members *have* to love us. That, as this story illustrates, simply isn't true. Bitterness festers and flourishes best in close quarters. And Jacob's older sons, violent characters to begin with, simply weren't allowed to get away from their cocky younger brother – or from their father's preference for him.

Fortunately, family irritations don't usually provoke murder plots! But they can touch off explosions that end in permanent estrange-ments. Although those blow-ups may seem abrupt, they are often fueled by years of our not taking those we love seriously.

WEARISOME WAITING

Audrey Stallsmith   November 11

Read Genesis 37:25-36

"So when the traders came by, his brothers pulled Joseph out of the well and sold him to them for twenty pieces of silver, and they took him along to Egypt." Genesis 37:28 (TLB)

When Joseph bragged about his dream of lording it over his brothers, he never guessed how much that vision was going to cost him. If so, he probably would have been happy to settle for far less!

Not only wasn't his dream being fulfilled, he found himself suddenly demoted from "favorite son" to "slave!" No doubt, Joseph at first fumed with schemes for revenge against his brothers. But the only Father to whom he had access in Egypt was far more loving, and therefore far less coddling than Jacob had been. So Joseph eventually had to emerge from his sulks and get on with things.

He still had certain advantages, after all. He'd inherited his mother's good looks and his father's shrewdness – not to mention a penchant for interpreting other people's dreams. But he must still have been somewhat baffled by how his own had failed to turn out.

We know, of course, that its fulfillment was still coming, just not nearly as rapidly or in the manner Joseph had expected. So, when we feel God has failed in what He promised us, we'd better stop harping on the injustice of it all and keep plugging away. For all we know, He may have something larger in store for us than we ever imagined!

TRICKY TEMPTATION

Audrey Stallsmith   November 12

Read Genesis 39:1-19

"How can I do such a wicked thing as this?
It would be a great sin against God!" Genesis 39:9b (TLB)

From his response to Potiphar's wife, we can deduce how much Joseph had changed during his time in Egypt. If he had faced this type of temptation while still in Canaan, we can envisage the 17-year-old righteously replying that fornication was beneath him.

Now we find his response based, not on what the transgression might do to his reputation, but on how it would affect others! It would be a betrayal of the faith placed in him by his master – and most especially a betrayal of the Heavenly Master who had preserved and blessed Joseph during his slavery. Although we don't like to look at it that way, for Christians, all sin is unfaithfulness to the One to whom we have promised ourselves.

Joseph's long dependence on God had obviously effected quite a change in the formerly cocky kid. He no longer saw himself as the center of the universe.

Unfortunately, Potiphar's wife hadn't experienced a similar transformation. When she didn't get what she wanted, she didn't care how many people she had to hurt to satisfy her vengeful fury.

Do we react as she did – caring only about what will satisfy our own immediate wishes? Or do we stop to ask ourselves how God and others are going to feel about our decisions?

DECIPHERING DREAMS

Audrey Stallsmith   November 13

Read Genesis 40

"Interpreting dreams is God's business," Joseph replied.
Genesis 40:8b (TLB)

Joseph seems to have adapted so quickly to prison that he shortly became a steward there, too. That was probably partly due to the genuine interest and sympathy he showed for the other prisoners. But we can guess it was also due to the confidence he must have radiated, an assurance based on his knowledge that he was never abandoned – even behind bars. "Interpreting dreams," he told the butler and baker, "is God's business."

Although he was referring to the explanation of their nighttime visions, we can take another meaning from that. All of us think we know what would make us happy. But God is much more knowledgeable than we are. He could see, for example, the weak and self-satisfied character Joseph would have become if he had remained forever a spoiled child in the ease of his father's house.

Instead, Joseph was shortly going to rise to much more power than he had ever envisioned. But the man who now knew what it meant to be a slave could handle the heights without their destroying his character. As one who was betrayed, sold, and eventually became a savior to those who tried to kill him, he would sometimes even be compared to Christ.

God actually has larger dreams for us than we have for ourselves. But we must be patient and allow Him to decide when we're ready for them.

CRITICISM

Joy C. Bradford   November 14

"Have I not commanded thee? Be strong and of a good courage; be not afraid, neither be thou dismayed: for the Lord thy God is with thee whithersoever thou goest." Joshua 1:9 (KJV)

Most felt the situation was questionable, but preferred to brush it under the rug. Not wanting to risk a backlash, they said things like, "Yes, it's wrong, but let's keep quiet. Just accept it and look the other way. We can learn from this. Let's quietly show how we feel by not taking part."

Others said, "It's not right, but I will participate."

Several responded, "I wouldn't have done it, but it's okay. Don't rock the boat."

A few said, "I see nothing wrong with it."

Sue had spoken up against something that – in her opinion – was unacceptable. Later, it was hard when others disagreed with her behind her back, in order to get their own points across. Those who repeated gossip concerning Sue's position added sin and hurt to the situation.

She learned that there is a price to pay for taking a stand. People have a tendency to shoot the messenger in hopes of avoiding the message! Will she be strong enough to speak up again? Yes, but only with God's help.

Dear Jesus, help Sue and others to understand that some people will disagree when she speaks. It doesn't mean that they are right. Help her to take a deep breath, be sure of the facts, and never compromise Your teachings. We all need Your strength as we seek to do Your will. Amen

OLD FRIEND AND COMPANION

Mary A. Koepke   November 15
"I have laid up thy word in my heart, that I might not sin against thee." Psalm 119:11 (RSV)

My old black RSV Bible is tattered and torn. I have repaired it with mailing tape, abused it by writing in the margins of its thin pages, underlined sentences in red, and highlighted passages in yellow.

Forty-two years ago, when it was new and pristine, it became my companion and friend. It has gone with me to church, adult Sunday School class, Bible studies, circle meetings, writing seminars and hospitals. It has traveled with me in cars, buses, trains, ships and planes throughout the U.S. and overseas. It has also sat with me on the back porch among flowers and bird songs; or in the rocking chair in the kitchen behind thermal glass doors as snow falls softly through winter silence.

Although I also read the King James Version and have referred to some of the many new translations, I feel most comfortable with my old friend, my RSV.

I never cease to find new insight, guidance, and peace rereading those marked-up wrinkled pages as we spend our quiet times together.

SNOWFLAKE

Chris Snow   *Haiku*   November 16

Snowflakes touch my skin
Reminding me of God's touch
His hand painted all

INTERRUPTIONS

Barbara Settle   (Missionary to Africa)   November 17

It was 5:00 p.m. I had returned to our hut from visiting and needed to get supper going when a woman arrived. We greeted each other, and I offered her a chair. After talking awhile, she told me why she had come. I helped her, and she returned to her own hut. When I looked at the clock, I saw that time was passing quickly. The menu was to be roasted potatoes, carrots, and onions. I also wanted to bake a cake. I started a good charcoal fire and had begun making the cake when another woman arrived with a baby on her back. The child had an awful case of scabies on his feet, legs, and hands. His mother and I greeted each other, and she sat down and chatted. It was hard to tell her I had no medicine to help. I was able to offer some suggestions, and she went her way. Meanwhile, my charcoal fire was beginning to die and, of course, time continued to fly.

Life is full of interruptions, and we are frustrated when our goals are blocked. I reflected on the words of Edward B. Pusey (1800-1862) in light of our situation in Africa: "To those, whose hope is in heaven … their irksome tasks, privations, sickness, heaviness of heart, unkindness of others, and all the sorrows which their Father allows them in this world, are so many means of conforming them to their Saviour's image."

Father, please help us to see interruptions as opportunities to become more like Jesus and show Him to others. Amen

ASSURANCE OF SALVATION

Joan Clayton   November 18

"But if we walk in the light, as he is in the light, we have fellowship one with another, and the blood of Jesus Christ his Son cleanseth us from all sin." 1 John 1:7 (KJV)

"Mawmaw," my granddaughter exclaimed enthusiastically over a long distance phone call, "Guess what! I gave my heart to Jesus and was baptized this morning at church – and Daddy did it. Now we can all go to Heaven!" Traci's excitement and faith was so contagious that we rejoiced with her.

Our Scripture reading today assures us that *"There is no condemnation for those who are in Christ Jesus."* (Romans 8:1) So, when I stumble and fall, I repent and go on with Jesus for He is all loving and forgiving. He knows my frame and He restores a penitent heart. I do not worry that I am saved one minute and lost the next.

So, if we love Jesus, we're going to Heaven. Let's be joyful and rejoice in our salvation today!

Dear Father, thank You for Jesus, Whose love and sacrifice makes eternal life possible. Amen

GOD STILL LISTENS

Teresa Wiedrick   November 19

""Save us, O Lord our God, and gather us from among the heathen, to give thanks unto thy holy name,, and to triumph in thy praise." Psalm 106:47 (KJV)

How often we call out to Him for forgiveness for yet another defiled day. Those "righteous" days are few. Repeatedly we recog-nize our folly – we see again that we missed the mark. Then we need to draw close to the One who is able to renew us.

"But they soon forgot what he had done and did not wait for his counsel." Psalm 106:13 (NIV)

We are a simple people. When we don't thirst, we don't drink. When we don't hunger, we don't eat. When we don't recognize our sin, we don't seek after His grace.

"Then they despised the pleasant land; they did not believe his promise." (Psalm 106:24 (NIV)

"Many times he delivered them, but they were bent on rebellion and they wasted away in their sin. But he took note of their distress when he heard their cry; for their sake he remembered his covenant and out of his great love he relented. He caused them to be pitied by all who held them captive." Psalm 106:43-46 (NIV)

His unfailing love reaches beyond our unfaithfulness. It is He who is the author and finisher of our faith, the beginning and end. He completes the work of our faith.

Dear Father, thank You for Your boundless, endless faithfulness. Your grace is mine on defiled days as well as holy days. Amen

A LESSON IN SECURITY

Karen Reno Knapp   November 20

My oldest son, Ethan, was a student in Jerusalem when the *Intifada* began in Israel. I prayed about his safety. I'd turn it over to the Lord – and then I'd worry some more. No matter how much I prayed, I seemed to have little peace.

I also have two younger sons, Eli and Andrew. While Ethan was in Jerusalem, Eli was working at a camp. Then he called to tell me he needed to go to Belize.

Great! I thought. *Now Eli is leaving the U.S., too.* I consoled myself that at least Andrew was safe. After all, he was still in college in Seattle. I didn't have to worry about him.

Soon Eli left for Belize. Now I fretted about him as well as about Ethan. One afternoon my phone rang. It was Andrew.

"Hi, Mom, the most exciting thing just happened! I was walking to class this afternoon when I fell down. I wondered if I had tripped. But I looked up and other people had fallen, too. Seattle just had a major earthquake!" Thankfully, Andrew was young and looked upon it as an adventure.

That earthquake was a blessing in disguise. It showed me that I couldn't protect any of my children. After that, I would check my e-mail or call if there was a suicide bombing in Jerusalem, but my heart was lighter. I *knew* God was in control. Finally, I had peace knowing that security is not in a *place* but in **Him**.

LONELY, YET NEVER ALONE

Evelyn Heinz   November 21

"Whom having not seen, ye love; in whom, though now ye see Him not, yet believing, ye rejoice with joy unspeakable and full of glory." 1 Peter 1:8 (KJV)

As a widow, my thoughts often turn to wishing my husband were here to share in those little conversations one has after a long day at work. Once, when I had that thought, at that instant, my eyes fell upon a goldfinch perching on the edge of the birdbath in the back yard. I smiled and my heart leaped for joy! To me, this was not co-incidence – it was "God-incidence." He sent that little bird just for me to see. When it flew away, I reveled in the gift that God had given me.

With God, I may be lonely, yet I am never alone. He gives me joy and blessings each day. In the 15 years of my widowhood, I have come to practice the presence of Jesus, spending many hours in solitude with

Him in prayer. He is with me just as He promised in Matthew 28:20.

I have found joy after my sorrows. He shows His presence in nature. Each little bird that comes seems to sing of His love for me. Each sunrise or sunset is colored with an unending joy. The dew on the grass, the changing seasons, the gentle breeze across my brow are all gifts of joy from our Heavenly Father. I'm grateful and alert to all the little joys He sends each day.

BEING THANKFUL IN ALL CIRCUMSTANCES
Nancy Dearborn   November 22
Read James 1:2-5
"And we know that in all things God works for the good of those who love him, who have been called according to his purpose."
Romans 8:28 (NIV)

At Bible study, our leader was sharing how he had been delivered from drugs over 17 years ago. He went on to relate how using drugs was destructive and devastating.

I thought about my own life. I'd grown up with a mother who was verbally, mentally, and at times, physically abusive. I spent years questioning how God could have used that for good in my life. Many times I felt alone, scared, and that my life was unmanageable.

It was not until this Bible Study – at 50 – that the revelation came. I realized that, because I always felt like my life was out of control when I was growing up, I never tried drugs or turned to alcohol! I had always been striving for control and wasn't tempted! For the first time in my life, I got down on my knees and *thanked the Lord* for the mother He had given me. I finally understood why God had allowed those specific circumstances in my life.

Sometimes it takes us years to understand how God was using something challenging in our lives for good.

Lord, help me to forgive others who have hurt me. Help me to be thankful even for the trials and difficult times in my life. Amen

HOW IS YOUR FAITH WALK?
Willie B. White   November 23
2 Corinthians 5:7; Hebrews 11:1

What is faith? ***"Faith is the substance of things hoped for, and the evidence of things not seen."*** Hebrews 11:1 (KJV) With a full understanding of faith, we humans have the assurance to ask the Lord anything in prayer, knowing that we will receive an answer.

2 Corinthians 5:7 tells us that we are to walk by faith and not by sight. What this verse means is that we are to believe the unbelievable, see the invisible, and receive the impossible. It was Abraham's faith that caused him to believe God. He obeyed His command to leave his home country and travel to a foreign land – not knowing where he was going! Now, that's real trust!

It was Abraham's faith that allowed him to believe God when he was told that he would have the son of promise in his old age. That assurance also allowed him to offer his son Isaac as a sacrifice, believing God would provide a substitute – which God did.

It was faith that caused Joshua and Caleb to bring a more excellent report, believing that the nation of Israelites could conquer the land of the giants.

It is our faith in Jesus Christ and God's grace that provides our salvation. Scripture encourages us to have faith the size of a mustard seed. If we did we could tell a sycamore tree to move from its place and into the sea and the tree would obey. What faith!

PROMISES

Paul E. Vander Wege   November 24

Read Romans 5:1-11
"We have been made right in God's sight by faith in His promises...." Romans 5:1a (Life Application Bible)

Once, when I was a child, my parents promised to come to a band concert. Then I did something to make them angry and they said that, as punishment, they wouldn't come. I was heartbroken. Yes, I did something wrong, but my parents broke their promise.

God makes so many promises in the Bible that they are almost impossible to count. He vowed never to leave His own, to forgive our sins, to provide for our needs, and to heal all our diseases. The most important promise, though, is that God would give us eternal life if we believe that Jesus' death on the cross makes us right with God.

When we believe that, then God begins to change us, to make us into what He has in mind. He even uses problems and trials we experience in our everyday life to build strength of character and patience – all of which helps us to trust God even more.

Unlike many parents (who are, after all only human!), God *always* keeps His promises to those who are His chosen children.

Father, I thank You for being faithful, loving, and caring for my family. Help me to keep my promises to You and those I love. Amen

Thought for The Day: God keeps all of His promises to all of His children.

A GRATEFUL HEART

Viola Ruelke Gommer   November 25

*"It is good to give thanks to the Lord, to sing praises to
Thy name, O Most High; ... For Thou, O Lord, hast made
me glad by what Thou hast done; I will sing for joy
at the works of Thy hand."* Psalm 92:1,4b (NASB)

Mother was humming. She always sang while she worked. But
today I couldn't see why. It had been hectic. The washer had over-
flowed. The car wouldn't start. There wasn't enough money to buy the
groceries we needed. Now, how would we get to the doctor's office?
Our plans for the day had been turned upside down.

A frustrated teenager, I asked, "Mother, how can you hum when
nothing has gone right today?"

"Ah," she said, "I'm counting my blessings. The Lord's been good to
us. He'll get us through today's problems." She went on with her work
… and her humming.

At dinner, Dad asked how our day had gone. Mother said, "We got
everything done."

She was right. We had finished the laundry after mopping up the
floor. The two of us *walked* to the store. We pared down our grocery
list. A friend took us to the doctor's. Now we were together, eating a
simple meal. Father said grace over it, adding, "Lord, You know our
needs before we do. Thank You for all Your gifts today. Amen."

Mother and Dad were right. I learned important lessons for then
and now. Many years later, I find myself humming as I count my blessings with a grateful heart!

"NO ONE IN PARTICULAR"

Bill Batcher   November 26

Lee Rudolph's prize-winning poetry collection, *A Woman and a
Man, Ice-Fishing* contains a poem, "Little Prayer in November." It has
been reprinted many times, read by Garrison Keillor, and has found a
wide audience. It begins "That I am alive, I thank/no one in particular."

In those opening lines, I think the narrator expresses the dilemma
many people face nowadays. We feel vaguely grateful for what we
have, but having killed off God (Nietzsche), we don't have someone to
whom we can express that gratitude. We want to just thank, not to
thank *anyone* or *anything.* Imagine how short the Oscar speeches
would be if "thank" were an intransitive verb!

We appreciate that we are alive, relatively healthy, and generally

194

happy. We might thank our lucky stars, or fortune, or some other usurper. Unfortunately, if we eliminate the one to acknowledge, we also eliminate any reason to be grateful. For in a random universe – controlled by impersonal forces – it truly does not matter whether we are living or dead, well or sick, happy or depressed.

This Thanksgiving, I am grateful not only for life, but for the Giver of that life! – *"For in Him we live and move and have our being."* Acts 17:28 (KJV)

When I give thanks, it is to "Someone in particular!"

A CHANGED HEART
Lisa Hill   *Thanksgiving Day*   November 27
"One of them, when he saw he was healed, came back, praising God in a loud voice." Luke 17:15 (NIV)

Our Lord is so merciful, gracious and generous with us! As Christians, we may have become numb to His many blessings and perhaps have taken them for granted. My cupboards are full, my children are healthy, and my family is intact.

In response to all He has done for me and continues to do, I seek to please Him, even if it's in a small way. The above verse tells us that thankfulness is pleasing to God – but sadly that sentiment is rare. According to the parable of the lepers, only10% of us are thankful!

Matthew 12:34b says, *"...for out of the overflow of the heart the mouth speaks."* (NIV) Sincere thankfulness comes from a changed heart – a heart surrendered to God that renounces sin and longs for the Master's touch.

Genuine gratitude lives here. Our circumstances may be difficult. But even so, the fact that our eyes have been opened to know Him and to glimpse, in part, His plan gives us a reason to be thankful.

While the leper received healing for his wasting flesh, he also received healing in his searching heart. I believe it was the latter that prompted his praise, as it should also prompt ours.

IF EVERY DAY WERE THANKSGIVING
Lanette Kissel   November 28
"That I may publish with the voice of thanksgiving, and tell of all thy wondrous works." Psalm 26:7 (KJV)

On Thanksgiving Day, we are reminded of all we have to be thankful for, and of the many ways God has blessed us. But, what about all the other days of the year?

I am a server in a buffet restaurant, and with an hourly wage of $2.13 per hour, I must rely heavily on gratuities from my customers to earn my living.

One evening, I felt irritated because I had earned only $39 in tips. I was feeling anything but grateful for the money I had taken in! But then, later that evening, I learned that the other girl who had shared the banquet room with me had taken in only $15. I felt ashamed when I realized how fortunate I had been in comparison. I then thanked God that I had been blessed with $39 that night.

I hope I can learn to thank God every day, in all things – even those situations which don't seem like a blessing at the time. Wouldn't it be wonderful if we could keep Thanksgiving in our hearts each day of the year?

Heavenly Father, help me always to remember to be thankful for Your many blessings in my life. Amen

THE BLOWS OF THE HAMMER

Daisy Townsend   November 29

"And we know that in all things God works for the good of those who love Him, who have been called according to His purpose. For those God foreknew He also predestined to be conformed to the likeness of His Son." Romans 8:28-29 (KJV)

Recently I visited a forge in our area where one can observe the process that each intricately formed item must go through to create the finished product. Mystified as to why it was necessary, I watched as an air hammer pounded relent-lessly on a piece of metal.

When the piece of metal was removed, I saw that underneath was a design created by raised surfaces. What had appeared to be sense-less blows from the hammer had been necessary to transfer the awesome design from the pattern to the piece of metal!

Last year a friend of mine encountered what seemed to be one senseless blow after another in her life. From our limited perspective, all we could see were the "blows of the hammer." However, a year later, my friend says that she wouldn't trade the experiences she went through for anything, because of the changes they have produced in her! She recognizes now that the blows of the hammer were needed to produce the imprint of Jesus more clearly in her character.

Thank You, Jesus, for loving us enough to continue the process of our transformation even when we don't understand why. Amen

"LORD, PLEASE HELP ME"

Alison Trenholme   November 30

"Love is very patient and kind ... It is not irritable or touchy.
It does not hold grudges and will hardly even notice
when others do it wrong." 1 Corinthians 13:4 (TLB)

Every thought of my estranged daughter is like an arrow in my heart. Sounds theatrical, but it's the truth. And I don't even know the reason for our estrangement. She hasn't responded when I've written to ask her. She returned my latest Christmas card, unopened.

"How can my only daughter be so cruel and hurtful?" I cried aloud when there was no one to hear me. Lately, I have been remembering an accusation my daughter made to me when she was six. "You never say anything about the good things I do, only the bad!" she exclaimed tearfully.

I find these words branded on my heart today, and I wonder if our estrangement started even then?

Sixty years since I was a single mother with three small children, I am now newly-married in my eighties to a kind, loving, generous man. Still, I find myself overlooking all the good things he continually does for me and harping on the "bad," which are only minor annoyances after all. Am I repeating myself, all these years later? Have I learned nothing at all?

Please, Lord, give me such a loving heart that I see only the good! Raise my eyes so that I do not see those actions I find so irritating. Help me, Lord, in this new relationship so that I do not spoil it with my poor vision. Amen

DECEMBER
ATTRACTED TO THE LIGHT

Joan Clayton   December 1

"The Lord is my light and my salvation; whom shall I fear?
The Lord is the strength of my life; of whom shall I be afraid?"
Psalm 27:1 (KJV)

It is not a coincidence that evil breeds in darkness. Unconfessed sins that are not brought to the "Light" will multiply. I find it interesting that unwelcome pests and rodents are more active at nighttime. Their destructive ways are hidden. So it is with sin: it steals, robs and kills.

Most crimes are committed in darkness – the perpetrator feeling that if no one can see the committed crime, the perpetrator cannot be identified. Yet God knows!

Every living thing must have the sun, including humans. People must have the "Son" also. "Jesus is the Light and if we lift Him up, He will draw all men to Him."

Each of us can be a lighthouse and guide others to the "Light."

Have you ever been traveling at night, tired and hungry? You pass a house with lights that suggest warmth, family, love, and comfort. It's the light and the warmth that draws us. Jesus is like that. He is the "Light" of all things.

He is the *"Light of the world!"* (John 8:12)

Dear God, thank You for Jesus, who is truly the Light of the World. Amen

PRAISE, LAUD AND HONOR
Megan Vance   December 2

To Thee, O Christ, the King may glory and praises flow
In Heaven and on earth, angels and men bow low.
You Who conquered death by rising that glorious day,
May we give You all our crowns and You alone obey.
You are our blessed Lord and there is none besides.
We give You all our hearts therein You may reside.
Oh, fill us with Your love and give us what we need –
Just more and more of You as on Your Word we feed.

NO PROBLEM TOO SMALL
Barbara Peer   December 3

Sometimes we wonder, *Does God have time for me? Maybe He's busy with more important things. Maybe my problems are too small for Him to be bothered with.*

We've often heard that there is nothing too difficult for God. Just as important is the fact that nothing is *too small* for Him to care about!

Look at this: *"And even the very hairs of your head are all numbered."* Matthew 10:30 (NIV) God is interested in all the details of our lives. He is never too tired or too busy with other concerns.

Many of the limitations we imagine God having are based on the limitations we are accustomed to seeing in one another. We get tired, we run out of time, we have obligations … we have to prioritize. But God never gets tired, He has eternity, and He can be everywhere all at the same time! He even keeps track of our hair! *Think of it – when you brushed your hair this morning, He knew exactly how many hairs came out in your brush and how many you had left on your head!*

Nothing is huge to God and neither is anything minute. He didn't need a giant telescope to place the stars in the sky; neither did He need a microscope to create the one-celled plants and animals. Whatever our circumstances, whether they seem to be a crisis of major proportion or a mere annoyance, God is here for us as our Counselor, Provider, Loving Father, and Best Friend.

WINTER STORM

Gloria Hillman   December 4

Wind blows roaring like a beast, snow blasted from nor'east,
Cold biting at my nose, freezing my hands and toes.
But it's good to feel alive and know that I'll thrive
Throughout this winter snow, shrouding what lies below.
When lovely spring brings leaves, I'll till the soil and plant my seeds,
Which scented flowers give, that grow and shout, *"He lives!"*
He came to vanquish death from this crusty earth,
To dry our tears that come from fruitless fears.
To show the meaning of love while preparing our place above.
My faith will keep me warm throughout this winter storm.

A PROMISE WE CAN COUNT ON

Shirley S. Stevens   December 5
*"And this is the promise that he hath promised us,
even eternal life."* I John 2:25 (KJV)

Some time ago, Tony Snow, President Bush's press secretary, returned to work after several days in the hospital because of a recurrence of cancer. As he met with the press corps, he became choked up because of the loving spirit they had showed him – so different from their usual adversarial relationship!

When a journalist asked Tony if he were discouraged since his cancer had returned, he told them that he was grateful that it was at least treatable. Then he added, "God doesn't promise us tomorrow; He only promises us eternity."

What a Godly way to look at life! I'm going to remember it!

THE RIGHT TO BECOME CHILDREN

Judy Barron   December 6
*"Yet to all who received Him, to those who believed in His name,
He gave the right to become children of God."* John 1:12 (NIV)

Father God,

I thank You this very day for the right to be Your child with all the blessings and privileges – as well as the responsibilities – that entails. I do not take this privilege lightly. I will remember it always. But I do not always accept the responsibilities easily and gracefully. To be a child is to be loved and cared for. But it means also to take care of brothers and sisters who need a helping hand. And so often I fall far short of my duties.

So, I thank You for the right to be called Your child, and I pray for the guidance and direction of the Holy Spirit to remind me of what I should be doing in love. Remind me of this often and forcefully, loving Father. Especially in this dreary, cold time of year, when all I wish to do is cover up and "hunker down" inside my warm home. Remind me of all of Your children who have no way to stay warm, dry, and free of hunger pains – and show me how I can be of help. Amen

LESSON FROM THE DEAD SEA

Jan Sady   December 7

"Then said He unto me, these waters issue out toward the east country, and go down into the Arabah, and go into the sea, and being brought forth into the sea, the waters shall be healed."
Ezekiel 47:8 (KJV)

The Dead Sea is so named because there is no living thing in the water. It has become symbolic of the deadness in our lives because of sin. It also represents someone who continually takes in, but never gives anything out. Its waters cannot quench our thirst.

Christ, however, has become the symbol of the "River of Life." When that river flows into our dead sea, He makes all things new! Just as in this passage in Ezekiel the waters were healed, so it is that our lives can be healed from pollution through the blood of Christ.

Father, I thank You for Jesus, the "River of Life." Fill me with Your Spirit so that I might become more alive in You every day. Amen

AWARENESS

Anna Dangerfield   December 8
Read Mark 12:28-34
"You shall love your neighbor as yourself." Mark 12:31 (NRSV)

On my way to the mall, I raced past a box turtle inching its way across the highway. I hoped other cars would slow down and let it reach the road's edge. In seconds, I cringed. Through my rear view mirror, I saw it hurled, disc-like, into the air by a speeding automobile. The driver raced on, unaware.

I'm like that speedy car and that turtle. I barrel through this busy season, hurling my children's and husband's needs aside while I shop for gifts and join in Christmas festivities. I speed past God's opportunities for service, while checking off one more name on my list. Like the turtle, I allow my blinder-like focus to envelop me. Like both of them, I am enclosed in a shell of self-absorption.

Jesus commanded us to love our neighbors. We show this love by helping and serving others. To do this, we need to be aware of their needs.

Dear God, Please open my eyes to the needs and the opportunities for Your service. Whatever my speed, may I show my love for You by being aware of Your people. Amen

Previously published in *The Secret Place* and *Spiritual Voice News*.

NURTURING OUR RELATIONSHIP WITH THE LORD
Connie Ansong   December 9
Read Matthew 4:17, Revelation 22:5

As we learn to be in agreement with the Lord (Amos 3:3) our relationship with family, friends, and other people gets better. We become responsible partners. We learn to be sensitive to the needs of others, and the Word teaches us how to live with people who are different from us. We learn to love because He is Love.

Lord, we thank You for making Jesus Christ our only role model. Give us the spirit of discernment to follow His path to Your Kingdom. Help us to focus on our steps so we do not slip. In Christ's name we pray with thanksgiving. Amen

MUSICAL INTERLUDES
Elizabeth M. Van Hook   December 10
"He gives strength to the weary and increases the power of the weak." Isaiah 40:29 (NIV)

In *Our Daily Bread*, David Roper notes that, "God writes the music of our lives. Our role is to follow His lead, humming, harmon-izing, blending, and singing in tune."

In longer musical compositions, there are *interludes*. Life is like that! In my thirties, I had one that lasted five months. Active in church, community, and job, my life was good! The tempo of my music never slowed, even as I existed on three hours' sleep a night.

Then, one morning, the melody nearly stopped. My life's composition had an *interlude*. "Walking pneumonia" became a complete physical break down. No more fast-paced music. Doctor's orders were "complete bed rest" in order to survive.

I pleaded with God for healing. Days, weeks, then months passed. It was difficult even to sit up. I searched the Scriptures for reassurance of healing. Every day I read Isaiah 40:31: *"...but those who hope in the Lord will renew their strength. They will soar on wings like eagles; they will run and not grow weary, they will walk and not be faint."*

Each day I expected a miracle. By May, with complete bed rest, medication, proper diet – and, most of all, prayers – I began to gain strength. The healing came! I felt better than I did before my illness! The crescendos of my life were now louder and more dramatic.

Father, we thank You for the attendance You give to our supplications. When Your answers come, the blessings are doubled! Amen

ADVENT

Kathy Johnson   December 11
"This is he who was spoken of through the prophet Isaiah: A voice of one calling in the desert, 'Prepare the way for the Lord, make straight paths for him.' "
Matthew 3:3 (NIV)

Advent has always been a season of the church year I anticipate. As far back as I can remember, my family used an advent wreath. And just as John the Baptist prepared the way for the Lord, so our family has used the wreath to prepare our hearts and minds for Christmas. Changes have been instituted in the design of advent wreaths over the years, but the one I remember from childhood is still the one I use in my home today.

The circle represents the eternal God. No beginning and no end.

The evergreen stands for eternal life.

Three purple candles represent penitence, a reminder of our sins and the reason Christ came to earth. The purple candles are lit on the first, second, and fourth weeks of advent.

The fourth candle is pink and represents joy. It is lit on the third week. In the midst of our sorrow over sin, we rejoice in the coming of our Lord. For by His birth, death, and resurrection, we by faith have eternal life.

A fifth candle is placed in the middle of the advent wreath. This candle is white and is lit on Christmas Day to indicate the birth of our

Savior. All other candles are extinguished, because the fulfillment of the promises represented by the purple and pink are fulfilled.

MARY'S SONG OF PRAISE

Lydia Harris   December 12

Read: Luke 1:46-56

"... for the Mighty One has done great things for me –
holy is his name." Luke 1:49 (NIV)

Our daughter and son-in-law invited my husband and me to dinner at a restaurant. As we finished, our daughter handed us a gift.

"What's this?" I asked. "It's not a special occasion."

"Open it and see." She and her husband both grinned.

Inside we found a photo frame inscribed with, "I love Grandpa and Grandma." This was an unfamiliar title for us! We learned it was indeed a special occasion – the announcement that we would become grandparents!

In Luke, Mary, the mother of Jesus, also received a surprise announcement. She, too, was expecting a baby, but her circum-stances appeared less than ideal. Since she was an unmarried virgin, rumors and stigma would be connected with her pregnancy.

How did Mary respond to this life-changing news? Did she ask, "Why me?" No, she glorified the Lord, and her spirit rejoiced in God her Savior (verses 46-47). She recognized God's sovereignty and acknowledged His plan to bless future generations through her. It was easy to praise God when our daughter announced her pregnancy. But how would I have reacted if Mary were my daughter? Do I praise God when He allows unexpected events to enter my life? May I grow in grace to respond like Mary!

Sovereign Lord, thank You for Your plan to redeem the world through Jesus. Like Mary, help me accept the things that enter my life and respond with praise to You. Amen

EVERY LAST DROP

Karen Reno Knapp   December 13

I was sitting in church ready to take communion. Sunlight streamed through the window directly onto the cups of grape juice waiting to be distributed to the congregation.

The words of Jesus came to my mind. *"Then he took the cup, gave thanks and offered it to them, saying, 'Drink from it, all of you. This is my blood of the covenant, which is poured out for many for the forgiveness of sins. I tell you, I will not drink of this fruit of the vine from now on until that day when I drink it anew with you in my Father's kingdom.'"* Matthew 26:27-29 (NIV)

Jesus sacrificially shed His life's blood for me, yet, how often do I nullify that death by not appropriating all that Jesus has for me?

Help me, Lord, as I drink the cup, to drink it fully. May I live each day in the light of Your death for me. Remind me that I am a sinner saved by grace, but saved for a high purpose. May I daily turn to You for guidance and, as much as I can, drink every last drop. Amen

GROWING PAINS

Jana Carman   December 14

"...You have taken off your old self with its practices and have put on the new self, which is being renewed in knowledge in the image of its Creator." Colossians 3:9-10 (NIV)

I've grown in body, yet I find
Myself still chained to childish ways:
Old habits fetter still my mind.
But growth, burgeoning, expands,
Exerting unimagined strength
To burst those cramping bands.
Growing means "the old won't fit,"
And like new shoes, the new,
So stiff at first, may chafe a bit.
Still, it's worth the pain to hear
The Father say with joyous tone,
"Good gracious, child! Look how you've grown!"

THE GREAT ANTICIPATION

Joseph M. Hopkins   December 15

"The seed of the woman (not man) will bruise the head of the serpent." (Genesis 3:15)

Centuries later the prophet Isaiah predicted, *"For a child is born to us, a son is given to us. And the government shall be on His shoulders. These will be His royal titles: Wonderful Counselor, Mighty God, Everlasting Father, Prince of Peace."* (Isaiah 9:6)

"Advent" means "coming." It is the season in which we "infanticipate" the birth of Jesus. For nearly 2,000 years the promise was repeated by God's prophets. They foretold that the Messiah would be a descendant of David, that He would be born of a virgin, that His birthplace would be Bethlehem, that He would be a "suffering servant" Who would preach good news to the poor, and that He would make a vicarious sacrifice to atone for the sins of the world.

In Advent, the millennia of "anticipation" are telescoped into the four weeks leading up to Christmas. What a time of joyful and grateful expectation it is as we look forward once again to celebrate the arrival of God's marvelous Christmas gift of Jesus!

Dear Father in Heaven, fill our hearts with the love, joy, peace, and hope that You covet for us and for all of Your children throughout the world. Thank You for making these gracious gifts available to us through Your Son, our precious Savior and Lord, Jesus Christ. Amen.

Originally appeared in *The 2006 Advent Booklet* of
the New Wilmington Presbyterian Church

THE BOOK

Mary A. Koepke   December 16
***"Thy word have I hid in my heart, that I might not
sin against thee."*** Psalm 119:11 (KJV)

I have always loved books. I have devoured fairy tales, myths, and legends, fiction and nonfiction. I have scoured "How To" books on everything from drawing, painting, sculpture, ceramics, calligraphy, writing, and poetry to theology – let alone struggling through com-puter manuals!

But if I were a castaway on a desert island with only one book, it would have to be my Bible. It is filled with wisdom, allegory, history, poetry, psychology and practical living advice – fraught with hope and inspiration in its many-layered collection.

No matter when I pick it up, my Bible teaches me something I need to know. Or opens the door to something new to be contemplated and absorbed! In this Book, God's true purpose is revealed in His Son, and those who keep the words of this Book are blessed.

As St. John wrote on the Isle of Patmos, ***"Blessed is he that readeth, and they that hear the words of this prophecy, and keep those things which are written therein...."*** Revelation 1:3 (KJV)

THE EAST GATE

Annie Bruening   December 17
Read Nehemiah 3
***"Moreover the spirit lifted me up, and brought me unto
the east gate of the Lord's house, which looketh eastward...."***
Ezekiel 11:1 (KJV)

One of the gates in the wall around Jerusalem is the *east gate*. This is the first one opened at the crack of dawn by the watchman.

It is also the gate Christians should be waiting – eagerly! – to open. Jesus said He was our "Bright and Morning Star." (Revelation 22:16) The Apostle Paul said that Jesus would descend from Heaven with a shout and we would meet Him in the air. (2 Thessalonians 4:17)

Doesn't this gate give us hope in this dark, unpredictable world in which we live? Despite the horror of terrorist attacks, hurricanes, tornadoes, floods, and forest fires we have a beacon of hope in God, who is still in charge of this world! Evil people cannot change the fact that God's Word is true, and Jesus is coming back!

Dear God, thank You for Your encouraging Holy Word. Please help us to read it every day and hear the message You want us to receive. Amen

DISCOURAGEMENT AND HOPE

Annie Bruening   December 18

Read Nehemiah 4:10-20

In one section of the story of Nehemiah's rebuilding of the walls around Jerusalem, the people have become discouraged because of all the decay and rubbish in their way as they worked.

Do we become discouraged because of all the obstacles in our way as we try to serve God at work? Maybe somebody forgot to order something, and we're short that item. Or someone didn't check the schedule and we're short of staff. The "no call/no shows," and those who simply quit on the spot and walk off the floor, cause discouragement. I face such things every day as I work in a nursing home, serving the sick, elderly and disabled.

In this story, the enemies of the Jewish people were planning a surprise attack. Anticipating this, Nehemiah has the men work close to their families so they don't have to worry about the safety of their loved ones. He arms them and says, ***"Don't be afraid, because our God will fight for us."*** Remember, our God will fight for us! We don't have to defend ourselves.

Dear God, we thank You for Your precious Word that gives us comfort and hope at trying times in our lives. Please help us to work with integrity and consideration of others. Amen

IT'S ALL ABOUT HIM

Donna Arndt   December 19

Christmas was six days away. As I was driving to work, I found myself becoming concerned about how I was going to accomplish everything left on my list. With baking to do, plus cleaning, laundry, shopping, and delivering fruit baskets to my two elderly neighbors, I wondered where to start.

I thought, perhaps, I should save the fruit baskets until last, since I already knew that one of my neighbors really likes to talk. I would have to spend some time (which I was short on) there with her.

While I was pondering all of this, a song by Michael W. Smith, a Christian singer and songwriter came on the radio. One of the lines said, "I'm sorry, Lord, for the things I've made it; it's all about You." These words spoke to my heart.

What was I making it? Christmas should be about remembering and thanking God for the love that was poured out to us through Jesus Christ, His son. How could I put insignificant things – like baking cookies, cleaning house and shopping for gifts – before two lovely ladies who needed to see the love of Christ displayed through me?

I thanked the Lord for reminding me that housework and all of these other "things" would always be there, but how much time would I have left with these dear senior saints?

Jesus is the most precious gift we will ever receive, and – not just Christmas Day – every day should be "All about Him!"

WHERE'S JESUS?

Angie K. Dilmore   December 20

"At that time Jesus said, 'I praise you, Father, Lord of heaven and earth, because you have hidden these things from the wise and learned, and revealed them to little children.'"
Matthew 11:25 (NIV)

One day during Advent, my mother babysat my young niece, Makayla. Mom thought Makayla would enjoy decorating the house for Christmas. They hung colored lights, door-adorning wreaths, and mistletoe. They placed red and green candles on the hearth and dangled stockings from the mantle. Then Mom carefully brought out the family's treasured manger scene. She and Makayla gently positioned the pieces. Mary, Joseph, shepherds, wise men, the angel, and stable animals were all put in place.

"But Grandma, where's Baby Jesus?" Makayla asked. "It can't be Christmas without Jesus."

"You're right!" Mom said, startled by her own oversight. Together, they looked in the crèche storage box. They searched through all the Christmas decorations and scoured the house over for the missing babe, but the figurine of Jesus was nowhere to be found.

How often do we become so obsessed with shopping, party planning, baking, and decorating that we forget what Christmas is really about? It is easy, in the midst of holiday busyness, to overlook our primary focus. How poignant that God can remind us through a small child that Christmas isn't complete without Jesus in the center. Where is Christ in your Christmas?

Dearest Jesus, help us to remember that You are the reason we celebrate. Amen

WATER FROM THE WELL

Robert McCreight   December 21
"...work out your own salvation with fear and trembling."
Philippians 2:12 (KJV)

Paul's admonition seems to run up against the doctrine that we are "saved by grace through faith" (Ephesians 2:8), and we get ourselves into trouble when we try to earn righteousness points.

In his book *The Kingdom Within*, John Sanford tells about a New Hampshire farmhouse well. The house had no plumbing, and all the clear and cool water came from the well that never ran dry – even during the hottest summers.

After a time the old house was modernized, along with indoor plumbing, and the well by the front door was boarded over.

Years later, on a warm summer's day, John decided he would like a cold drink from the well. Removing the cover, he let down the bucket to find – the well bone dry!

Why? Curious, Sanford inquired. He learned that it was fed by hundreds of tiny underground rivulets. After water was drawn out, the well was refilled by these tiny streams. When no longer tapped, those tiny streams closed up.

The well had failed – not through lack of water – but through lack of *use!* The well that once supplied clear, cool water became only a deep hole in the ground.

There's a close parallel here between the subterranean water-ways of that New Hampshire farm, and the unseen system of faith which nurtures all human life. It would behoove us to keep the "water" of life flowing through channels enlarged by frequent use!

NO ROOM AT THE INN

Kathy Johnson   December 22

"And she gave birth to her firstborn, a son.
She wrapped him in cloths and placed him in a manger,
because there was no room for them in the inn." Luke 2:7 (NIV)

We were driving from California to Minnesota, trying to make it in three days, hoping to camp along the way. The first night was so hot, none of us slept. The second night we not only could not find a campground, we could not find a motel or hotel. *Everything* along the interstate was booked across the state! We needed to sleep – and we still had one more day to drive.

Eventually we followed others into a city welcome center and slept in our car for the night.

Even in our modern society, to be without a place to lay your head for the night is traumatic. Just think what it would have been like also to give birth and care for a newborn without a place to stay! Doesn't this make you appreciate all Mary did for each of us as she held the Savior of the world in her arms that night long ago in the stable?

Lord, thank You for coming to earth to seek and to save us. We would also like to thank You for the woman chosen to be Your mother. She endured much for us all, and, by her obedience, secured her own salvation. In Your holy name, Amen

WHAT WILL HE BECOME?

Bill Batcher   December 23

Read Matthew 1:18-25

"She will bear a son, and you shall call his name Jesus,
for it is he who will save his people from their sins."
Matthew 1:21 (NASB)

This Child sleeping in His crib, what will He become?
Will He Who told Isaiah, Joel, and Daniel what to say
and from beginning knows the end,
be a prophet proclaiming hope
and bring His erring people back to God?
This Child sleeping in His crib, what will He become?
Will He Who rules the nations, to Whom kings bow down,
Who moves the clouds and Whom the storms and winds obey,
will He – like great King David's son – wear a crown?
This Child sleeping in His crib, what will He become?
Will He Who from eternity could enter God's reality,

will He assert Melchizadek's entitlement to be as one
of Aaron's sons, of Levi's tribe, a priest?
This Child sleeping in His crib, what will He become?
Will He Who built the universe, and fashioned sun and stars,
the earth, the hills, the sea, the animals, the birds, the fish —
will He be a carpenter –
like me?

HOLY BREAD

Marjorie Gray   December 24

"Is not the bread that we break a participation in the body of Christ?" 1 Corinthians 10:16 (NIV)

As we were celebrating communion, I overheard a six-year-old ask his mother, "When can I start taking the magic bread?" In our hushed circle around the table, I pondered those words.

The minister broke, lifted for God's blessing, and passed the bread, repeating solemnly, *"the body of Christ, the bread of heaven."* When his hand rested on the child's head in blessing, I prayed that the little one would realize our love and overflowing joy.

As we stood and chewed that bite silently and simultaneously, I prayed that throughout the days and weeks ahead we would share our lives, worship God, sing, pray, and work together in the name of the One who gave up His life for us. I gave thanks that the child knew this bread was special. I prayed that all of us would distinguish between *magic* and *miracle*, between mysterious ritual and grateful, humble living.

At home I looked in the dictionary and found that the words *bread* and *break* were related. It reminded me that part of our participation in the Body of Christ is being broken, sharing our brokenness, coming before God as sinners, equally in need of Christ's atoning sacrifice.

Lord Jesus, thank You for Your love for children. May we come to You as children today. Amen

GOD'S CHRISTMAS GIFT TO THE WORLD

Joseph M. Hopkins   December 25

"For God so loved the world that He gave His one and only Son, that whoever believes in Him shall not perish but have everlasting life." John 3:16 (NIV)

Dr. E. Stanley Jones has written, "Jesus is not man at his highest, but God at His lowliest. He is not man reaching up, but God reaching down." Jesus *"made Himself nothing, taking the very nature of a servant, being made in human likeness."* (Philippians 2:7) *"The Word became flesh and lived for a while among us."* (John 1:14)

We are born with an instinctive belief in the supernatural. Unaided efforts to understand life's origin, meaning, purpose, and destiny have spawned hundreds of religions. But only partial truth can be attained by human exploration and insight. That is why our Creator has revealed Himself to us supernaturally through His prophets and through His Son, Jesus Christ.

If the baby Jesus had not grown up to live the perfect life, teach the perfect truth, make the perfect sacrifice to atone for our sins, and rise from the dead to validate His claims and promises, we would not be celebrating His birth. Were it not for Good Friday and Easter, there would be no Christmas.

Dear Lord Jesus, how thankful we are that You came into the world to be our precious Savior, Lord, and Friend. Help us to exult with Zechariah, the father of John the Baptist, **"Praise the Lord, the God of Israel, because He has come and redeemed His people."** (Luke 1:68)

"DO EVERYTHING IN LOVE"

Joy Bradford   December 26

"Let all that you do be done in love."
I Corinthians 16:14 (NASB)

Lord, I read this Scripture again this morning. Why is it so hard to do everything with love? The things I like to do are easy, but there are times I don't feel loving toward others. Help me to stop and think on this verse before I speak with body language and the words of my mouth. I fall short.

Lord, I try to use my talents and gifts to show others that I love You. But I fail miserably when I respond to unkindness directed toward me or to those I care about. As You know, I want to lash back. I become defensive and want to talk about the situation with those who are not even involved. Forgive me! Help me hold my silence.

Thank You for Your Word that continues to encourage me to be formed in Your image. I want to do better. Please let my life count for you. You are a gracious forgiving God and I need You every moment of my life. Keep reminding me that You do all things in love. You are a constant encourager and friend. I want to be more like You. Amen

"THE HOUSE OF FALLEN PERSIMMON"

Shirley S. Stevens December 27

Therefore, take no thought, saying, What shall we eat? ...
But seek ye first the kingdom of God and his righteousness;
and all these things shall be added unto you.

Matthew 6:31,33 (KJV)

When I visited Japan, I went to the hut of a pupil of Basho, the famous haiku poet. As I looked at the tiny, thatched-roof house called *Rakshisha*, I wondered about its name: *The House of Fallen Persimmon.*

In America, the wild persimmon is a small fruit loved by wildlife; however, in Japan the persimmon is the size of a tomato and much tastier.

It seems that the poet had counted on harvesting the sweet, orange persimmons the following day. Then he would have funds for his pilgrimage. But a strong wind came up in the night and knocked down all of the fruit. The poet commemorated it in a well-known haiku.

This made me think of the passage from *The Sermon on the Mount* in which Jesus warns us about laying up treasures on earth. Ill winds are going to blow. If we, however, seek first the Kingdom of God and His righteousness, we need not fear loss.

Lord, help me to remember to value the true riches You offer which cannot be destroyed here on earth. May I not be anxious about filling my storage bin or bank account. Amen

READY FOR GIANTS

Jana Carman December 28

"It is not by sword or spear that the Lord saves."
1 Samuel 17:47 (NIV)

The first of David's five stones sailed straight to its target: Goliath's head. But why *five* when only one was needed?

Gath, Goliath's hometown, seemed to grow giants. Scripture mentions four others: Sippai, Lahmi, Ishbi Benoth and an unnamed one. Five giants, five stones. The danger was greater than it appeared. But so was the power to defeat them.

"The battle is the Lord's!" David shouted.

We face giants too: illness, broken relationships, new situations, fears. Like David, we can rely on God for help and go forward in His name. Victory comes *"not by might nor by power, but by My Spirit, says the Lord of hosts."* Zechariah 4:6 (NIV)

Thank You, Lord, for this day's promised victories. May we do our part. Amen

HE WAS AMAZED

Norm MacDonald   December 29
"And he was amazed at their lack of faith" Mark 6:6a (NLT)

He was amazed – I don't know why
That's such an odd thing from one on high.
He was amazed – I don't know why
He knows the heart of both you and I.
He was amazed – I don't know why
Is it something human, or just a lie?
He was amazed – I don't know why
That's such an odd thing from one on high!
He was amazed – I *do* know why –
So He could love both you and I.

HOPE – A REMEDY FOR DISCOURAGEMENT

Thomas Dallio   December 30
**"Now hope does not disappoint, because the love
of God has been poured out in our hearts by the
Holy Spirit who was given to us."**
Romans 5:8 (NKJV)

All of us can relate to encountering people who are actively in-volved in their attempts to discourage us. Whether it's from the mean things they do or what they say, sometimes they succeed in causing us to feel disappointed and discouraged. Maybe life's circumstances overwhelm us – or perhaps the seemingly absent ray of sunshine has that effect. Whatever it is, there has got to be a remedy – and quick! – because discouragement can result in alcohol and drug abuse, suicide, criminal behavior, or any of thousands of types of devastating effects.

I can personally understand these feelings and results because I am serving a lengthy prison sentence in solitary confinement without any visitation and the very unlikely possibility that I will ever be released. What's more, officers who work here seem to enjoy going out of their way to try to make prison miserable with un-remedied officer miscon-duct.

I've noticed that one of the effects of being discouraged is a cold and hardened personality, unwilling to live because of prolonged mistreatment and abuse.

God offers a valuable remedy in the gift of the Holy Spirit pouring God's love in our hearts by His abiding presence within as Comforter and Friend.

Whenever you feel discouraged, please remember that God is greater and the love God gives will wipe away every tear from our eyes and minister a love that brings hope – which never disappoints! *Now that is good news!*

HE CAME AS A CHILD

Evelyn Minshull   December 31

"And she gave birth to her first-born son; and she wrapped Him in cloths, and laid Him in a manger, because there was no room for them in the inn." Luke 2:7 (NASB)

He came as a child, an infant – helpless, dependent, loved ... perceiving as though for the first time a world He had seen created.

When did He first recall His Heavenly roots?

At what age did He first sense the call to do His Father's work?

Like every child, He gradually learned to stand, to speak, to undertake simple tasks. His infant hands reached to touch His mother's face, to stroke a wayside flower. Later, He touched – with healing – the crusted sores of lepers, the twitching of the palsied, the distortions of the paralyzed.

Once, His baby footsteps left prints among shavings in Joseph's workshop. Later, He walked the hillsides, the village streets, the shores of Galilee to speak peace and promise to those who suffered.

Once, His childish love filled only the small circumference of family. Later, the perimeters expanded, enclosing the whole world in His caring.

But first, He came as a child – our Brother, our Savior, our Lord.

Lord, even as we marvel at Your coming, may we remember the power of Your ministry and the price You paid for our salvation. Amen

Our Gifted Writers/Contributors
For Volume XIV

May we have a round of applause for these insightful, Godly writers who, through their devotionals, shine light into varied aspects of the Christian life for the rest of us! Without them, there would be no **Penned from the Heart**. It is clear from what we've read that the following writers have truly "penned their work from their hearts!" Thank God for them all!

Connie A. Ansong, RN, began with a professional understanding of human behaviors, which encouraged her to seek a closer relationship with God. Now she wants to share all she's learning. Writing is another step in her exciting spiritual journey. 3-27, 10-19, 11-8, 12-9

Donna Arndt, in the mountains of Oakland, Maryland, works for Area Agency on Aging and helps husband Leslie with his Christian bookstore. Her work has appeared in *The Upper Room, Secret Place, Women Alive, and Purpose.* To her, writing is a gift from God and she hopes to continue using it for His glory and honor. 3-28, 12-19

Ruth Baldwin's Christian parents were 40 and 52 years of age when she was born. Their teachings have been called old-fashioned, but the Lord's Words are everlasting and never-changing. That's what she proclaims! Always! 1-20, 3-30, 6-3, 8-20

Judy Barron attends Trinity Lutheran Church, McKean, Penn-sylvania, where she is active as a Council Representative for worship, communion lay assistant, and altar care helper. Her grandchildren are her great joy. 1-22, 2-22, 3-31, 5-12, 10-3, 12-6

Bill Batcher, "a poet under construction" taught 35 years, is retired, and leads a writers' group in Riverhead, NY. Two poems were published in *Decision* and several others won awards from *Bylines* and *Writer's Digest*. In 2003, "Upside Down" won the Higher Goals in Christian Journalism award from the Evangelical Press Association. Bill's book of Easter poems, *Footsteps to the Resurrection*, was published in 2005 by Winepress. 3-29, 5-3, 6-7, 7-19, 11-26, 12-23

Florence Biros, wife of James Biros, wears many hats. Her passion is to uplift Jesus wherever she can – and she's found lots of ways! Without Florence there would be no *Penned from the Heart,* and no *Dog Jack* book and movie. It is said that she knows just about everyone in this country and beyond. They aren't far wrong. She is a dear friend to many. 9-14, 10-18

Esther Bordwell is a resident of a Presbyterian retirement center in Washington, Iowa. She takes part in church and other volunteer activities. Creative writing is her favorite activity, next to time spent with children and grandchildren. 1-18, 5-15

Joy C. Bradford has been the wife of George for 45 happy years, mother, and grandmother. She earned a Bachelors Degree from the University of Texas. While active in her church, she is blessed to serve in Prison Ministry by teaching writing skills to men at the Collin County Jail. 2-2, 5-18, 6-4, 9-24, 11-14

Annie Bruening married George 43 years ago. They have five children and six grandchildren. Annie is a CNA, CMA, and Realtor. She writes devotions for the nursing profession and Christian fiction. 3-18, 4-1, 5-31, 9-7, 10-15, 11-6, 12-17

Barbara Major Bryden is married to Ken, a former Navy man, and has a daughter, Liz. She is from Olympia, Washington and loves roses. 5-21, 8-22

Annettee Budzban is an author, freelance writer, and religion columnist. Her column *Inspirations* is featured each week in the *Daily Herald* and *Zion-Benton News* in Lake County, Illinois. She has been published in various e-zines and magazines. ahrtwrites2u@aol.com 5-16

Helene Burgess and her 94-year-old mom are living in Passaic, New Jersey, and are enjoying her retirement time with the family. 5-9, 6-2

Charlotte Burkholder is a free-lance writer from Harrisonburg, Virginia who enjoys writing devotionals and personal experience stories. Her work has been published in *The Secret Place, The Family Digest, Celebrate Life*, and others. 4-4, 5-25, 8-15

Jana Carman, Salem, New Jersey, is a pastor's wife, musician, teacher, and writer. She writes in many genres, including a book of performance poetry and monologues, *People of Faith*, Lillenas Drama. 2-4, 4-15, 5-13, 6-1, 8-8, 9-1, 10-23, 10-27, 12-14, 12-28

Debbie Carpenter takes great joy in being a wife, mother, and grandmother. She loves to write and to work part-time on the Children's Ministry Staff at her church in Tucson, Arizona. 1-28, 1-29, 2-15, 3-4, 5-8, 5-23, 7-28

Jason Carpenter is from Celina, Texas – home of the Bobcats. He was born on September 26, 1971 and Born Again in October of 1995! and wants to tell the world about his Lord. 7-3

Amelia Chako, 72, is a grandmother from Hermitage, Pennsyl-vania, taking classes in writing from Evelyn Minshull, and this is her first publication! She says, "The Lilac Bush is now 9 feet tall and just lovely!" 5-4

Valerie J. Chambers is a graduate of Baptist Bible Institute, Graceville, Florida. As an author of short stories and poetry, she is fulfilling a lifelong desire and call to ministry. Valerie resides in the Daytona Beach, FL area, and works in the medical field. She is a member of Calvary Christian Center, Ormond Beach, FL. 1-9, 3-20, 5-26, 6-30, 7-21, 8-1, 10-12

Lisa Christine has a master's degree in professional writing from Regent University, and experience as an editor for educational publishers, a magazine contributor, a newspaper journalist, and as an online author for Webservant Ministries. She has samples of her writing at www.writingbylisa.com 8-24

Kay Clark is retired from teaching English at Ball State University, and currently supervises student teachers at Anderson University. A widow of a Disciple of Christ pastor, she is the mother of four, grandmother of eight, and great-grandmother of two. 11-1

Joan Clayton is a retired educator. Joan's passion is writing. She is presently Religion Columnist for her local newspaper and is also working on her next book. She has been published in many anthologies and in five *Chicken Soup* series. 4-9, 5-28, 6-26, 9-2, 10-16, 11-18, 12-1

Carol Cleal from Cortland, Ohio, is a Manager of a Mental Health Unit. She serves on her church's praise and worship team and attends a small group Bible study. She is married with two sons and three grandchildren. 8-7

Gloria Clover, former 10-year editor of *Penned from the Heart*, lives in Hadley, PA with her husband (and dog), and writes Christian romances and cozy mysteries. Her romantic novella is available in a Barbour anthology, *Race to the Altar*. 1-1, 7-5, 7-6, 7-7, 9-10

Pat Collins, mother of three, grandmother of seven, and great-grandmother, writes children's stories and poems. Her poems have been adapted to music, appear in church bulletins, and have been published by International Library of Poetry. 1-17, 6-23, 9-12, 10-17

Basle Cox was born in Dallas, but claims the hometown of Archer City, Texas, home of several movies. It is also home of Larry McMurty, author of "Lonesome Dove." Basle is a distant relative of Edgar Alan Poe. 3-5, 6-6

Debbie Crawford is from Southern Illinois. She has had a love for writing since her grade school days. Debbie enjoys writing about what God has shown her through life experiences, and is delighted to be a part of this devotional. 7-13

Jean L. Croyle, who, according to her mother, has been talking non-stop and writing since toddler age has always been moved by words and their images. She is a columnist and photojournalist for several newspapers as a feature writer, poet, and contributes to Internet sites. She is working on her second novel. 10-9

Thomas Dallio of New York, tells a haunting story of his life in "Hope – A Remedy for Discouragement." He shares his complete love and trust in the Lord Jesus – and the Good News of the Gospel. 12-30

Anna Dangerfield, Aiken, South Carolina, enjoys writing spiritual and secular work. She writes a column for a magazine honoring older women. Anna is happily married, has three sons, a beautiful daughter-in-law and a handsome grandson. She enjoys reading, traveling and beach activities. 12-8

Barbara Vath Dawson considers herself a "late bloomer." After her children were grown, she graduated from Clarion University. She's had two Monologues performed at the Little Theater in Franklin, Pennsylvania where she and her husband, Earnie, reside. In addition to caring for her family, she feels called to write for the Lord. 5-17

Nancy Dearborn has been a part-time freelance writer for over 25 years. Publication credits include *Christian Standard, Woman's Touch, Evangel, Alive, Church of God Evangel, Spirit-Led Writer*, etc. She says, "God is so awesome! Currently, I am having the privilege of spending my days reading God's Word and writing on a full-time basis." 1-14, 7-23, 9-16, 11-22

Penny Deary lives in Irvine, California with her husband, Kevin, along with 2 dogs, 2 cats, and a horse. Blessed by the Lord, she enjoys quilting, writing, walking with her dogs, and riding her horse. 3-24

Leigh DeLozier is a Christian writer and speaker where her family lives in Georgia. She has had two devotional books published, and a third will be released in 2008. To learn more about Leigh's speaking and writing ministries, visit www.soulrestministries.net and www.godlygirlplace.com. 4-18, 6-9, 9-6

Angie Dilmore enjoys writing for children and inspirational devotions. She is currently working on a year-long devotional for kids. She lives in Lake Charles, Louisiana with her husband and twin sons. 3-3, 10-4, 12-20

Eric Dilmore, age 13, writes poetry and short fiction stories from his home in Lake Charles, Louisiana. He enjoys chess, soccer, and math. 1-31

Shannon Dubois is a freelance writer and parenting columnist. Her work appeared in Christian magazines and devotional guides. She and her husband enjoy traveling and living abroad, having spent two years each in Japan and England. They now reside in a rural area overlooking the Cascade Mountains in Redmond, Washington with their three children, and the occasional bobcat. 4-21

Lorena Estep and her husband, Chuck, have moved from their home with many gardens to a place in the mountains where she hopes to have more time to write and travel. In addition to having articles published in magazines, she writes a ten-page bi-monthly newsletter for her church, and is currently seeking an agent for a novel. 1-4, 3-8, 4-3, 5-2, 5-30, 6-13, 10-6

Dave Evans has had nearly 100 poems and articles published in previous editions of *Penned from the Heart*. He enjoys riding and training his horse, Conagher. His Australian Shepherd-mix dog, Matt, and he visit several skilled nursing facilities, bringing cheer and comfort to patients. 4-17, 7-24, 8-12, 9-23,

Marjorie K. Evans is a freelance writer with many published articles. She enjoys her family, church, writing, reading, and needlework. She lives in Stanton, CA. 11-7

Neil C. Fitzgerald, retired teacher, presently free-lances. His work has appeared in over 200 publications including *Christian Science Monitor, Decision, New York Herald Tribune,* etc. An A.B. from Stonehill College and a M.Ed. from Bridgewater State College, he was Massachusetts Teacher of the Year in 1968. 2-25, 4-10, 9-15

Rose Goble has taught preschool, second, and sixth grades. For eight years she visited the 48 states and Canada with her truckdriving husband. Now she dispatches him around the Midwest. She writes articles and fiction for Sunday school papers. 4-19, 5-27, 6-21

Viola Ruelke Gommer, RN, MSN, is the mother of two, grandmother of six, and wife of a retired United Methodist pastor. She has been involved in mission work in the US, Bolivia, Haiti, Guyana, Zimbabwe, Dominican Republic, Russia, and Cuba. 1-25

Marion E. Gorman, Manns Choice, Pennsylvania, and her husband have six married children and 19 grands. She enjoys sharing God's love through her writing, gardening, and scrapbooking. Her new project is a church newsletter. 10-14

Marjorie Gray, of Greenbelt, Maryland, is a Holy Spirit–formed poet, non-fiction writer, and lover of God's revelation in Scripture and Creation. A teacher, she is also an instructor with Crossroad Bible Institute. Her work has appeared in Mustard Seed Ministries and Judson Press, *Christian Communicator, Echoes, Evangel, Everyday Blessings, Faith@Work,* and *Penwood Review.* 3-15, 4-16, 12-21

Stefanie Smith Grennek, McAllen, Texas, is originally from Indiana. In 2007 she graduated from a Christian university with a degree in Journalism. She now works with her new husband (as of July!) at a missionary language school in south Texas. 2-29, 6-10

Christopher Wayne Griffin, 25, of McKinney, Texas, loves to write. He loves the Lord, his dear wife, Earnestine Dashield, and their six children. 1-6

Judy Gyde of Toledo, Ohio, has had several devotional series published, as well as many magazine articles such as *Decision, Dr. D. James Kennedy's Multiply Newsletter, Family Magazine*, etc. Her work has also been published in books and anthologies. She served as president of Northwest Ohio Christian Writers and attended several ACW writers' conferences. 9-19

Roy D. Hall, from Diboll, Texas, is a freelance writer and adjunct professor of Bible at Angelina College in nearby Lufkin. His work has appeared in many publications. 5-7

Charles E. Harrel lives with his family in Portland, Oregon where he directs *HisPlaceOutreach*. He served as a senior pastor for 30 years before pursuing a writing ministry. Charles enjoys writing, teaching, and family camping trips. 4-20, 4-29, 5-20, 10-5

Janice May Harris is a teacher, illustrator/writer living in Portland, Oregon. She is a member of Oregon Christian Writers. 1-13. 7-11, 8-11

Lydia E. Harris writes devotionals, articles, book reviews and the column, "A Cup of Tea with Lydia." A former school teacher, she also teaches at writers' conferences. She has been married 40 years and has two children and four grandchildren. Contact her at: LydiaHarris@Qwest.net. 1-30, 4-22, 6-24, 7-29, 8-16, 10-26, 12-12

Delores Hartman received international recognition for her artwork on the 2006, Series A, $500 Peace Bond; has illustrated book covers, copy-edited books, written for the Altoona Mirror Newspaper, been published in *Mature Living, The Standard* and *Winner of Byline Writers of Humor*. One of her photographs appeared on the cover of *Penned from the Heart 2007 Edition*. 7-12, 10-24

Evelyn Heinz, of McHenry, Illinois, loves her birds at her window – especially the goldfinches. They give her joy! An artist, she has been a widow for 15 years, and practices the presence of Jesus. 4-24, 11-21

Violet Herlocker lives in Fancy Gap, Virginia, on the Blue Ridge Parkway. She has been published in several volumes of *Penned from the Heart, Guideposts*, and other magazines. Her works in progress include a ghosted memoir and a motivational book co-written with Sam Bartlett, CEO of Family Friendly Schools. 4-14, 6-8

Mary Herron, of Meshoppen, Pennsylvania, is the wife of a retired United Methodist minister. They have three children and seven grandchildren. She does Home Health part-time, writes, and works among her flower gardens as a hobby. 1-25

Lisa Hetzel is a freelance writer, songwriter, comedienne, storyteller and kindergarten teacher. She lives with her husband and their son in Conyers, GA. Her current projects involve devotionals, articles and an anthology with her fellow authors in EMACW. 10-20

Albert S. Hickey hails from Torrington, Connecticut. He has authored a book of poetry, *Who Art in Heaven*. 7-2

Lisa Hill resides in Elmira, New York with her husband, Terry, daughter, Victoria, and her sons, Jesse and Beau. Please feel free to contact her at TLHILL@pkFamily.com. 4-12, 11-27

Gloria Hillman is a graphic artist on Long Island, New York, who normally works in water colors. But through a writers group in her church, she was inspired to begin painting pictures with words as well. 6-25, 8-26, 12-4

Dorothy Holley, Pittsburgh, spent years caring for others. She now devotes her life to writing and gardening. Her book, *A Whole Quart Jar*, tells of living on a 167-acre farm during the Depression and the necessity of neighbors helping one another. 1-19

Joseph M. Hopkins, New Wilmington, Pennsylvania, is a musician, missionary, teacher, and Presbyterian minister who has spent his life promoting the Gospel all over the world. 2-3, 4-11, 7-4, 8-14, 8-31, 11-2, 12-15, 12-25

Donna J. Howard is a free-lance writer from Orfordville, Wisconsin. She and her husband have been married nearly 52 years. They have three children and five grandchildren. Her published credits include: *Today's Christian Parent, My Devotions, PrayerWorks, Victory Herald, Long Story Short E-zine for Writers, Taj Mahal Review (Anthology)* and *other publications*. 1-8, 4-26, 6-27, 7-30

Elouise H. Hults has enjoyed writing since high school days in Canton, Pennsylvania. She and her husband, Lew, reside in New York's Central Southern Tier. Their treasures: five adult children; 10 grandchildren. She feels "blessed." 4-25, 7-27

Annette M. Irby is a wife and mother who lives in Washington state and enjoys writing songs, articles, and novels. Her articles have appeared in *Northwest Christian Author*, *The Christian Journal* and the devotional *The Secret Place*. 2-6, 4-28

Kathy Johnson lives in Minnesota with her husband and six children. Publishing credits include *Christmas in the Country*, *Lutheran Woman's Quarterly*, *Woman's World*, *Portals of Prayer*, and *My Devotions* for children. Published under the name of Susan St. Clair for Wild Rose Press, she is a freelance writer, editor, and speaker. 2-8, 4-30, 6-29, 7-18, 12-11, 12-22

Helen Kammerdiener of New Bethlehem, Pennsylvania, is a retired teacher, church association co-coordinator, food pantry site manager, community choir narrator, lay speaker, Sunday School and Bible study teacher, and children's Bible club helper. She finds life hectic – and says writing is relaxing. 1-16, 6-5, 10-25

Jennifer Kanode is an English-as-a-Second Language teacher and an announcer on a Christian radio station. She has a Bachelor's degree in Communications and has been writing short stories since she was in elementary school. 1-11, 2-9, 5-1, 6-15, 8-28

Ray Kantowski, former pastor, and CBN associate, lives in Virginia Beach, Virginia with his wife, Patsy, and is currently writing four books, one of which was just published, *"Is Something Missing?"* He is blessed that their large, loving family lives just minutes away. 8-27

Betty King has authored three published books, and is a Devotional and Life Style newspaper columnist and speaker who lives with multiple sclerosis. Visit her website www.bettyking.net or email her at baking2@charter.net 2-11, 6-20, 7-20

Lanette Kissel, wife, mother, and writer, lives in Evansville, Indiana. She enjoys writing short stories, novels, and traditional rhyming Christian poetry. Once again this year she has shared her devotional writing with *Penned from the Heart*. 2-14, 6-17, 7-25, 11-28

Karen Reno Knapp is a free-lance writer whose work has appeared in *Decision*, *The Christian Reader*, *Power for Living* and other publications. She and her husband, John, spend six months in Florida and six months in Pennsylvania. They both like to write and travel, as do their four adult children. 11-20, 12-13

Mary A. Koepke is a free-lance writer/illustrator. She lives with her husband of 57 years at the Passavant Retirement Center in Zelienople, Pennsylvania. She is active in the Arts Program which includes painting, sculpting, journaling, poetry, and needlework workshops. 1-15, 2-28, 7-9, 9-4, 10-11, 11-15, 12-16

Jesse Justin Koontz Sr. writes from Texas, is 31, and the father of three girls and two boys. In addition to his writing, he is a meat salesman. 2-12

Tonya LaCourse who lives in Appalachin, New York says she is "in my early 20's, love to read, and am studying writing every chance I get. Recently, I started riding horses and now dream of writing about them." 1-23

Christian Lagow, from Hurst, Texas, is honoring God with his writing skills. He believes the quote "nothing is too foolish if it is done out of the love of God." 8-19, 9-5, 10-30

Carey Anne Meyer-LaSor calls herself "a blessed woman whose calling in life is as mother to two boys, Nathan and Matthew, daughter, sister, aunt, owner of Kenzie (a little Westie), fortunate friend of some amazing people, and colleague of some true Titans on the campus of Westminster College in New Wilmington, Pennsylvania." 6-7

Carol J. Lee, a retired clinical social worker, is living in rural Montana with husband of 26 years. She has 4 stepchildren and 9 grandchildren. Began writing in l990s; self-published poetry devo-tional in l998, *Dine With The Master.* Poems appeared in *Montana Woman* and *The Journal of Pastoral Care & Counseling.* She enjoys watercolor, fishing, time with family, friends, and raising raspberries and blueberries. 2-16, 6-22, 8-21

Rick Leland of Three Rivers, Michigan, writes a column, *Inspiration Point,* which appears in newspapers in nine states. He has been married for 25 years to Nancy, who edits his writing and is a faithful ministry partner. 6-18, 8-25

Janelle Howard Leonard tells us that she and her husband were married in July of 2002, two weeks after she graduated from high school. Currently, they have two wonderful boys, ages one and three. The family lives in Vestal, New York. 6-12

Lillian Lewis, at 85, is still a S.S. teacher, church organist and mission chair for her church, as well as a lay speaker! She's been writing "forever," and been published in many publications. A widow with 3 children, 6 grands, and one great, she now writes "with the hope her articles will help someone." 4-13

Lizzie Joy Lukens of Canton, Ohio, is the editor of Lachryma: Modern Songs of Lament (www.lachryma.com). She spends her days singing, writing, and painting. 2-23

Norm MacDonald and his wife of 24 years live in Monroe, North Carolina. An alumnus of Trinity Evangelical Divinity School (TEDS) and Wayland Baptist University, he served 20 years in Adult Edu-cation and Training and seven years as Senior Pastor. He has written his own Adult Bible study and Discipleship curriculum. 4-8, 7-8

Robert McCreight, Mercer, Pennsylvania, a fourth-generation Presbyterian pastor who loves the Lord, has a wife, two daughters and two grandchildren. Twenty years in parish ministry was followed by serving as interim pastor for eight congregations where he has met many delightful saints. 6-19, 12-21

Sandra McGarrity lives and writes in Chesapeake, Virginia. She is the author of three Christian novels. Visit her web page at:
http://hometown.aol.com/mygr8m8/myhomepage/books.html 11-4

Jane Miller writes *Heart Stories* for *Gardeners and Families* columns. Her work also appears in *Pittsburgh Professional Maga-zine*. Jane lives in Pittsburgh, Pennsylvania with her psychologist husband, Rick. They are the parents of 3 children, ages 26, 21, and 10. 8-13

Evelyn Minshull, author of 26 published books, has taught creative writing workshops to all ages. She and Fred have been married for 56 happy years. While they were at home, their three daughters were her "first readers" – her "on-target" critics. 2-1, 4-6, 5-14, 6-11, 7-15, 8-3, 9-3, 9-26, 10-1, 10-21, 10-29, 12-31

Brad Nelson is the pastor of the Princeton Bible Church in Plainsboro, New Jersey. He has penned several insightful devotions you won't want to miss**.** 3-17, 7-14, 9-21

Scott Noble, of Falcon Heights, Minnesota, is a former assistant editor of *Decision Magazine* and has had articles published in a variety of periodicals. Currently, he is the director of operations and communications for a Christian non-profit ministry. 2-17

Derrick K. Osorio, Huntingdon, Pennsylvania, writes of his early years when he was unaware of his need for God. His "A Fool for Christ" is a must-read. He finds he has "had to harness prayer under the unlikeliest of conditions." He hopes to encourage others by his writing. 1-26, 7-17

Barbara Peer is a freelance writer living in Cape Coral, Florida with her husband and three cats. She writes articles and devotionals for Christian publications, and is currently working on her Ed.D. in Pastoral Community Counseling. 2-18, 8-2, 12-3

Debra J. Phenes, New York, says she is **"a 30-something female," enjoys southern gospel music and has had a desire to write for some time. She has put more focus on her writing lately and loves to encourage both believers and non-believers by her written word and song. 2-13, 3-10**

Sarah Lynn Phillips and her husband, Barry, reside in Clarks Green, Pennsylvania and have three daughters. Besides being a full-time homemaker, Sarah enjoys writing, reading, encouraging others, and editing a bi-monthly newsletter for women in her church. 3-12, 5-5

Julie Pollitt worked for a small Colorado newspaper in the late 1990s. She is now married, has two little boys, and lives in Clearwater, Florida. She is currently the coordinator of MOPS (Mothers of Preschoolers) at her church in quaint Safety Harbor. 2-10

Evelyn Quinby, Youngstown, Ohio, is a mother of two, who loves the Lord and music. She writes music she receives from Him, as well as the verses. Originally from West Virginia, she spent many years in the secretarial workplace. She's a pushover for stray kitties, but took time to write two devotionals. 5-29, 7-1

Glenda Joy Race, Pennsylvania, enjoys teaching, writing, and singing. She teaches writing skills and GED preparation through Luzerne County Community College. She is involved in children's and music ministries. She enjoys sharing her singing and writing talents with others. 1-5, 2-19, 6-28

Betty Redmon, a former resident of New York, employed in millinery design, now lives in Stanton, California. She enjoys friends, writing, and finds life to be an exciting adventure. 1-21

Debbie Rempel is active in her church in Dallas, Oregon, and volunteers at the school affiliated with it. She is an active member of Oregon Christian Writers and loves to write poetry about nature, Heaven and her walk with the Lord. She has put together several compilations as gifts to others. 3-6, 11-3

Angelicia Roberts, a Minnesotan, has established herself as a writer, and has published her first book: *The Way, The Truth & The Life*. She's written, performed, and facilitated workshops for different events and businesses. 2-20, 9-27

Micki Roberts is a member of ACFW, RWA, and FHL. She writes Inspirational Fiction, devotions, poetry, and songs. Micki and her husband of 30 years live in Florida and have two grown children. 2-24

Joanna Ronalds, Warragul, Australia, sent several devotions which she authored. They have appeared on daily devotional blog sites. 2-7, 3-25, 8-17, 9-8

Jan Sady, Mayport, Pennsylvania, President, Writers Fellowship; Editor, *The Path*; Author, *God's Lessons from Nature*. Published in *Small Town Life*, *Upper Case*, *Cross & Quill*. Articles accepted in *Ideals* and *The Writer Magazine*. Certified lay speaker for UMC. janfran@alltel.net. 2-26, 8-4, 8-29, 9-9, 10-22, 12-7

Pan Sankey, Vienna, Ohio, and Bob, have three children, and ten grands! She began writing in 1985 and creates Bible study guides and skits, and mentors a women's group. Pan delights in poetry about God's creation, His Word, and His provision. 3-11, 5-10, 9-11

Barbara Settle, her husband Brad, and their three children have been missionaries in Tanzania, East Africa since 1997. They live among a people group who never knew the name of Jesus before the Settles and other missionaries arrived. Today, there are a community of believers and a primary school. 11-17

Darryl Sherlock of Smethport, Pennsylvania is a poet who loves to share his work with others. 8-30

Joseph Smart is a graduate of Mountain View High School and is the father of a wonderful little girl, Maja Smart. He is the son of two wonderful, caring, loving parents, Ron and Kathy Smart of Weatherford, Texas. 1-12

Columba Lisa Smith lives in Ben Lomond, California and wanted to share her "View from Heaven." 1-27

Chris Snow is from Frisco, Texas. He is thankful to God for the blessings in his life and claims Psalm 20: **"Some boast in chariots, and some in horses; but we will boast in the name of the Lord...."** (Verses 7-8) 6-14, 11-16

Paul Soderberg resides in Dallas, Texas and is a lover of the great outdoors. He has three children, Brittany, Zechariah and Matthew. Paul thanks God for His "anointing touch." 1-10, 3-2, 4-5, 6-16

Walter Stadler, of Melissa, Texas, is a carpenter by trade, and loves to write. He grew up on the shores of Lake Lavon in North Central Texas, is a graduate of Princeton High School, and

attended East Texas State University. He and his wife, Nancy, have a daughter, Kellye Jo, and a son, Walter IV. 5-11

Audrey Stallsmith, Hadley, Pennsylvania, is the author of the *Thyme Will Tell* mystery series from WaterBrook Press. She also writes articles on "Historical Plants" and "Christian Thought: Lewis, Chesterton, et al" for her web site, thymewilltell.com. 11-9, 11-10, 11-11, 11-12, 11-13, 11-14

Margaret Steinacker is an organist/keyboardist for two Sunday services at a vibrant United Methodist Church in Indiana. She works with her husband, Gerry, who serves as the Director of Music and Worship Arts. An Adult Education teacher, she centers her life, whether at church or in school, on being Christ to those in need and sharing His love. She has two sons and seven grand-children. steinmag@gmail.com 1-2, 2-21, 3-13, 4-2, 8-9

Christy Stenger has been married for 19 years to a USAF officer and has three children. After writing for about 5 years, she got serious last year, writing devotions, poems and fiction. She has been published on two web sites and in *Reflections* – a Christian magazine for women. 8-6

Shirley S. Stevens leads a Christian Writers' Group, The First Word, in Sewickley, Pennsylvania. She serves as teacher in residence and mentor for The Writing Academy. Currently secretary of the St. Davids Christian Writers' Conference, she enjoys receiving e-mail: poetcat@earthlink.net. 3-1, 8-5, 9-22, 10-7, 11-5, 12-5, 12-27

Susan Stitch, Florissant, Missouri, got her inspiration for "Kicked in the Teeth" from her twin boys, Chris and Kevin, who'd been wrestling. Kevin was excited about his tooth quarter and it gave her inspiration for this delightful devotional. 1-3

Eunice Tan, hails all the way from Australia! She has a background in accounting and English literature, with a Masters degree in Creative Writing. Recently, she found herself drawn back to her passion for writing for God. 8-10

Kris Thayer, from Placerville, California, has written a 365-day Christian Devotional entitled *Fellowship with Jesus.* She has sent us two samples which are based on 1 and 2 Corinthians, Galatians, Ephesians and Philippians. She hopes they will further the good news of Jesus Christ. 3-7, 5-6

Pamela S. Thibodeaux is a member and co-founder of Bayou Writers' Group in Lake Charles, Louisiana. Multi-published in romantic fiction as well as creative non-fiction, her writing has been tagged as, *"Inspirational with an Edge!"* Email: pthib-7@centurytel.net 3-16, 9-25

Daisy Townsend, Pennsylvania, has been writing for some years, and has appeared in many publications. She and her husband, Donn, are missionaries to Japan and will be going there to live in 2008 for several years when he retires. They leave behind two children, and three grandchildren. 3-9, 4-23, 8-18

Alison Trenholme, *Greenport, New York, writes that "it's been* 60 years since I was a single mother with three small children. I am now newly-married in my 80s to a kind, loving, generous man. *11-30*

Deborah J. Tune resides in a small, Ozark town in Missouri; beauty is everywhere. Wife, mother, evangelist, gospel singer, and home-schooling mom of 12 years, her motto is: "Life is to be lived – so keep your money and spend yourself. The story that your life tells will live on after you." 5-24, 7-22

Michele Tune, of the Missouri Ozarks says, "When I came across your website, I knew it would be a great honor to be published in one of your books! God's done a great many things for me and I would love to share, encourage, and inspire through my writing!" Learn more at www.michele-tune.com. 3-19, 4-7, 9-17, 10-8

Stanley Tune also lives in the Ozarks with his wife of 33 years, daughter (above), and son, Matthew. Facing disabilities and challenges after a tragic motor vehicle accident, Stanley continues the Lord's work as a singer and songwriter. 2-5

Risa L. Ulmer, Avis, Pennsylvania, writes that recently she found "a fantastic lady, Shirley Stevens, at a St. David's Christian Writers' Conference." She was encouraged to submit some of her writings to Penned from the Heart. We used her poem on 9-28.

Megan Vance, Natrona Heights, Pennsylvania 12-2

Paul E. Vander Wege writes from Oskaloosa, Iowa. He recently attended the Colorado Christian Writers' Conference where he was motivated to submit his work. He says that *Penned from the Heart* caught his eye "because this poem and these devotionals come from my heart." A teacher for 35 years, he later became a landscaper. 3-14, 5-22, 9-13

Elizabeth M. Van Hook, is retired and has moved back to New Jersey to be closer to her family. She continues to photograph butterflies and flowers when she is not busy at her church or doing historical research of her aunt's family who came to America with the Puritans, bought fruit trees from Johnny Appleseed, and received land from President Andrew Jackson. 4-27, 9-20, 9-30, 10-10, 12-10

D. Jonean Walton of Kermit, Texas, has written her devotional for those who question if we are missing out on the abundant life. She completed a Masters program where she wrote for the academic fraternity newsletter. 7-16

Charles A. Waugaman, poet, was an art director, college art teacher, conference and workshop leader, editor, and served churches in Maine, Connecticut, and Pennsylvania. Retired in Vermont, he delights in long morning devotions where many of his writings begin. 1-24, 3-26, 9-18, 10-2

Karen Welborn, Columbia, Illinois writes a devotional opinion column for the *Monroe County Clarion Journal Newspaper*. Her work is also being published in Wesleyan Sunday School material. Karen is a graduate of Central Bible College, Springfield, Missouri. and has been a pastor's wife for 32 years. 1-7

Chet Weld lives in Tucson, Arizona with his wife, Susan. Chet is the Director of Counseling at Casas Church. He recently earned his Ed.D. in Counseling Psychology at Argosy University. He enjoys ministering Christ to hurting people, writing music, reading, and going for walks. 2-27

LaDonne Weyman, Pennsylvania, and her husband are motorcycle enthusiasts who love to travel. Her passion is to seek God's will and see His blessings come alive through their grandchildren. She writes a monthly article for her home church. 9-29

Teresa Wiedrick, hails from Alberta, Canada. She is a busy mother of three daughters who has always enjoyed writing. She is a free-lance writer, formerly in fictional pursuits. Lately she has a passion for writing devotional material. 10-28, 11-19

Willie B. White, Michigan, wears many hats including teaching, having spent years in study at various universities, and now serves in sundry services for the Lord. She has three grown sons and when she isn't writing, she enjoys many hobbies. She is working on her second book. 3-23, 11-23